Bridging the Gaps

Bridging the Gaps

Linking Research to Public Debates
and Policy-making on Migration
and Integration

Edited by Martin Ruhs, Kristof Tamas,
and Joakim Palme

OXFORD
UNIVERSITY PRESS

OXFORD
UNIVERSITY PRESS

Great Clarendon Street, Oxford, OX2 6DP,
United Kingdom

Oxford University Press is a department of the University of Oxford.
It furthers the University's objective of excellence in research, scholarship,
and education by publishing worldwide. Oxford is a registered trade mark of
Oxford University Press in the UK and in certain other countries

Published in the United States of America by Oxford University Press
198 Madison Avenue, New York, NY 10016, United States of America

British Library Cataloguing in Publication Data
Data available

Library of Congress Control Number: 2018962583

ISBN 978–0–19–883455–7

Printed and bound in Great Britain by
Clays Ltd, Elcograf S.p.A.

Foreword and Acknowledgements

This book is the outcome of a project carried out within the auspices of the Swedish Migration Studies Delegation (Delmi). The mission of Delmi, which was set up as a government committee, is to serve as a bridge between social science research, on the one hand, and public debate and policy-making, on the other. The initial motivation for this book was the idea that Delmi would benefit from analyses of the experiences of other initiatives and projects aimed at linking research to public debate and policy-making processes, not only in other countries, but also in international settings. The work on the book thus became an important tool for Delmi in terms of self-reflection and self-evaluation, serving as a sounding board for critical reflections of the work of the committee.

The idea for this book project came from Kristof Tamas, who then engaged Joakim Palme and Martin Ruhs as co-editors. These three editors had once been brought together by a politician, the late Jan O. Karlsson, who in so many ways was dedicated to the mission of bringing research closer to policy-making, not least as co-chair of the Global Commission for International Migration and, before that, as Minister of Migration. We are happy that his successors as Ministers of Migration have shared his engagement in research. As Minister, Tobias Billström was responsible for setting up Delmi as an independent committee—which we, also in retrospect, believe was a wise decision. Later, his successors as responsible ministers, Morgan Johansson and Heléne Fritzon, have continued to support the work of the committee. We see this support as being part of a quest for more knowledge and respect for the value of pursuing this work in an independent format.

The source of inspiration for this anthology was a book published in 1993 by Alexander L. George, *Bridging the Gap: Theory and Practice in Foreign Policy*. George examined US foreign policy strategies and explored ways to bridge the gap between the two cultures of academia and policy-making. He advised policy-makers to reinforce their use of academic knowledge while inviting scholars to produce more policy-oriented knowledge. This piece of advice is also useful for the study of migration and integration, and the relations between academia, media/public opinion, and policy-makers. Over the past couple of decades, the notion that policy-makers should rely on research to form evidence-based policies has been challenged. Liberal democratic governments are increasingly feeling threatened by the rise of populist parties. Academic knowledge and expert views are increasingly being questioned by post-truth advocates.

Our overall concern is the question of how we could help in bridging the gaps between academic research and media/public opinion, academic research and government policies, and government policies and public debate. What are the opportunities and pitfalls of trying to produce policy-relevant research? What lessons can be learnt from past experiences of efforts to use research to inform public debate and policy-making processes? These are highly timely and topical questions in a large number of countries across the world.

We are very grateful to all the chapter authors for their contributions. We are pleased that we could gather and persuade such a knowledgeable group of scholars and practitioners from Europe and beyond to contribute to this book. The contributors have a wealth of knowledge and experiences with linking research to public and policy debates on migration and integration across a wide range of different institutional settings and countries.

We would also like to extend our gratitude to the Royal Swedish Academy of Letters, History and Antiquities (*Vitterhetsakademien*), who provided generous financial support for a workshop in May 2017 which enabled this book's contributors to gather in Stockholm. This workshop proved exceptionally helpful for facilitating discussions among our contributors and for shaping the book in a way that makes it appealing to a wide-ranging audience, including academics, policy-makers, civil society and media, and the general public. We would also like to thank the following commentators who provided very helpful discussions of the draft chapters presented at the workshop: Alessandra Venturini, Kerstin Brunnberg, Tom Nuttall, Michele Levoy, Eskil Wadensjö, Bernhard Perchinig, Peter Webinger, and Johan Hassel.

The editors have benefited greatly from the support of the Delmi secretariat throughout the project. Associate professor Henrik Malm Lindberg has, in many ways, been an important engine for the project and his input has been extremely valuable. Dr Constanza Vera-Larrucea has provided a stream of useful comments about the various chapters in this volume that greatly improved a number of the contributions, not least our own. We are also grateful for the support of Dr Erik Lundberg and Dr Sara Thalberg.

We would like to acknowledge the excellent support from Oxford University Press, not least by Adam Swallow who believed in the book project—his enthusiasm has been truly appreciated and has spurred us forward—and by Katie Bishop who helped us complete the project. Keith Povey has done an excellent and expedient job as copy-editor, for which we are truly grateful. Elakkia Bharathi did a great effort in helping us finalize the book.

International migration and integration are among the greatest challenges of our time. Well-balanced policies can make a great deal of difference to promoting the considerable benefits and positive outcomes that migration can generate while, at the same time, reducing any potential risks and adverse consequences. Wise policies are not designed by default, which is why it is so important to feed knowledge into policy-making processes. We hope that the theoretical reflections, case studies and policy analyses in this book will be helpful in building more and stronger bridges across research, public debate and policy-making processes on migration, integration, and related public policies.

Contents

Contents

List of Figures and Table

Figures

Table

List of Figures and Table

Figures

Table

List of Abbreviations

ACOM	Advisory Commission on Minorities Research, The Netherlands
AER	Swedish Labour Policy Council
AfD	Alternative for Germany party
AFIC	Africa Intelligence Community
AMID	Academy for Immigration Studies, Denmark
BAMF	Federal Institute for Migration and Refugees, Germany
CARIM	Consortium for Applied Research on International Migration
CBS	Netherlands Statistics
CDU	Christian Democratic Union of Germany
Ceifo	Centre for Research in International Migration and Ethnic Relations, Sweden
CEPR	Centre for European Policy Research
COMPAS	Centre on Migration, Policy and Society, University of Oxford
CSU	Christian Social Union in Bavaria
DCI	Development Cooperation Instrument, European Commission
Deifo	Delegation of Immigration Research, Sweden
Delmi	The Migration Studies Delegation, Sweden
DFID	Department of International Development, UK
DHS	Department of Homeland Security
DIAMINT	Science–Society Dialogues on Migration and Integration in Europe
DIW	German Institute for Economic Research
EASO	European Asylum Support Office
EBA	Expert Group for Aid Studies, Sweden
ECRE	European Council on Refugees and Exiles
EEA	European Economic Area
EEAS	European External Action Service
EIFO	Expert Group for Immigration Research, Sweden
ELIAMEP	Hellenic Foundation for European and Foreign Policy
EMN	European Migration Network

EMSC	European Migrant Smuggling Centre
ESO	Expert Group on Public Economics
ESRC	Economic and Social Research Council, UK
ETF	European Training Foundation
EU	European Union
EUI	European University Institute
EWS	Early Warning System
FRONTEX	European Border and Coast Guard Agency
GAMM	Global Approach to Migration and Mobility
GDP	gross domestic product
GLO	Global Labor Organization
GMG	Global Migration Group
ICE	Immigration and Customs Enforcement
ICMPD	International Centre for Migration Policy Development
ICT	Information and Communication Technologies
IDPs	internally displaced people/persons
ILO	International Labour Organization
IMER	International Migration and Ethnic Relations
IMISCOE	International Migration Integration and Social Cohesion in Europe
INTCEN	Intelligence Analysis Centre, EU
IOM	International Organization for Migration
IPCR	Integrated Political Crisis Response, EU
IRC	International Rescue Committee
IRCA	Immigration Reform and Control Act
ISAA	Integrated Situational Awareness and Analysis
ISC	Metropolis International Steering Committee
IT	information technology
IZA	Institute for the Study of Labor
JHA	Justice and Home Affairs
KCMD	Knowledge Centre of Migration and Demography
LPF	List Pim Fortuyn party
LSE	London School of Economics
MAC	Migration Advisory Committee
MAFE	Migration Between Africa and Europe
MIF	Migration Impacts Forum
MigObs	Migration Observatory

MIPEX	Migrant Integration Policy Index
MMP	Mexican Migration Project
MPI Europe	Migration Policy Institute Europe
NAPI	National Action Plan for Integration
NGOs	non-governmental organizations
NOU	Norwegian Official Commissions
NPV	net present value
OECD	Organisation for Economic Cooperation and Development
OPT	optional practical training
ÖVP	People's Party (Austria)
Pegida	Patriotic Europeans Against the Islamization of the West
PVV	Party for Freedom, The Netherlands
REF	Research Excellence Framework, UK
RESOMA	Research Social Platform on Migration and Asylum
SCIFA	Strategic Committee on Immigration, Frontiers and Asylum
SCP	The Netherlands Institute for Social Research
SDG	Sustainable Development Goals
SNS	Centre for Business and Policy Studies, Sweden
SOAS	School of Oriental and African Studies, University of London
SOU	Swedish Government Official Reports, Sweden
SPÖ	Social Democrats Austria
SSHRC	Social Sciences and Humanities Research Council, Canada
STEM	science, technology, engineering, and mathematics.
SVR	German Expert Council for Migration and Integration
SVT	Swedish Television
TRIEC	Toronto Region Immigrant Employment Council (Canada)
UN	United Nations
UNDESA	United Nations Department of Economic and Social Affairs
UNDP	United Nations Development Programme
UNGA	United Nations General Assembly
UNHCR	United Nations High Commission for Refugees
VPRO	Dutch Public Broadcasting Association
VVD	People's Party for Freedom and Democracy, The Netherlands
WRR	Scientific Council for Government Policy, The Netherlands

List of Editors and Contributors

Editors:

Joakim Palme is Professor of Political Science at Uppsala University. He has published extensively on the welfare state and inequality as well as social investment. Joakim is the co-editor of *Welfare and the Great Recession* (Oxford University Press 2019). He was the Director of the Institute for Future Studies in Stockholm 2002–2010. Since 2013 he is Chairman of Delmi, the independent Swedish Migration Studies Delegation (www.delmi.se) appointed by the Swedish government in 2013 and actively engaged in migration policy discussion.

Martin Ruhs is Professor of Migration Studies and Deputy Director of the Migration Policy Centre (MPC) at the European University Institute in Florence. Martin is the author of *The Price of Rights: Regulating International Labor Migration* (Princeton University Press 2013) and co-editor (with Bridget Anderson) of *Who Needs Migrant Workers? Labour Shortages, Immigration and Public Policy* (Oxford University Press 2010). He was a Member of the UK's Migration Advisory Committee during 2007–2014.

Kristof Tamas is Director of Delmi, the Migration Studies Delegation. He has held positions as senior adviser in the secretariat for the Swedish chairmanship of the Global Forum on Migration and Development, Swedish national expert at the EU Commission, independent research consultant at the Institute for Futures Studies in Stockholm, and special adviser and later deputy director at the Ministry of Foreign Affairs and the Ministry of Justice. He has over twenty-five years of experience in international collaboration in the field of migration and development. He is the co-editor (with Joakim Palme) of *Globalizing Migration Regimes* (Routledge 2006).

Chapter authors:

William Allen is a Fellow in Political and Development Studies at Magdalen College, University of Oxford, and Research Officer at the Centre on Migration, Policy and Society (COMPAS). His main research areas are in political communication and public opinion, particulary how media relate to immigration attitudes and policymaking. He also has interests in developing theories of knowledge exchange among migration researchers and the wider public, in order to inform more effective practice. His recent publications on these subjects have appeared in journals including The International Journal of Press/Politics, International Migration Review, and Public Understanding of Science.

Scott Blinder is Assistant Professor of Political Science at the University of Massachusetts Amherst. His research focuses on public opinion toward migration and its impacts on elections and policy. Recent publications include 'Imagined Immigration: The Impact of Different Meanings of "Immigrants" in Public Opinion and Policy Debates in Britain' (*Political Studies* 2015) and 'The better angels of our nature: How the anti-prejudice norm affects policy and party preferences in Great Britain and Germany' (with Robert Ford and Elisabeth Ivarsflaten, *American Journal of Political Science* 2013).

Christina Boswell is Professor of Political Science at the University of Edinburgh. Her research explores the relationship between knowledge and public policy. Recent publications include *Manufacturing Political Trust: Targets and Performance Measurement in Public Policy* (Cambridge University Press 2018) and *The Political Uses of Expert Knowledge: Immigration Policy and Social Research* (Cambridge University Press 2009/2012).

Grete Brochmann is Professor of Sociology at the University of Oslo. She specializes in international migration, European immigration policies, comparative integration policies in welfare states, and historical studies of immigration to Norway. Recent publications include *Europe's Immigration Challenge. Reconciling Work, Welfare and Mobility* (co-edited with Elena Jurado, I.B. Tauris 2013) and *Immigration Policy and the Scandinavian Welfare State 1945–2010* (with Anniken Hagelund, Palgrave Macmillan 2012).

Elizabeth Collett is the Founding Director of Migration Policy Institute (MPI) Europe and Senior Advisor to MPI's Transatlantic Council on Migration. She is based in Brussels, and her work focuses in particular on European migration and immigrant integration policy. Ms. Collett has produced dozens of working papers, policy briefs, and memos focused on the future of EU immigration and asylum policy, as well as national-level policy developments, most recently "After the Storm: Learning from the EU response to the Migration Crisis" (2018) and "All at Sea: the Policy Challenges of Rescue, Interception and Long-Term Response to Maritime Migration."

Howard Duncan is Executive Head of the 'Metropolis' Project and Secretariat, based at Carleton University in Canada. Howard has been Editor of the journal *International Migration* since 2015. He has published extensively on issues related to migration, integration, and cities. Howard is a frequent speaker on the management of migration and integration.

Han Entzinger is Professor Emeritus of Migration and Integration Studies at Erasmus University Rotterdam. Before that, he was Professor at Utrecht University and affiliated to the Dutch Scientific Council for Government Policy and the United Nations in Geneva. Publications include *Integrating Immigrants in Europe: Research–Policy Dialogues* (with Peter Scholten et al., Springer 2015) and *Migration between States and Markets* (with Marco Martiniello and Catherine Wihtol de Wenden, Ashgate 2004).

Monique Kremer is Professor of Active Citizenship at the University of Amsterdam. Her research focuses on citizens in the welfare state. Monique has served as a senior academic staff member of the Scientific Council for Government Policy in the Netherlands since 2004, working on such research projects as 'How unequal is the Netherlands?' (2014) and 'Making Migration Work' (2014). She also co-authored 'Identifications with The Netherlands'.

Katy Long is a researcher and a writer whose work explores the causes and consequences of migration for migrants, citizens and communities. Katy is a Research Associate at the Overseas Development Institute in London and a Senior Research Associate at the School of Advanced Studies, University of London. Recent books include *The Point of No Return: Refugees, Rights, and Repatriation* (Oxford University Press 2013) and *The Oxford Handbook of Refugee and Forced Migration Studies* (co-edited, Oxford University Press 2014).

Philip Martin is Professor Emeritus of Agricultural and Resource Economics at UC Davis. He has published extensively on global labour migration. Recent books include *Merchants of Labor* (Oxford University Press 2017) and *Managing Labor Migration in the 21st Century* (with Manolo Abella and Christiane Kuptsch, Yale University Press 2006).

Robert McNeil is Researcher for COMPAS in Oxford, examining the social environments from which news stories and narratives about migration and migrants emerge; how media debate affects migration policy decisions (and vice versa); and how information gaps affect the way these issues are discussed. He lectures on migration and the media for Oxford's MSc in Migration Studies. He is also the Head of Media and Communications at the Migration Observatory.

Peter Scholten is Professor of Public Administration at Erasmus University Rotterdam. Recent publications include *Mainstreaming Integration Governance* (Palgrave 2018) and *The Politics of Immigration and Migration in Europe* (with Andrew Geddes, Sage 2016).

Agnieszka Weinar is Adjunct Research Professor at the Institute for European and Russian Studies, Carleton University, Ottawa. She is also a Marie Curie Senior Research Fellow at the Robert Schuman Centre for Advanced Studies, EUI, Florence. Publications include the edited volumes: *Migrant Integration Between Homeland and Host Society* Vol 1 (2017), *Emigration and Diaspora Policies in the Age of Mobility* (2017), *The Routledge Handbook of the Politics of Migration in Europe* (2018) with Saskia Bonjour and Lyubov Zhyznomirska, and the recent article 'Cooperation on Migration and the Revised European Neighbourhood Policy' (2017).

Klaus F. Zimmermann is Professor Emeritus of Economics at Bonn University and President of the Global Labor Organization (GLO); Co-Director of POP at UNU-MERIT; and Honorary Professor at Maastricht University, Free University of Berlin, and Renmin University of China, Beijing;. He is also the Editor-in-chief of the Journal of Population Economics. Recent publications include *Labor Migration, EU Enlargement, and the Great Recession* (co-edited with Martin Kahanec, Springer 2016).

1

Introduction

Making Linkages Between Research, Public Debates, and Policies on International Migration and Integration

Martin Ruhs, Kristof Tamas, and Joakim Palme

Evidence-based Policy-making versus Post-truth Politics?

International migration and integration are among the most important and controversial public policy issues in many high-income countries. The global economic downturn in the late 2000s and the sharp increase in the number of refugees and other migrants making their way to Europe in 2015 have intensified what, in many countries, were already highly charged debates about the impacts of immigration on the host economy and society. Concern about immigration has been a major driver of the rise of Donald Trump in the United States, Britain's referendum vote to leave the European Union, and the growing support for right-wing populist parties across various European countries.

Public debates and policy-making on migration and integration are often ill-informed and based on myths, rather than facts. The common lack of evidence in debates and policy-making is frequently lamented, but not particularly surprising. Personal beliefs and public opinion on migrants and refugees can clearly be shaped by a range of different factors that have little or nothing to do with facts, data, and evidence, such as the frequency of actual contact with migrants, perceived competition and threats from immigration, education, age, and the media (e.g. OECD 2010; Blinder 2011). Similarly, policy-making on migration can be influenced by a range of interests, institutions, and ideas which may or may not be based on realities of the scale, processes, causes, and effects of migration (e.g. Boswell et al. 2011; Hampshire 2013). Third, while advances in measurement and research have generated important insights about migration and integration, there are important limits to the existing data and analyses. The available 'evidence base' is characterized by considerable gaps and mixed results around key migration issues (such as the impact of immigration on diversity and solidarity among residents of the host country—see, e.g., Demireva 2015). All this means that there are many reasons why facts, data, and research may—and, in practice, often do—play a relatively minor role in public debates and policy-making on migration and integration.

The disconnect between migration policy debates and migration realities has encouraged many people, including policy-makers in many countries, to advocate more 'evidence-based' debates and policy-making. This approach stresses the need for 'rational' and 'depoliticized' migration and integration policies that are based on data and knowledge, rather than on anecdotes, fears, and misperceptions about migration and integration. A wide range of initiatives have been launched in different countries, including 'independent expert committees' that provide policy advice and recommendations to governments (see, e.g., Martin and Ruhs 2011) and 'fact-checkers'—that is, individuals or organizations that check the factual accuracy of, for example, media reports and/or politicians' speeches on migration and integration (see, e.g., Graves and Cherubini 2016). While the impacts and effectiveness of these initiatives have varied, it is clear that, since the turn of the millennium, their presence has grown in many countries. Until recently, it seemed, at least superficially, that a desire for more evidence-based policy-making had become the norm in many countries.

Recent political events and developments have complicated this picture— for example, the sense of 'crisis' in many European countries sparked by the inflows of refugees and other migrants since 2015, the UK's referendum vote to exit the European Union, and the election of Donald Trump as US President. Many populist parties that have grown in strength across Europe in recent years have been openly critical of the roles of evidence and 'experts', who are often portrayed as representing elite views rather than the interests of 'the people' (see Boswell 2018). In the UK, high-profile figures of the campaign to leave the European Union ('Vote Leave') explicitly rejected the usefulness of 'experts' in public policy debates and policy-making. In early June 2016, Michael Gove, a Conservative Cabinet Minister at the time, declared that 'people in this country have had enough of experts' and Gisela Stuart, a Labour MP and Vote Leave campaigner, argued that 'there is only one expert that matters, and that's you, the voter'.[1] At the same time, the rise of Donald Trump in the United States was accompanied by an apparent increase of a similar scepticism about the role, motivations, and usefulness of so-called 'experts' in public debates and policy-making. *The Economist* called Trump a 'leading exponent of "post-truth" politics—a reliance on assertions that "feel true" but have no basis in fact'.[2] While scepticism about the role of research and experts in public policy-making is not new, proponents of the idea of a general shift towards 'post-truth politics' suggest that the status of 'facts' in public debates and policy-making processes has been fundamentally transformed in the twenty-first century. Davies (2016) suggests that, as politics has become more adversarial and the number of providers of 'facts'—a contested notion and concept—has expanded rapidly, 'rather than sit coolly outside the fray of political argument, facts are now one of the main rhetorical weapons within it'.

Both ideas—'evidence-based policy-making' and 'post-truth politics'—are, to a considerable extent, caricatures of much more nuanced and messy realities of what are typically highly politicized processes of (de)linking data/research, public debates, and policy-making. Evidence-based arguments and approaches to policy-making are never free of subjective decisions and normative judgements about, for example, what exactly constitutes 'evidence' (and who decides on that issue), how to separate 'reliable' from 'unreliable' data and analysis, what to do about processes and effects that are hard or impossible to measure and so on. At the same time, while there are clearly many recent (and older) examples of public policy debates and policy-making processes in different countries that pay little or no attention to facts and evidence, the much-hyped shift to an 'age of post-truth politics' is clearly not inevitable, ubiquitous, or necessarily permanent. Perhaps more than ever before, there is a need to study and understand how and why data, facts, and research affect—or do not affect—public debates and policy-making in different countries and contexts. This clearly (and obviously) requires consideration of how data and research relate to the politics of public policies and to the characteristics of processes of policy-making and implementation, all of which can, and often do, vary across countries and over time.

Aims and Contributions of this Book

This book explores the interplay between social science research, public debates, and policy-making in the area of international migration and integration. It has three core aims. First, the book seeks to contribute to the conceptualization and theorization of the potential relationships between research, public debates, and policy-making on migration and integration (Part I of the book, comprising Chapters 2–4). In doing so, it explicitly builds on existing research in this field, including the rapidly growing number of studies that investigate the links between social science research and public policy in general (e.g. Bastow et al. 2014), as well as the smaller number of analyses that focus on the research–policy nexus in the specific fields of migration (e.g. Boswell 2012) and integration (e.g. Scholten et al. 2015).

A second aim of the book is critically to discuss and identify the reasons for the failure or success of a range of initiatives aimed at using research to inform public debates and/or policy-making on migration and integration, both within national contexts and at supra-national levels of governance. In Part II of the book (Chapters 5–10), senior scholars and researchers with extensive experience of engaging in public debates and policy-making provide critical reflections on efforts to use research to inform migration/integration debates and policy-making in different national contexts. These reflections and assessments cover 'impact-oriented' research projects and initiatives aimed at informing *national* debates and policy-making in the UK, the Netherlands, Norway, Germany, Sweden, and the United States. Part III of the book (Chapters 11–14) then focuses on research and analysis aimed at informing migration debates and policies across countries and/or at supra-national levels of governance. This includes critical reflections on the role and use of research and researchers in EU policy-making; the experiences of the long-standing 'Metropolis' project, which aims to bridge migration research and policy in different countries; and the contributions of researchers and 'experts' to global governance processes relevant to international migration.

A third core goal of the book is to identify effective strategies and institutional designs for linking research to public debates and policy-making on migration and integration in different national and institutional contexts. Part IV (Chapter 15) provides a synthesis and critical discussion of the implications of the research in this book for how to think about, manage, and strengthen the links between research, public debates, and policy. One focus of the discussion will be on whether and how the nature of these interrelationships varies across countries and issue areas, and the implications for the 'transferability' of particular approaches across borders and institutional settings. While the specificity of the case studies does not allow for a systematic cross-country analysis, the different chapters provide a rich and diverse collection of case studies that clearly highlight the importance of paying attention to cross-country differences in the politics and institutions that mediate the interrelationships between research, public debates, and policy-making on migration and integration.

Overall, *Bridging the Gaps* contributes to existing research and knowledge in at least two ways. First, the theoretical and empirical analyses in the book go beyond the focus on the two-way relationship between research and policy-making explored by most existing studies. This is achieved by conceptualizing and analysing *triangular* interrelationships between data/research, public (including media) debates, and policy-making processes, set in the broader context of the politics of public policies. The book thus inserts 'public debates', including the role of the media, into the theoretical and empirical analysis.

A second key feature and contribution of this book is that, rather than aiming for comprehensive 'impact assessments' of particular initiatives, the authors of the various 'case studies' in Parts II and III of the book provide reflections and insights that are strongly based on their personal professional experiences with informing migration and integration policy debates and policy-making processes. The case studies are not meant to be attempts to provide systematic impact evaluations. Instead, they constitute a diverse set of structured explorations of successes and failures (including determinants and policy lessons) of initiatives aimed at linking research to public debates and policy-making on migration and integration across different national contexts and levels of governance.

Analytical Framework

All the chapters of the book are written within a common basic analytical framework. The framework is intentionally broad and rudimentary. Its key purpose is modest but important: to provide a common point of reference for analysis that the individual chapters elaborate, illustrate, and develop further in a variety of ways.

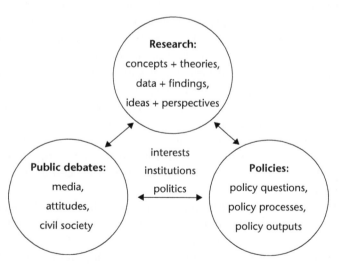

Figure 1.1 Triangular relationships between research, public debate, and policies

We suggest that it is helpful to consider triangular relationships between research, public debates, and policies. Figure 1.1 is meant to illustrate the inter-dependencies and potential two-way causalities between the key variables of interest to this project (keeping in mind that there are, of course, many other factors that are related to and have an impact on public debates and policy-making).

We use the term 'research' as shorthand for concepts and theories, data, and empirical findings, as well as ideas and perspectives. So, our approach to conceptualizing and studying research is fairly broad and covers a range of different types of knowledge. Since we are also interested in how different forms of knowledge travel between country contexts, this broad approach is of strategic importance. 'Public debates' is broadly understood, too. It specifically includes public attitudes and media reporting on migrants and refugees, as well as the arguments made by various public and civil society organizations. Some of these components, such as media and public opinion, are likely to be correlated in important ways. Finally, our understanding of 'policies' relates not only to policy outputs (such as the formulation of new immigration laws and policies), but also to the emergence of policy questions and the characteristics of policy processes.

A first basic point to make about this conceptualization is that research, public debates and policies can all influence each other. This means that any assessment of the role of research in debates and policy-making processes must consider the existence and potential implications of two-way causalities; for example, whether and how the focus of research questions and the types of data collected were affected by politics, policies, and public debates.

Second, researchers can influence public debate and policy-making by producing research, and/or by providing 'expert' commentary in public debates (e.g. through commenting on migration issues in the media) and 'expert advice' to policy-making processes (e.g. as short-term advisors or longer-term 'seconded experts'). Expert commentary and advice does not necessarily require the production of new research. The relative influence exerted by these two types of activities (production of new research and expert commentary/advice) on debate and policy—and the relationships between them—can be expected to vary across countries and institutional settings. Who qualifies as an 'expert' and what exactly constitutes 'evidence' can also be specific to place and time.

Third, Figure 1.1 makes clear that research can impact policy-making directly and/or indirectly through public debate (especially public opinion, media reporting, and civil society organizations). Public opinion is often—but not always—an important factor in the development of new migration and integration policies. In some cases, policy-makers consider public attitudes as a hard constraint on what they consider to be feasible policy options. In other cases, policy-makers propose, defend, and sometimes implement new policies that are not completely in line with current public attitudes. As migration and integration have become major politicized issue areas, ministers or whole governments can be out of office if they do not take account of public attitudes and balance their policies or policy statements in an appropriate way. Evidence—including how it is presented and contextualized—can play an important role in this process as policy-makers can, and often do, ignore or use research selectively to strengthen their arguments and justify their policy choices in public debates.

The media can correct or reinforce individuals' misperceptions and stereotypes about migrants and refugees. While the relationship between public opinion and the media (e.g. in terms of who influences whom and to what extent) is an open empirical issue that can be expected to vary across countries and national media cultures, it is clear that research can potentially influence both. While research can produce different and conflicting results depending on the scientific discipline, methods, and/or data used, evidence and facts have the potential to correct public misperceptions and shift public attitudes, at least to some extent (keeping in mind that facts are not the only driver of public attitudes to immigration and integration, often being of quite marginal relevance). Similarly, researchers can become an important resource for civil society organizations and journalists concerned with migration/integration— although one clearly cannot assume that all media outlets are interested in publishing evidence-based reports rather than, for example, articles that are in line with their readers' views.

Fourth, whether and how research affects policy-making and public debates will always be critically influenced by institutions, interests, and the broader politics of immigration, integration, and related policy areas (such as education, labour markets, welfare states, and so on). There can be important interactions between research and other policy determinants, such as the economic interests of employers and the political orientation of the government in power. Christina Boswell's book *The Political Uses of Expert Knowledge* (2012) shows that, in addition to playing an instrumental role in policy-making, research can have important political functions which are often more symbolic than instrumental.

The potential interrelationships between research, debate, and policy, and the likely interactions with other policy determinants, can make it difficult to isolate and assess the effects of research on migration and integration policies. The rapidly growing research literature on how to measure the wider societal 'impact' of social science research makes clear just how difficult this can be in practice (see, e.g., Bastow et al. 2014).

Outline of the Book

Part I: Concepts and Theories

The book begins with three chapters that provide theoretical analyses of different parts of the three-way relationships between research, public debates, and policy-making on migration and integration. Chapter 2, by Christina Boswell, focuses on the relationships between research, experts, and the politics of migration. Boswell's starting point is that research and expert knowledge can have different uses in immigration politics and policy-making. It can play an *instrumental role* (i.e. it can help with the development of policies to achieve certain outcomes, or to address perceived policy problems), perform a *substantiating* function (i.e. it can act as a resource for lending credibility to particular preferences or claims), or be valued as a source of *legitimacy* to the organizations taking policy decisions (i.e. research and expert knowledge can help signal authority and competence of the decision-maker). The chapter then identifies three sets of conditions that, Boswell argues, influence the extent to which research is used and for what purpose, and that can help explain cross-national variations and fluctuations over time in patterns of knowledge utilization on immigration policy. These conditions include the level of contestation and political salience over the issue, the 'mode of settlement' (democratic or technocratic) that is seen as appropriate in political deliberation, and the mode through which policy-makers derive legitimacy (whether through symbolic gestures or through outcomes). The chapter goes on to explore how this theoretical approach and analysis can help make sense of the current scepticism about expertise in debates on immigration.

Chapter 3, by Han Entzinger and Peter Scholten, analyses the relationship between research and policy-making on *integration*. Drawing on a large, cross-country, empirical research project conducted during 2011–2014 (see Scholten et al. 2015), the chapter considers how research and policy-making in the field of migrant integration have developed over time, and how their relationship functions under the present conditions of strong politicization of the issue in Europe. Entzinger and Scholten propose a theoretical framework that distinguishes between three aspects of research–policy dialogues in the domain of immigrant integration: *dialogue structures* (including the formal and informal arrangements created for the exchange and communication of knowledge and research); knowledge *utilization* (i.e. the cultures and practices of knowledge utilization in policy processes); and, taking the perspective of researchers, knowledge *production*. The chapter then considers—first theoretically and then empirically drawing on the results of Scholten et al. (2015)—how the increasing politization of the issue of integration in Europe can affect the various dimensions of research–policy dialogues in different countries. One of the findings from the empirical analysis is that increasing politization of integration has been associated with more symbolic forms of knowledge utilization (i.e. a rise in the *substantiating* and *legitimizing* functions of knowledge, to use the concepts developed by Boswell in Chapter 2). Another development has been a gradual broadening of research–policy dialogues to what Entzinger and Scholten call 'science–society dialogue', a term that is meant to reflect a diversification of methods of mutual influencing to include various forms of public debates. The chapter thus makes clear the need for moving theoretical and empirical analyses beyond the relationships between research and policy to include various forms of public debates, including the role of the media. Entzinger and Scholten argue that the media can play an important and effective role when the gap between researchers and policy-makers widens.

Chapter 4, by William Allen, Scott Blinder. and Robert McNeil, then focuses on the relationships between research and public debates with a focus on public perceptions and the media. One of the chapter's key messages is that we need to be highly critical of what the authors call a 'naive model of research impact' that focuses only on the ways in which research and data can flow into and affect public debates, whether through direct engagement between researchers and publics, or through mediated channels. The chapter explains why and how the relationship between research evidence and public debate is not only uncertain, but also bi-directional, in the sense that media and public discussions affect research as well as being affected by it. For example, engagement with media and other users of research can shape the kinds of questions researchers ask in the first place. The chapter makes a similar point about the relationships between media and public perceptions. While media can affect how and what people think about migration and integration, the causality can also run the other way, as public perceptions and popular opinion can sometimes influence what kinds of media content are produced. The chapter authors argue that, in market-driven media systems typical of Anglo-American democracies, media organizations can be understood as creating 'products' that they try to sell to audiences, which requires an understanding of who their audiences are, what they think, and what kinds of stories will motivate customers to access their 'products'. The authors thus argue that effective communication of research for public impact involves much more than presenting facts and figures. Instead, it requires awareness of both the conditions and the contexts in which researchers supply information, as well as the ways that media and members of the public generate demand for certain kinds of research or data.

Part II: National Experiences

Following the largely conceptual and theoretical discussion in Part I, the five chapters of Part II provide critical reflections on experiences with different efforts and strategies to use research to inform migration/integration debates and policy-making in different national contexts. Chapter 5, written by Martin Ruhs, discusses the experiences of the Migration Advisory Committee (MAC) and the Migration Observatory (MigObs) in providing independent analysis to inform immigration debates and policy-making in the UK. The MAC was established by the UK government in 2007 and MigObs was launched by the University of Oxford in 2009 as an 'impact project' to inform public and media debates. Ruhs provides critical reflections and personal assessments based on his role as one of five members of the MAC during 2007–2014 and as the first Director of MigObs during 2009–2012. He shows how the specific institutional design of an impact initiative such as MigObs, or of an expert advisory body such as the MAC, has important implications for its credibility, political acceptability and, thus, long-term impacts on debates and policy-making. The chapter argues that it is important to recognize and emphasize, as MAC and MigObs have done in the UK, that it is neither feasible nor desirable to 'take the politics out' of migration debates and policies. Policy-makers sometimes present and justify expert advisory bodies in terms of their alleged function of 'de-politicizing' migration debates and policy decisions. Ruhs argues that this impression should be avoided and resisted by the experts involved whenever possible. Ultimately, all policy decisions are inherently normative, in the sense that a decision needs to be made about whose interests to prioritize and how to evaluate the inevitable trade-offs. Experts can advise and suggest policy options but they cannot, and should not, identify the one 'optimal' policy solution that, for most questions, does not exist.

Chapter 6, by Monique Kremer, reflects on the public reception and controversies surrounding the publication of *Identificatie met Nederland* (Identification with the Netherlands), a major report by the independent Netherlands Scientific Council for Government Policy (WRR). In the report, the WRR advised against an immigrant integration policy that promotes 'the [Dutch] national identity' in favour of a strategy focusing on processes of identification in education, in the labour market and in the community. This message incensed many people, including politicians, scientists, and royalists. The chapter uses the case of how this report was received to discuss more broadly how scientifically informed policy advice is made in the context of a rapidly changing relationship between science, policy, and politics, characterized by the growing significance of public opinion. Kremer considers how social scientists can better advise policy-makers in this new reality. She argues that scientifically informed policy advice needs to go beyond the simple model of 'speaking truth to power', and requires much greater collaboration and stakeholder involvement than in the past. The chapter suggests that, if social science has less authority and credibility than it once had and politicians can 'shop around for convenient truths', researchers and academics cannot always operate on their own to advise government. Consequently, 'knowledge coalitions' have become increasingly important. Kremer suggests that, partly as a consequence of the experience with the 'Identification with the Netherlands' report, different stakeholders are now more likely to be drawn into the process of producing WRR reports, including a variety of academics (including critics of the WRR), policy-makers, and civil society organizations such as employers' associations and trade unions. She argues that the WRR has increasingly taken on the role of an 'honest broker' in the process of production and exchange of knowledge and research for policy-debates and policy-making.

Chapter 7, authored by Grete Brochmann, focuses on the role of research in policy debates about immigration and the sustainability of the welfare state in Norway. The contribution of experts to policy-making processes in Norway was formalized in 1972 through the establishment of the Norwegian Official Commissions (*Norges offentlige utredninger*—NOU). The Official Commissions have been important in policy-making in Norway, playing a significant role in the 'consensual Norwegian governance'. The chapter draws on the author's experience with two specific commissions, which Brochmann chaired, on the relationship between international migration and the sustainability of the Norwegian welfare state. Brochmann argues that, while these commissions did have some impact on actual policy changes, they had fundamental effects on public discourse. In the early 2000s, immigration became one of the most emotionally charged issues in public debates in Norway. Public discourse became quite polarized, first with regard to issues related to refugees and then, following EU enlargement in 2004, also with regard to the free movement of EU workers. The chapter discusses how the first of the two commissions analysed played an important role in promoting public understanding of the diversity of immigrants in Norway, thus reducing existing stereotypes and prejudices among the population at the time. According to Brochmann, the first Commission also played a key role in moving public discourse in the direction of accepting more open discussions of the impact of immigration on the welfare state, thus also encouraging more conscious policy-making in the field of immigrant integration. The second, more recent Commission was established in the wake of the large inflows of refugees and migrants into Europe in 2015. The Commission recommended an institutional approach to integration and cultural adaptation, emphasizing the importance of long-term processes of inclusion and socialization through the educational system and the labour market. While it is too early to assess its policy impacts,

11

Brochmann suggests that the public reception of the Commission report so far reflects a general trend toward a situation where policy-making based on research and facts has become almost common sense in Norway in the field of immigrant integration.

Chapter 8, written by Klaus Zimmermann, discusses Germany's evolving migration policy challenges and developments from the perspective of a scientific observer and academic policy advisor over a period of several decades. It reviews the major migration policy debates in Germany since World War II to discuss the difficulties encountered by researchers when trying to convey key research messages and findings to society and politics. The core policy issues discussed in this chapter include accepting the status of Germany as an immigration country, the creation of an immigration law for admitting skilled migrants based on Schröder's 'Green Card', the debate about transitional employment restrictions on workers from the new EU member states in the context of EU Eastern enlargements in 2004 and 2007, the fight against misperceptions about 'welfare migration', the debate about the need for internal labour mobility in Europe, the challenge of openness to high-skilled labour migration to Germany, and the 2015 'refugee crisis'. Zimmermann explains why, in his experience, the media are the most important channel for policy advice. He argues that a fundamental problem with traditional media is that they are committed to balanced reporting which, he argues, can lead to a bias against mainstream scientific findings, as the importance given to minority findings within the research literature is too great. The chapter emphasizes the importance of promoting successful migrant role models as one of the key tools for influencing public debates and policy-making on migration and integration in Germany.

Chapter 9, by Kristof Tamas, discusses the Swedish experience with government-funded committees to discuss critically the potential opportunities, benefits, and pitfalls when attempting to bridge the gap between research and policy-making. The chapter reviews the Swedish committee system, in general, and the functioning of migration and integration committees working in the 1970s through to the 1990s, in particular. It provides a detailed discussion of a specific case of a committee—the Integration Policy Power Commission set up in 2000 to investigate integration, including discrimination issues, in Sweden—where this form of research became heavily politicized and led to a major public controversy. Tamas compares the experiences of government committees with those of two other types of research–policy interactions: think tanks—which receive funding from, for example, the private sector or various interest groups, but which might nevertheless be selectively interpreted and politicized by various political interest groups; and a more independent form of government-funded committee without direct political involvement—such as the Migration Studies Delegation (Delmi).

Tamas concludes that politics-based evidence can easily undermine the legitimacy of policy-making. This is why, Tamas argues, there is a need for more transparency in the committee system when formulating the terms of reference and selecting the researchers tasked with an enquiry. Committees need to operate at a measured distance from the government, permitted to be both critical and supportive of government policies.

Chapter 10, authored by Philip Martin, focuses on the United States. The chapter discusses examples of government-funded efforts to develop consensus among researchers on the number and impacts of migrants in the United States, including the Bi-National Commission on Mexico–US Migration and National Academy of Sciences studies released in 1997 and 2016. Martin argues that the US experience demonstrates that, even when researchers achieve consensus on the socio-economic impacts of migrants, the results can be interpreted very differently by what Martin calls *admissionists* (who favour more immigration and the legalization of unauthorized foreigners) and *restrictionists* (who oppose amnesty and want to reduce immigration). The chapter suggests that the overall effect of economic research on policy-making in the United States has been muted because migration's major economic effects are (re)distributional, with migrants and owners of capital the major winners. Martin argues that admissionists generally stress the positive net effects of migration for individual migrants, the minimal costs to US workers and other benefits of immigration ranging from preserving industries to repopulating cities and increasing diversity. In contrast, restrictionists highlight migration as a key reason, along with technology and trade, for depressing wages and hurting low-skilled Americans, increasing inequality, and reducing social trust. The chapter argues that, as the numbers of migrants have risen, the debate over migration policy has become increasingly dominated by the most extreme admissionists and restrictionists. According to Martin, researchers are also tugged towards these 'no borders' and 'no migrants' extremes by the funders who support and publicize their work. Martin argues that migration research risks joining other issues where links between funders and researchers make research findings suspect, reducing the credibility of experts and research in a wide range of fields.

Part III: International Experiences

Having discussed the links between research, public debates, and policy-making in different national contexts in Part II of the book, Part III shifts the analytical focus to research aimed at informing migration debates and policies across countries and/or at regional, supra-national levels of governance. Chapter 11, written by Elizabeth Collett, provides a critical discussion of the role of evidence in EU policy developments. It reviews the formal and informal modes of research–policy interactions at EU level that have developed since the late 2000s, and assesses the relative merits of each. The chapter concentrates particularly on the events of 2015–2018—including the so-called 'refugee crisis'—to reflect on how the relationships between data, research, and policy are changing, and what lessons might be learned for European policy-makers and researchers. Collett sees a strong correlation between how far EU institutions are actively seeking to engage with external expertise, and how far that expertise can then influence its own policy work. She suggests that proximity to policy-makers (how far experts are embedded in policy-making networks at EU or national level), reputation (the canon of expertise that researchers bring to the table), and familiarity (whether the research framing fits within the pre-existing views of policy-makers) are all factors affecting influence. The chapter also identifies an important paradox: policy-makers are, according to Collett, ready to hear from civil society and academic actors who can offer a first-hand account of policy effects, or raise issues that otherwise do not reach Brussels. At the same time, however, access to EU policy-makers is greatly advanced by regular presence in the policy-making environment, whether in Brussels or in a national capital. Researchers who are undertaking new fieldwork tend to have limited access to the policy-making environment. Thus, Collett argues, as the scope of EU interest in migration broadens to non-EU countries and the implementation of EU policy at local level, the gap between knowledge production and access to EU policy-makers is likely to broaden. The chapter thus suggests that the role of effective interlocutors who can distil information and draw relevant policy conclusions from the latest research has become ever more important.

To inform and help develop its external migration policies, the EU has funded a wide range of different research projects and cooperations. Chapter 12, by Agnieszka Weinar, discusses the experiences of one of these EU-funded projects and 'knowledge-brokers': the Consortium for Applied Research on International Migration (CARIM) Observatories at the European University Institute (EUI), funded by the European Commission between 2004 and 2013. The Observatories were given the task of building a knowledge base on migration in the southern and eastern neighbourhoods of the EU, and also in India. The chapter focuses mainly on the case of the CARIM-South and CARIM-East Observatories. It provides a critical analysis of the experiences of these two projects, to identify key insights and lessons for consideration regarding the relationship between research and policy-making in cross-country settings. Weinar discusses the Observatories in the wider context of EU policy developments and reflects on the challenges of collaborative research in a complex international environment. She reflects on the various risks that can hamper such cross-country collaborations, including the language of knowledge production and variations in research culture. The key challenge, according to

Weinar, is how to create and sustain a genuine partnership in collaborative research and research–policy communications that includes and effectively engages academics from different academic cultures, policy-makers from different institutional settings, and actors from other sectors that bring their own perspectives. She argues that effective partnerships rely on the acknowledgement of diversity, understood as linguistic, cultural, and institutional diversity that impacts on research goals, its execution, and on the policy–research dialogue. Echoing some of the arguments made by Elizabeth Collett in Chapter 11, Weinar suggests that collaborative research in such a context requires a team of knowledge translators (or brokers) that have the trust of the policy-makers and the researchers from the countries where the data collection and research is taking place.

Chapter 13, written by Howard Duncan, provides critical reflections on the experiences of the Metropolis project, including Metropolis Canada and Metropolis International. Founded in 1995 and part-funded by the Canadian government, the aim of Metropolis has been to 'enhance policy through research' by making connections between and within academic disciplines, government ministries, and civil society organizations. The chapter first discusses the workings of the Metropolis Project in Canada, with its university-based Centres of Excellence and a broad partnership of agencies of government at all levels and civil society organizations across the country, followed by an account of how it has worked—and continues to work—internationally. Duncan reviews the reasons for the various successes of Metropolis and identifies key challenges that remain. He argues, for example, that the academic reward structure that favours publication in academic journals and rarely recognizes work in support of policy has been a significant barrier discouraging participation of some researchers, especially early-career scholars. He also argues that academics working from a critical theory perspective remain largely ignored by the policy world, but those engaged in empirical and statistical studies often find a much more receptive policy audience. At the same time, Duncan argues, governments can be conservative in their range of interests and slow to embrace new fields developed by the research community. The chapter also discusses the challenges Metropolis has encountered when trying to reach countries in the Global South. Duncan suggests that this is partly because the relation between migration and cities—a long-standing focus area for Metropolis—is quite different in the North than it is in the South. The agenda of most Metropolis discussions has primarily tended to reflect the interests of the countries of the Organisation for Economic Co-operation and Development (OECD), and those are the interests of destination societies: integration and social cohesion, economic effects, demographic trends, smuggling and trafficking, and managing undocumented migration.

15

Chapter 14, written by Katy Long, discusses the role that both research and researchers have played in (re)forming the global governance of international migration, with a special focus on refugees. The chapter considers the motivations for researchers engaging in global governance reform, surveys the historical role of research in defining policy and considers some of the problems faced by researchers working in this area today. Long argues that, while research has played a vital role in identifying and systematizing the weaknesses within migration's global governance systems, research has an extremely limited ability to shape or effect reform directly, except where it fits with pre-determined political agendas. She suggests that researchers often play an important role in conferring legitimacy on processes of migration reform, as global governance 'experts'. But Long questions whether this type of engagement has much impact in shaping global agendas, rather than simply legitimizing existing political platforms. There is a clear risk, Long argues, that the experts who are invited to the table are those whose conclusions best fit the policy preferences of key policy-makers and stakeholders. Long argues for 'fewer experts and more research', precisely because the latter does not offer any 'quick fixes' to what are typically very difficult and complex policy challenges. The chapter makes the case for research that is policy-relevant without being policy-driven, calling for more innovative collaborations between researchers and policy-makers where researchers play an active role in helping design and in building policy projects. Critically, Long argues that for researchers to become policy innovators, new policy ideas must be given room for failure, which requires a major change in the way many researchers, policy-makers, and policy reviewers think about and evaluate new policy initiatives.

Part IV: Conclusions, Lessons Learnt, and the Way Forward

Chapter 15 concludes the book by identifying key insights and lessons that can be learnt from the diversity of national and international level experiences with efforts to link research to public debates and policy-making on migration and integration. The conclusion returns to the conceptual framework outlined in this introduction—focusing on three-way relationships between research, public debates, and policy-making—and highlights what we have learnt about these relationships from the different types of analyses in this book. It includes a number of recommendations for researchers, policy practitioners, and other participants in public debates (such as journalists) that are aimed at strengthening the links between them. The concluding chapter argues that, when the different actors contributing to research, public debates, and policy-making understand and appreciate each other's constraints, such common understandings can pave the way for improved policy-making processes and better public policies that deal more effectively with the real challenges of migration and integration.

Notes

1. See Deacon 2016, www.telegraph.co.uk/news/2016/06/10/michael-goves-guide-to-britains-greatest-enemy-the-experts/
2. See The Economist 2016, www.economist.com/leaders/2016/09/10/art-of-the-lie

References

Bastow, S., Dunleavy, P., and Tinkler, J. 2014. *The Impact of the Social Sciences*. London: SAGE.

Blinder, S. 2011. UK Public Opinion Toward Migration: Determinants of Attitudes. *Migration Observatory Briefing*, University of Oxford. Oxford: COMPAS.

Boswell, C. 2012. *The Political Uses of Expert Knowledge*. Cambridge: Cambridge University Press.

Boswell, C. 2018. *Manufacturing Political Trust: Targets and Performance Indicators in Public Policy*. Cambridge: Cambridge University Press.

Boswell, C., Geddes, A., and Scholten, P. 2011. The Role of Narratives in Migration Policy-making: A Research Framework. *British Journal of Politics and International Relations* 13: 1–11.

Davies, W. 2016. The Age of Post-Truth Politics www.nytimes.com/2016/08/24/opinion/campaign-stops/the-age-of-post-truth-politics.html

Deacon, M. 2016. Michael Gove's Guide to Britain's Greatest Enemy . . . the Experts www.telegraph.co.uk/news/2016/06/10/michael-goves-guide-to-britains-greatest-enemy-the-experts/

Demireva, N. 2015. Immigration, Diversity and Social Cohesion. *Migration Observatory Briefing*, July 2015, University of Oxford. Oxford COMPAS.

The Economist, 2016. Art of the Lie, www.economist.com/leaders/2016/09/10/art-of-the-lie

Graves, L., and Cherubini, F. 2016. *The Rise of Fact-Checking Sites in Europe*. Oxford: Reuters Institute for the Study of Journalism, University of Oxford.

Hampshire, J. 2013. *The Politics of Immigration: Contradictions of the Liberal State*. Cambridge Polity Press.

Martin, P., and Ruhs, M. 2011. Labor Shortages and US Immigration Reform: Promises and Perils of an Independent Commission. *International Migration Review* 45(1): 174–87.

OECD (Organisation for Economic Co-operation and Development). 2010. *Public Opinions and Immigration: Individual Attitudes, Interest Groups and the Media*. Paris: OECD.

Scholten, P., Entzinger, H., Penninx, R., and Verbeek, S. (eds). 2015. *Integrating Immigrants in Europe: Research–Policy Dialogues*. Heidelberg: Springer.

Part I
Linking Research, Public Debates, and Policy-Making

2

Research, 'Experts', and the Politics of Migration

Christina Boswell

Introduction

It has frequently been observed that immigration politics and policy-making are far from 'evidence-based' (Florence et al. 2005; Boswell 2009a; Caponio et al. 2010; Jørgensen 2011; Scholten et al. 2016). In many areas of policy—ranging from asylum and refugee policy, through to immigration control and enforcement, and immigrant integration—policies often appear to be based on somewhat simplistic, or even populist, assumptions about migration dynamics. Public political debates on immigration tend to be even less informed by expert knowledge or research, with an apparently widening gap between evidence about the dynamics and impacts of immigration, and media and political claims (Boswell 2009b; Balch and Balabanova 2011; Boswell et al. 2011; Caponio et al. 2014). Thus, while there has been huge growth in the field of migration studies since the turn of the millennium, public political debate and policies appear to be largely reactive and short-termist, often running counter to broader economic and social goals.

A classic explanation for this lack of take-up of research locates the problem in the dynamics of politics. Politicians do not base their claims on 'evidence' about the effects of immigration, as this is not a vote winner. Immigration is a famously emotive issue and, as we have seen recently with the surge in support for populist movements in many democracies, the most compelling narratives are not based on technocratic arguments about economic costs, skills shortages, or demographic trends. Instead, they are informed by more visceral concerns about identity, belonging, fairness, and entitlement (Sides and Citrin 2007; Brader et al. 2008).

However, this dismissal of the relevance of research is made too quickly. For a start, research and expertise *are* often invoked in public debates about immigration, and most ministries dealing with immigration have their own research unit or department. Governments and international organizations have spent substantial sums of money commissioning research on immigration, and constantly reaffirm the necessity of filling information gaps about the causes, dynamics, and effects of migration (Boswell 2009a). Moreover, the politicization of migration is not necessarily correlated with a decline in interest in research. Indeed, research is often mobilized as part of political contestation; and research findings themselves can become the object of controversy (Boswell 2009b; Caponio et al. 2014; Scholten et al. 2016). Thus, expertise and research are far from irrelevant to immigration policy-making and political debate; the relationship between expert knowledge and policy in this field is considerably more complex.

In my research on the political uses of knowledge, I have shown how research is highly valued by politicians and public officials involved in policy-making. It is far from irrelevant to the politics of migration.[1] However, we need to be more clear-sighted about how we understand its relevance. Research is not valued exclusively—or even predominantly—for its role in 'problem-solving'. It is not simply invoked to make adjustments to policy with the aim of achieving particular outcomes, as most accounts would hold. Indeed, this 'instrumentalist' or 'problem-solving' account offers an overly simplistic view of the value of expert knowledge. I have shown, instead, how research can have an important symbolic function.

In my work on the use of research in immigration policy (Boswell 2009a), I distinguish between two such symbolic functions. First, expert knowledge may be seen as a resource for lending credibility to particular preferences or claims—what I term the 'substantiating' function of knowledge. Politicians and officials may be keen to invoke particular research findings to bolster their arguments—a form of research as 'ammunition' (Weiss 1979). They may do so through commissioning research from their own research department or from an external source, through drawing on existing independent research, or through setting up an expert committee or commission to produce research.

Second, expert knowledge may be valued due to its providing a source of legitimacy to the organizations taking decisions—what I call the 'legitimizing' function of knowledge. In this second case, knowledge provides a signal that the actor in question—whether an individual, a committee, or an organization—is competent to make well-founded decisions, as they possess epistemic authority (Herbst 2003). Policy actors may signal this authority through hosting their own research unit, or establishing mechanisms to draw on external expertise—for example, in the form of a research network, expert group, or scientific advisor. What matters in this case is not so much the ability to invoke particular findings but, rather, the fact that policy-makers are in a position to mobilize and deploy authoritative research, implying that their decisions are sound.

When we seek to understand the role of research in immigration politics and policy-making, we need to bear this three-way distinction in mind: is research valued for its instrumental, substantiating, or legitimizing function? Each of the three different uses of knowledge is associated with somewhat different conditions. In the discussion that follows, I shall explore three sets of conditions that influence the extent to which research is used and for what purpose. These three conditions are:

- the level of contestation and political salience over the issue;
- the 'mode of settlement' (democratic or technocratic) that is seen as appropriate in political deliberation; and
- the mode through which policy-makers derive legitimacy (whether through symbolic gestures, or through outcomes).

I suggest that these factors help explain cross-national variations in patterns of knowledge utilization on immigration policy, as well as fluctuation over time and across sub-areas of immigration policy. The chapter goes on to explore how this account can help make sense of the current scepticism about expertise in debates on immigration.

Understanding the Political Uses of Expert Knowledge

Expert Knowledge and Political Contestation

A number of studies on the use of research in immigration policy have shown how political salience and political contestation can influence the extent and nature of knowledge utilization (Scholten et al. 2016). Here, political salience refers to the level of attention devoted to the issue in political debate (as measured by, for example, mass media coverage and political claims-making), as well as the importance of the issue for voters. Political contestation implies the existence of conflict over the nature of policy problems, or how best to address them through state interventions. Where both conditions are present—where an issue is seen as important to the public and is the object of competing policy claims—then we would expect political actors to be keen to mobilize resources to bolster their rival claims.

Expert knowledge is frequently one of the resources invoked by those engaged in political debate. Protagonists may be keen to deploy research findings and expert knowledge to bolster their claims. Such expert knowledge often takes the form of quantitative data, such as statistics on levels of immigration, estimates of the economic impact of migration, or projections of future migration flows. Quantitative data are often favoured due to their presumed authority: they convey objectivity, precision, and rigour, and such data are compact and portable across contexts (Espeland and Stevens 2008).

Such research utilization can be characterized as 'substantiating' research. Research findings or statistics are selectively deployed to underpin claims or preferences that are contested. Thus, political salience and a high level of contestation are likely to generate a strong demand for substantiating knowledge, providing political actors with resources to support their pre-given preferences.

This form of substantiating research use can also be identified in more technocratic policy-making settings. Civil servants may draw on research findings to reinforce the case for pursuing a particular policy, or adopting a preferred programme. Again, this is more likely to be the case where the issue is seen as politically significant, but where the preferred course of action is contested. Knowledge may be deployed in this way in wrangles between departments or ministries, or in attempts to justify particular approaches or spending decisions to the core executive.

Modes of Settlement

There is a second important condition that influences modes of knowledge utilization in political debate and policy-making: the 'mode of settlement' that is seen as appropriate for adjudicating between claims. By this, I mean the sorts of claim that are considered legitimate or authoritative in weighing up the desirability of different policy options. We can distinguish between two main modes of settlement. The first comprises what can be termed 'democratic' modes of settlement: a procedure through which contestation is legitimately resolved by deferring to the interests or preferences of voters. In this case, we could expect the views of each participant to count equally—each voter or participant in the debate is equally qualified to give their (non-expert) assessment, based on their interests or values. Such contestation is often associated with more normative debates about justice, shared values, and identity. Many areas of immigration policy meet this description: debates over multiculturalism and diversity, citizenship, or distributive aspects of asylum policy are often seen as legitimately resolved with reference to popular notions of fairness, or by invoking the national 'interest'.

The second procedure for assessing rival claims is what can be termed a 'technocratic' mode of settlement. According to this mode, expert claims have particular authority in settling contestation. This may be because the nature of the policy problems requiring resolution are viewed as highly complex and technical: decision-making is thus dependent on expert methodologies or empirical knowledge, so that the impacts of different interventions may be gauged. Indeed, as sociologists studying risk have argued, expert knowledge is more likely to be invoked in political contestation where the future implications of decisions taken now are difficult to predict. In such contexts, experts and their claims have greater weight than those of 'lay' or non-expert participants. Such modes of settlement are also associated with 'post-ideological' debates (Fischer 1990), in which the fundamental orientation of policy has already been agreed (for example, the importance of reducing unemployment or improving health care); what remains contested is the most appropriate means of achieving these goals.

In the field of immigration policy, technocratic modes of settlement are most typically associated with debates on labour migration. Here, economic and demographic analyses are often seen as having particular authority in political debate and policy-making (see also Chapter 10 in this volume). This is in contrast to more value- or interest-based issues, such as integration and diversity, which may be more appropriately resolved through democratic modes of settlement. It should be noted that the technical complexity of an issue does not determine its mode of settlement. Issues that are extremely complex may be settled through value- or interest-based debates (the UK's debate on leaving the EU being a prime example of this). The mode of settlement reflects dominant views about the legitimate basis for settling political conflict, rather than an 'objective' assessment of what types of considerations are most valid in settling the matter. Thus, for example, although the issue of managing asylum is immensely complex, in many national debates it has been discussed in terms of values and interests, with little consideration of specialized or technical knowledge about how best to reduce asylum flows.

Political debate will rarely—or, perhaps, never—be resolved exclusively by technocratic modes of settlement. Different value judgements and interests will invariably have a role in shaping preferences. Indeed, recourse to expert knowledge and statistics as a mode of settlement is often largely ritualistic. Politicians have already fixed on their preferred course of action and are deploying expert research to bolster their claims; also, their political rivals may feel equally compelled to draw on research to substantiate their counterclaims. Where this happens, expert knowledge may become discredited. Once it is clear that protagonists are selectively marshalling data to support political claims, evidence may lose its scientific authority, effectively becoming contaminated or 'politicized' (Weingart 1999) (see also Chapter 9 in this volume).

However, even if such technocratic modes of settlement are ritualistic, they still imply that expert knowledge is seen as a relevant resource in political debate. This is in contrast to democratic modes of settlement, in which expert knowledge may be seen as irrelevant, out of touch or even elitist: this will be

25

discussed more fully later on in this chapter. Thus, while political salience and political contestation imply that participants in policy debates will be seeking resources to strengthen their claims, it is not necessarily the case that expert knowledge will be seen as an appropriate resource to marshal. This will depend on the second condition: which mode of contestation is seen as appropriate for weighing up rival claims. This, in turn, may vary over time, across policy fields and across different countries.

Modes of Legitimation

Thus far, we have concentrated on how expert knowledge may be drawn on in political debate. But our third condition is more relevant to knowledge utilization in public administration: the ministries and agencies involved in elaborating and implementing immigration policy. Following literature on organizational institutionalism, I understand organizations in the public administration as preoccupied with securing legitimacy from their environments (March and Olsen 1983; DiMaggio and Powell 1991). They are keen to meet expectations about appropriate behaviour through ensuring their rhetoric and actions meet the approval of key actors on whom they are dependent for support. However, as Scott and Meyer (1991) have argued, organizations may go about seeking legitimacy in two distinct ways, depending on the type of 'sector' in which they operate.

First, where organizational outputs have tangible effects on the objects of their intervention—in other words, where policy interventions are monitored on an ongoing basis—then organizations will need to adjust their interventions to ensure they achieve the right outcomes. Thus, they will need to draw on resources to ensure the policies they adopt have the desired effects, in order to meet the expectations of voters or stakeholders. Their mode of legitimation is based on tangible outputs or outcomes. Examples of such areas may include numbers of asylum seekers or net migration figures, which are measured through reliable bureaucratic data on a regular basis. Voters are likely to reward incumbents based on how far they are able to influence these measured outcomes.

Yet, in many areas of policy the effects of organizational interventions are diffuse, difficult to measure and may not be easily attributable to particular policies. There may be limited information about social problems or dynamics, or the effects of policy interventions may only be felt in the longer-run, or be difficult to attribute (Boswell 2012). In this second type of case, organizations cannot derive legitimacy through their outputs. Instead, they fall back on rhetoric and symbolic actions to derive support (Scott and Meyer 1991; Brunsson 2002). This is what can be termed a 'symbolic' mode of legitimation.

Typical areas where this is likely to be the case include policies on immigrant integration and diversity, or on irregular migration. Policy is often symbolic in the sense of comprising cosmetic adjustments. Such gestures substitute for adjustments that achieve substantive change, given the difficulties in monitoring the effects of such interventions (Slaven and Boswell 2018).

These two different modes of legitimation are also linked to distinct patterns of knowledge utilization. As shown in previous work (Boswell 2009a), where policy outcomes are observable and attributable, policy-makers are more likely to draw on expert knowledge to adjust policy outputs. Thus, they are likely to use knowledge instrumentally, to adjust their policy interventions. By contrast, where they derive legitimacy through symbolic adjustments, they are more likely to use knowledge symbolically. Indeed, they may well deploy expertise to signal that their department or government is taking sound and well-grounded decisions—in other words, we are likely to see expert knowledge being used as a source of legitimation.

As discussed in the previous section, we should note that expert knowledge or research is not always deemed an appropriate resource for adjusting policy, or for signalling commitment to certain goals. Such resources are likely to be most relevant where the policy area is associated with a technocratic mode of settlement. And, indeed, even in bureaucratic decision-making, not all forms of expertise will be valued as authoritative. My research on the Home Office suggested that officials working in the operational wing of the Home Office often felt their practical understanding of immigration and asylum dynamics was more reliable than research studies based on small samples or more abstract theoretical presuppositions (Boswell 2009a). So, again, the mode of settlement will shape what sorts of knowledge are considered pertinent, and these may vary across issues or countries, even in more specialized decision-making venues.

Bringing these three points together, we can summarize the conditions shaping different forms of knowledge utilization.

- In public debates and policy-making, expert knowledge is most likely to be used as a resource where the issue is salient and contested.

- The degree to which expertise and evidence is seen as relevant to such debates also depends on the mode of settlement: how far expertise and research is seen as an appropriate resource for evaluating competing options.

- Knowledge utilization also depends on how policy-makers derive legitimacy. Where support is contingent on observable outputs, expert knowledge is likely to be deployed to inform policy interventions. Where support is derived from rhetoric or cosmetic adjustments, it is more likely to be marshalled to signal authority and commitment.

Immigration, Expert Knowledge, and Populism

I initially developed this theoretical approach in the 2000s, in an era when many industrialized immigration countries were keen to marshal research about the economic benefits of immigration, especially with regard to highly-skilled workers. Debates on labour migration in particular were characterized by a technocratic mode of settlement, with economic and demographic research exerting influence in framing debates and justifying policies to recruit labour migrants. Debates on immigration in many European countries and the United States appear to have shifted since then, as illustrated most strikingly by the anti-immigrant rhetoric of the UK campaign on the EU referendum and the ensuing 'Brexit' vote; the campaign and election of Donald Trump in the United States; and rising support for populist anti-immigration parties in a number of European countries, including Austria, Denmark, Finland, France, Hungary, the Netherlands, and Sweden.

One common feature of the claims-making strategies of populist anti-immigration movements is their eschewal of expertise. Populist movements mobilize support through claiming to articulate the interests of 'the people' as opposed to established institutions and elites (Taggart 1996; Canovan 1999; Mudde 2004). Frequently, their claims are targeted at a discredited ruling elite and its values: not only those seen as part of the political and economic establishment, but also the media, academics, and other experts (Canovan 1999). While populism does not necessarily imply the rejection of technocratic measures (Mudde 2004: 547), populist styles of mobilization tend to reject complex, technical arguments in favour of simple claims and spontaneous action. Unlike other ideological movements that may sideline evidence that runs counter to their claims, for populist movements, the rejection of expertise is a core part of their political identity and strategy of mobilization.

This has interesting implications for the conditions set out earlier in this chapter. On the one hand, populist parties are keen to put immigration issues at the centre of their political claims-making strategies. They tend to achieve electoral success in contexts where immigration issues are salient, and they advance policy proposals that are often highly contested by other political parties. Through their rhetoric, populist parties may also play an important role in expanding and consolidating anti-immigrant sentiment, thus increasing the salience of such issues in political debate. Thus, populist anti-immigration movements are clearly associated with the politicization of immigration issues, implying that rival political parties will be keen to marshal resources to bolster their claims about immigration.

However, populist narratives do not derive credibility from being backed up by expert knowledge; indeed, such narratives are often premised on a rejection of the methods and claims of experts. This implies that populist claims are not typically backed up with 'evidence' or specialized experience. Part of their appeal may derive precisely from their defiance of such expertise. As Michael Freeden puts it, populist claims are characterized by their simplicity and urgency, and should not be 'adulterated by reflection and deliberation' (2017: 6). Part of this is what Clarke and Newman describe as a different 'sense of time', evident in populist campaigns. While the knowledge claims underpinning conventional mainstream politics rely on expert analysis and economic forecasts, acknowledge complexity and some degree of uncertainty about the future, and factor in temporal delays to implementation, populist claims effectively efface time. They promise immediate fulfilment—a capacity to dispense with planning and negotiation, to achieve instantaneous results. And the knowledge they appeal to is often experiential, harking back to a 'celebrated and imaginary past' (Clarke and Newman 2017: 12).

This could imply that populist parties are shifting debate away from techno-cratic modes of settlement. They are the defenders par excellence of sup-posedly 'democratic' modes of settlement. They want to let 'the people' decide. Yet, moderate parties do not necessarily embrace this purely demo-cratic mode of settlement. They may continue to evoke more technocratic or expert sources to substantiate their claims. In this sense, the 'mode of settle-ment' may not be settled: there may be a co-existence of rival understandings of what constitute relevant modes of evaluating competing claims. In other words, there may be a divide between protagonists who continue to invoke expertise as relevant to deliberation on immigration policy issues, and those who see it as irrelevant. This type of fracture appears increasingly evident in public political debates across liberal democratic countries experiencing a rise in populist parties. It implies that political contestation goes beyond substan-tive claims about appropriate policies, to more radical disagreement about what constitutes legitimate and appropriate modes of settling political debate.

This is not just a challenge for public political deliberation. It also creates a number of challenges for policy-making. As I argued earlier, incumbents are likely to use research to adjust outputs where they anticipate their perfor-mance will be appraised and rewarded by voters. Yet, one of the features of populist claims-making is that it is not constrained by evidence or expert knowledge about the causes and dynamics of social problems, or about the sorts of interventions that may be effective in steering them. Thus, the populist rejection of expertise creates an awkward gap between the types of claim grounding pledges, and prevalent modes of knowledge use within the administration. Populist politics invokes varying causal stories about policy problems and responses, drawing on quite distinct sources of know-ledge (such as anecdote, public myths, or dystopian scenario-mapping). The gap is likely to be especially pronounced where populist movements offer up specific pledges, or commit themselves to precise outcomes which can be measured. Incumbents seeking to mobilize support through signalling commitment to populist goals will face substantial challenges when it comes to implementing them.

This clearly creates political risks for populist parties that achieve political power. In many ways, such movements will be more comfortable in opposition than as incumbents. Once in power, they risk being exposed as unable to deliver their simplistic and overly ambitious pledges. This creates what I have termed a 'populist gap'—a discrepancy between what opposition parties may claim, and what they can feasibly achieve once in government (Boswell 2003). Indeed, this is a well-rehearsed issue in political science studies of immigration. How populist-oriented governments manage this risk depends in part on how far they can sustain their narratives about policy problems and their government's performance to address these, in the face of contradictory evidence. Where the impacts of interventions are diffuse and difficult to measure and attribute, populist governments may evade exposure—and this may well be the case in areas such as immigration control and immigrant integration, where there is a lack of reliable data on government performance. But where their performance is subject to observation and measurement, then they may be exposed as unable to achieve their goals—as may be the case with, for example, reducing asylum or immigration inflows. In such areas, voters are likely to be disillusioned at the failure of governments to deliver. Thus, the unfeasibility—and potentially damaging effects of—populist immigration policy may be more evident in some policy areas than others, depending on how easy it is to measure policy impacts.

The gap between populist narratives and more expert and technocratic narratives also creates serious tensions in the relations between political leaders and their public administrations. Bureaucratic modes of reasoning are firmly grounded in technocratic modes of settlement, which employ a well-established repertoire of rationales, methods, and modes of appraisal. The implication is that the internal modes of constructing and responding to problems within bureaucracies will be starkly out of kilter with the narratives emanating from populist politics (Boswell and Rodrigues 2016). Where this happens, populist policy goals may simply not be translatable into meaningful courses of action for the bureaucracy.

Conclusion

This chapter has explored the conditions under which expert knowledge is deployed in political debate and policy-making. It started by distinguishing between the different ways in which research and expertise can be used: instrumental, substantiating, and legitimizing. It then set out three conditions influencing the extent and function of expert knowledge utilization in political debate and policy-making: political salience and contestation, mode of settlement, and mode of legitimation. In the second part of the chapter, I explored what this theoretical approach could tell us about the current rise in populist movements across liberal democratic countries. I suggested that while populist movements are associated with the greater salience of, and contestation over, immigration issues, they also eschew technocratic modes of settlement. Yet, rather than shift debates to wholly democratic modes of settlement, political contestation in such settings may well be characterized by second-order contestation: conflict over what types of claim constitute legitimate grounds for assessing policy options. Thus, current debates on immigration involve not only contestation about the nature of immigration dynamics and impacts and appropriate policies to address these, they also involve contestation about what sorts of knowledge or other claims are appropriate resources for settling such debates. This partly explains widespread observations about how fractious and divided polities appear to be in such settings.

Finally, I explored what the rise of populist, anti-expertise political movements implied for modes of legitimation. The eschewal of research and expert knowledge by populist movements exposes them to a number of risks once in government. It implies that their policy interventions are likely to be based on popular and often simplistic narratives about social problems, and appropriate modes of steering them. Given this, populist governments are likely to try to sustain legitimacy through rhetoric and symbolic interventions. But where the effects of their policies can be monitored and attributed, voters are likely to be disappointed in their failure to deliver. At the same time, the pronounced gap between such populist narratives, and the more technical forms of deliberation and reasoning that prevail in public administration, are likely to create acute tensions between political leaders and their civil servants.

The implication is that we are likely to see serious rifts not just in terms of claims-making in the arena of public debate, but also between different logics of deliberation in politics and public administration. The rise of populist parties does not just threaten progressive approaches to immigration policy, it also fundamentally questions the role of knowledge in public debate and policy-making, which raises serious challenges for governance.

Note

1. See Boswell (2009a) for the fullest exposition of this research. The first part of this chapter draws on the theory developed in this work.

References

Balch, A., and Balabanova, E. 2011. A system in chaos? Knowledge and sense-making on immigration policy in public debates. *Media, Culture & Society* 33(6): 885–904.

Boswell, C. 2003. *European Migration Policies in Flux. Changing Patterns of Inclusion and Exclusion*. Oxford: Blackwell.

Boswell, C. 2009a. *The Political Uses of Expert Knowledge: Immigration Policy and Social Research*. Cambridge: Cambridge University Press.

Boswell, C. 2009b. Knowledge, legitimation and the politics of risk: The functions of research in public debates on migration. *Political Studies* 57(1): 165–86.

Boswell, C. 2012. How information scarcity affects the policy agenda: Evidence from immigration policy. *Governance* 25(3): 367–89.

Boswell, C., and Rodrigues, E. 2016. Policies, politics and organisational problems: Multiple streams and the implementation of targets in UK government. *Policy & Politics* 44(4) (October): 507–24.

Boswell, C., Geddes, A., and Scholten, P. 2011. The role of narratives in migration policy-making: A research framework. *British Journal of Politics & International Relations* 13: 1–11.

Brader, T., Valentino, N. A., and Suhay, E. 2008. What triggers public opposition to immigration? Anxiety, group cues, and immigration threat. *American Journal of Political Science* 52(4): 959–78.

Brunsson, N. 2002. *The Organization of Hypocrisy: Talk, Decisions and Actions in Organizations*. Copenhagen: Abstrakt.

Canovan, M. 1999. Trust the people! Populism and the two faces of democracy. *Political Studies* 47(1): 2–16.

Caponio, T., Thränhardt, D., and Bommes, M. 2010. Italy—Migration research coming of age. In *National Paradigms of Migration Research*, eds D. Thränhardt and M. Bommes. Göttingen: Vandenhoeck & Ruprecht.

Caponio, T., Hunter, A., and Verbeek, S. 2014. (De)constructing expertise: Comparing knowledge utilization in the migrant integration 'crisis'. *Journal of Comparative Policy Analysis: Research and Practice* 17(1): 26–40.

Clarke, J., and Newman, J. 2017. 'People in this country have had enough of experts': Brexit and the paradoxes of populism. *Critical Policy Studies* 11(1): 101–16.

DiMaggio, P. J., and Powell, W. W. 1991. Introduction. In *The New Institutionalism in Organizational Analysis*, eds Walter W. Powell and Paul J. DiMaggio. Chicago: University of Chicago Press, 1–38.

Espeland, W. N., and Stevens, M. L. 2008. A sociology of quantification. *European Journal of Sociology* 49(3): 401–36.

Fischer, F. 1990. *Technocracy and the Politics of Expertise*. Newbury Park: Sage.

Florence, E., Martiniello, M., Adam, I., Balancier, P., Brans, M., Jacobs, D., Rea, A., Swyngedouw, M., and Van der Straeten, T. 2005. Social science research and public policies: The case of immigration in Belgium. *International Journal on Multicultural Societies* 7(1): 49–67.

Freeden, M. 2017. After the Brexit referendum: Revisiting populism as an ideology. *Journal of Political Ideologies* 22(1): 1–11.

Herbst, S. 2003. Political authority in a mediated age. *Theory and Society* 32(4): 481–503.

Jørgensen, M. B. 2011. Understanding the research–policy nexus in Denmark and Sweden: The field of migration and integration. *British Journal of Politics & International Relations* 13(1): 93–109.

March, J. G., and Olsen, J. P. 1983. The new institutionalism: Organizational factors in political life. *American Political Science Review* 78: 734–49.

Mudde, C. 2004. The populist zeitgeist. *Government and Opposition* 39(4): 542–63.

Scholten, P., Entzinger, H., Penninx, R., and Verbeek, S. (eds). 2016. *Research-Policy Dialogues on Migrant Integration in Europe*. Dordrecht: Springer.

Scott, W. R., and Meyer, J. W. 1991. The organization of societal sectors. In *The New Institutionalism in Organizational Analysis*, eds Walter W. Powell and Paul J. DiMaggio. Thousand Oaks, CA: Sage: 108–40.

Sides, J., and Citrin, J. 2007. European opinion about immigration: The role of identities, interests and information. *British Journal of Political Science* 37(3): 477–504.

Slaven, M., and Boswell, C. (2018). Why symbolise control? Irregular migration to the UK and symbolic policy-making in the 1960s. *Journal of Ethnic and Migration Studies*. Early online (9. April 2018).

Taggart, P. A. 1996. *The New Populism and the New Politics: New Protest Parties in Sweden in a Comparative Perspective*. London: Macmillan.

Weingart, P. 1999. Scientific expertise and political accountability: Paradoxes of science in politics. *Science and Public Policy* 26(3): 151–61.

Weiss, C. H. 1979. The Many Meanings of Research Utilization. *Public Administration Review* 39(5): 426–31.

3

Research–Policy Dialogues on Migrant Integration in Europe

The Impact of Politicization

Han Entzinger and Peter Scholten

The social sciences have played an important role in shaping public understanding of processes of immigrant integration in Europe, and often also in shaping governmental policies. The reverse, however, is also the case: policy-makers play a role in shaping the production of knowledge. Policy-makers, including politicians, may solicit the knowledge they wish to have in many ways and with differing degrees of openness. Although major differences exist between European countries in the way relations between policy and research on immigrant integration have evolved, many of these countries have witnessed a substantial increase in the body of scientifically based knowledge on immigrant integration. At the same time, in many countries public authorities seem to have become less interested in making use of the assembled knowledge. Politicians and policy-makers often use scientific research for symbolic rather than instrumental purposes (see Chapter 2 in this volume; Boswell 2009; Scholten and Timmermans 2010). Clearly, in parallel with the increasing politicization of the field, the belief in rational societal steering with the help of academic expertise has yielded to a growing cynicism about the validity of research and the credibility of researchers—a phenomenon confined neither to the field of migrant integration, nor to Europe. At the same time, researchers in academia seem progressively more disenchanted about the policy orientation of research on immigrant integration and the lack of theoretical development of this research field. They see this as an effect of the intense contacts between researchers and policy-makers that have existed in several countries.

This chapter aims to develop deeper insights into how research and policy-making in the field of migrant integration have developed over time, and how their relationship functions under the present conditions of strong politicization of the issue in Europe. We define politicization as the phenomenon whereby, in the process of decision-making, political arguments and considerations gain precedence over other arguments, particularly scientifically based arguments. The discussion in this chapter is based on a comparative research project carried out between 2011 and 2014 under the auspices of IMISCOE, the largest European network of migration research institutes.[1] The project, named Science–Society Dialogues on Migration and Integration in Europe (DIAMINT), was coordinated by the authors of this chapter at Erasmus University Rotterdam, and funded by the Volkswagen Foundation in Hannover. Seven EU member states (Austria, Denmark, Germany, Italy, the Netherlands, Poland, and the United Kingdom) plus the European Union, as such, were involved in the study, to which research teams in each of the participating countries contributed.[2]

Conceptualizing Research–Policy Dialogues

In the DIAMINT project, research–policy dialogues are defined broadly as all forms of interaction between researchers and policy-makers in the domain of immigrant integration. The term 'dialogues' reflects the reciprocal nature of research–policy relations; we are not just looking at how research is used in policy-making, but also how the policy context and the dialogues influence research in terms of size, orientation, and content. We distinguish three aspects of research–policy dialogues. First, we explore and analyze the *dialogue structures*. These are the formal and the informal arrangements that have been created or have come into existence through which knowledge itself, decisions on knowledge production, and the relevance of knowledge for policy are communicated and exchanged. Second, we look at cultures and practices of knowledge utilization in policy processes (*knowledge utilization*). Here, we take the perspective of policy-makers or the process of policy-making and analyse what role has been assigned to researchers and what function attributed to knowledge and research. Third, taking the perspective of researchers, we look at cultures of *knowledge production* in the field of migration research itself. Figure 3.1 shows the three aspects of research–policy dialogues and how these are interconnected. In the next section, we will elaborate on all three elements—and also their interrelationships—and further develop the major hypotheses that have guided us throughout the project.

Prior to the DIAMINT project, these three aspects of research–policy dialogues had been dealt with separately in the migration literature.

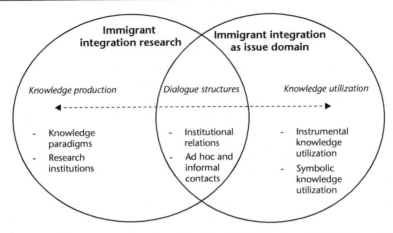

Figure 3.1 The three main aspects of research–policy dialogues and their interrelationship: the project's conceptual model

A considerable number of scholars have written on research–policy structures and their various channels of communication, such as research institutes, advisory bodies, expert committees and more informal networks (Bommes and Morawska 2005; Florence and Martiniello 2005; Geddes 2005; Penninx 2005; Thränhardt and Bommes 2010; Scholten 2011). Christina Boswell (2009, and see also Chapter 2 in this volume) has focused on knowledge utilization. The impact of policy on migration research has been treated by various other scholars, such as Favell (2003); Penninx (2005); Vasta and Vuddamalay (2006); and Thränhardt and Bommes (2010). However, the interconnections between these three aspects were not dealt with. The key objective of the DIAMINT project was to bring together these literatures and explore how the relations between these three aspects could be conceptualized and analysed empirically.

Dialogue Structures

Our first key question here is how research–policy dialogues are structured. How are dialogues organized, in what venues do they take place, what types of actors are involved, what type of knowledge is communicated, and what issues are discussed?

In the sociology of sciences and in policy sciences, a number of ideal models of research–policy structures have been defined (Hoppe 2005; Scholten 2011). The *enlightenment model* ('speaking truth to power') is perhaps the one that comes closest to the typical ideal image of the role that scientific research should have in policy-making. The enlightenment model postulates sharp boundaries between research and policy, and assumes that scientific knowledge will eventually 'creep' into the policy-making process, thus (indirectly) determining how policy-makers interpret and act upon policy problems. In contrast to the sharp boundaries of the enlightenment model, Hoppe (2005) formulates a *technocratic model* of research–policy relations, where researchers ('experts') are more directly involved in policy-making. In a technocracy, researchers do more than just provide knowledge; they also frame policy problems and develop solutions; they come much closer to taking on the role of policy-makers themselves.

Whereas both the enlightenment and the technocratic models assume that research–policy relations should be structured to give research a primary role in policy-making, alternative approaches such as the engineering model and the bureaucratic model firmly believe in the primacy of politics in policy-making. The latter two models assume that research provides input to policy-making and political decision-making, while recognizing that the outcomes of policy-making are also determined by other considerations, including values, norms, and power. In the *bureaucratic model*, research is supposed to provide data ('facts') that are required by policy-makers to develop policies and to reach decisions. This model assumes a sharp Weberian fact–value dichotomy between research and politics. The *engineering model*, by contrast, allows researchers a more far-reaching role in policy-making, while assuming, however, that politics keeps its primacy and is at liberty to select ('pick-and-choose') those strands of expertise that it sees fit.

Although these models are primarily based on the function that research and knowledge may have for policy and policy-making, they may also be used as heuristic devices for mapping differences between forms of dialogues, or even for comparing types of research–policy dialogues between countries. Several studies have already indicated that significant differences exist between countries in terms of such structures, as well as in their degrees of institutionalization. Scholten, for instance, found that the Dutch research–policy nexus was strongly institutionalized between 1980 and 1992, implying a very significant influence of research on policy-making (in the logic of the technocratic model) (Scholten 2011). The French research–policy nexus, by contrast, involved more informal and personal networks between researchers and policy-makers, with a much stronger primacy for politics (the bureaucratic model).

Knowledge Utilization

The second aspect of research–policy dialogues focuses specifically on the question of how knowledge is utilized in policy-making. As explained in her 2009 book and in Chapter 2 in this volume, Christina Boswell distinguishes between different types of practices of knowledge utilization. The most basic type involves the *instrumental* utilization of knowledge and expertise, where research outcomes are directly taken as input for policy-making. It is this type of knowledge utilization that is assumed in the notion of 'evidence-based policy-making'. In addition to the instrumental use of knowledge, Boswell distinguishes two *symbolic* types of knowledge utilization. Rather than being used as input for decision-making, knowledge can be used to provide authority to policies that have already been decided by *substantiating* these through relevant (and supportive) knowledge and expertise. Besides substantiating policy decisions, research can also be used for the plain *legitimization* of policies and policy institutions. This legitimizing function of research and expertise does not refer to substantive research findings themselves, but to the mere symbolic act of having knowledge and expertise to claim authority over a particular policy domain or policy issue.

Knowledge Production

The third aspect focuses on the relationship between knowledge production and the structures of research–policy dialogues: how does knowledge production influence such dialogues and, vice versa, how do dialogues affect migrant integration research itself? Research–policy dialogues can create opportunity structures for specific researchers, research programmes, and institutes to emerge and influence policy-making (Penninx 1988; Jasanoff 2005; Entzinger and Scholten 2014). In the longer run, however, there may also be a significant influence in the opposite direction. Strongly institutionalized relations with policy-making institutions may affect the structural characteristics of migration research as a research field; for example, the extent of consensus or fragmentation. The strongly institutionalized relationship between research and policy-making in the Netherlands and Sweden in the 1980s, for instance, provided a dominant position for specific dialogue structures and their participants—such as the Advisory Commission on Minorities Research (ACOM) and the Expert Group for Immigration Research (EIFO), respectively—and thereby created a 'consensus' in migration research in that period (Hammar 2004; Penninx 2005; see also Chapter 9 in this volume). In contrast, recent studies show that the rapid politicization of this domain has created much more diverse opportunity structures, thus facilitating the fragmentation of the migration research field (Bommes and Morawska 2005; Scholten et al. 2015).

Beyond such effects on the structure of the research field (which have received relatively little attention so far), various scholars have pointed to more substantive impacts on 'knowledge production', recognizable in methodological, theoretical, and disciplinary developments. Thränhardt and

Bommes (2010), for example, claim that research–policy dialogues have hampered the theoretical development of migration research. They argue that migration research uses the nation-state as a 'constitutive frame'. This has hampered the rise of a more critical approach to the role of the nation-state and has stressed 'the social importance' of solving integration as a problem of the nation, rather than conceptualizing and theorizing immigration and integration from a more scientific perspective (Favell 2003; Thränhardt and Bommes 2010: 30). Wimmer and Glick Schiller (2002: 301–2) refer to comparable biases in migration research, coining the term 'methodological nationalism'. In their view, 'nation-state building processes have fundamentally shaped the ways immigration has been perceived and received. These perceptions have in turn influenced social science theory and methodology and, more specifically, discourse on immigration and integration'. The strong orientation on integration within the nation-state has (co)produced specific national models of integration.

Partly as a reaction to the tendencies of migration research to confine itself within a national framing, there has been an undeniable upsurge of international comparative studies in the field of migration and integration, especially since the mid-2000s. Emerging international research networks such as IMISCOE have triggered this, but it has also been supported strongly by policies of the EU's Directorate-General Research and Innovation (for instance, through the Framework Programmes and Horizon 2020) and other EU funds (the Asylum, Migration and Integration Fund and its predecessors, as well as the European Social Fund). This new direction of research has, in turn, led to more explicit criticisms of national models of integration, and to the rise of transnationalist and post-nationalist perspectives on immigrant integration.

The Effects of Politicization: Three Hypotheses

Migrant integration has clearly evolved into a highly politicized topic throughout Europe since the early 2000s. This also has implications for research–policy dialogues (Scholten and Verbeek 2014). In the DIAMINT project, we seek to theorize the impact of politicization on research–policy dialogues, developing and examining a number of hypotheses, based on more generic literature from the sociology of sciences (Scholten et al. 2015).

Our first hypothesis is that the politicization of migrant integration would contribute to a de-institutionalization of existing research–policy dialogues. Dialogues will become less direct, more open to diverse participants and more ad hoc. By contrast, institutional relations will persist in places with a relatively low level of politicization.

Our second hypothesis focuses on knowledge utilization. While instrumental knowledge utilization involves the direct use of knowledge in policy formulation and political decision-making—as in 'evidence-based policy-making'—symbolic knowledge utilization refers to more indirect functions of knowledge for policy-makers, either to substantiate policy choices that have already been decided or to legitimize policy actors. Following Boswell's analysis of knowledge utilization in the UK, Germany, and the EU, we expect that politicization generates more symbolic forms of knowledge utilization (Boswell 2009).

The third hypothesis refers to the effect of research–policy dialogues on developments within the field of migration research itself. Trends such as the de-institutionalization of research–policy dialogues and the internationalization of academia challenge the container view of 'national models of integration', and can be expected to contribute to academic fragmentation, or diversification in terms of knowledge paradigms (see also Favell 2003; Thränhardt and Bommes 2010).

In the following sections, we assess the evidence for each of the three hypotheses on the basis of the data collected in the DIAMINT project. Each research team participating in this project collected original material through a systematic study of relevant policy documents and literature, particularly those published since the year 2000. Furthermore, in each country in-depth interviews were held with twenty to thirty stakeholders and experts. All activities were based on a commonly based research outline and used the same methodology. The research teams held regular meetings to exchange experiences and to discuss and interpret the outcomes. The remainder of this chapter gives a presentation of some of the most important findings of the project and attempts to draw parallels between the DIAMINT project and the main research questions that lie at the basis of this book (see also Table 3.1.).[3]

Changing Structures of Research–Policy Dialogues?

Our first hypothesis dealt with the relationship between the politicization of migrant integration and the de-institutionalization of research–policy dialogue structures. We have found mixed evidence when comparing the findings from the various cases. Generally speaking, we have found evidence of changes in the institutional set-up of research–policy dialogues, rather than a clear de-institutionalization of dialogue structures. Politicization appears to change, rather than impede, research–policy dialogues. Interestingly, in some cases we have found that institutionalization followed *after* a period of politicization, as in Germany and Austria.

Table 3.1 Summary of findings on the development of research–policy dialogues on migrant integration in the context of politicization[a]

	Hypothesis I De-institutionalization of research–policy dialogues	Hypothesis II More symbolic knowledge utilization	Hypothesis III Diversification of knowledge paradigms
Austria	Institutionalization follows politicization in the late 2000s	Substantiating knowledge utilization	Knowledge production has always been diverse
Denmark	Modest de-institutionalization since the 2000s	From instrumental to legitimizing knowledge utilization	Diversification of knowledge claims
Germany	Institutionalization follows politicization in the 2000s	Instrumental as well as legitimizing knowledge utilization	Knowledge production has always been diverse
Italy	Failed attempt to institutionalize in the 1990s	Substantiating knowledge utilization	Knowledge production has always been diverse
Netherlands	Change of institutional nexus from technocracy to bureaucracy	From instrumental to legitimizing knowledge utilization	Clear diversification of knowledge claims
Poland	First efforts to institutionalize dialogues in 2000s in response to EU efforts	Legitimating knowledge utilization	Dialogues promote knowledge production
United Kingdom	Periodic attempts at institutionalization tend to fail	Especially substantiating knowledge utilization	Clear diversification of knowledge claims
European Union	Institutionalization because of politicization (research as 'politics by other means')	From legitimizing to substantiating knowledge utilization	Promoting a single comparative orientation

[a] This table is adapted from Scholten and Verbeek (2014).

Only in the Netherlands, Italy, and Denmark have we found modest direct evidence in favour of the original de-institutionalization hypothesis. In the Netherlands, the strongly institutionalized technocratic research–policy nexus that had been built around the Ethnic Minorities policy was dismantled in the 1990s and 2000s, in a context of increasing politicization. However, this de-institutionalization was also spurred by developments within the research community. Furthermore, it led to a re-institutionalization of a different type of nexus, of a more bureaucratic nature, that focused not so much on conceptual research but rather on data-driven studies, carried out by the Social and Cultural Planning Office (SCP) and Netherlands Statistics (CBS), two government agencies. In Italy, attempts were made to institutionalize research–policy dialogues in the 1990s, particularly by setting up a Commission on the Integration of Migrants. Given the politicization of migration at that time, the Commission did not have a great impact and was dismantled. In

Denmark, researchers were directly involved in the genesis of policies in the 1980s and 1990s, but less so thereafter. However, as in the Dutch case, a certain re-institutionalization of research–policy dialogues also took place in Denmark, although it was different in character.

We have found that in various cases—Germany being the most prominent example—the politicization of migrant integration may have spurred the establishment of research–policy dialogues, rather than impeding them. In contrast to, for example, the Dutch case, the development of migration research in Germany followed a more autonomous path with very limited dialogue between researchers and policy-makers, especially at an institutional level. The politicization of migrant integration at the end of the 1990s and in the early 2000s provided various opportunities for researchers to become more actively engaged in policy-making and in political debate. This led to the establishment of various 'boundary organizations', such as the Council for Migration and the Expert Council for Migration and Integration (SVR) (Entzinger and Scholten 2014). The Austrian case, reflecting to some extent the German experience, even reveals evidence of efforts to institutionalize research–policy relations in the aftermath of politicization. In Austria, at the end of the 2000s, the grand coalition between the Social Democrats (SPÖ) and the People's Party (ÖVP) involved researchers and research-based commissions as well as non-governmental organizations (NGOs) and other stakeholders in formulating a National Action Plan for Integration (NAPI). At the same time, more informal dialogue structures emerged in Austria, outside institutional channels.

The more bureaucratic dialogue structure that emerged in the Netherlands in the late 1990s—with a preference for statistics-driven research oriented towards specific government policy priorities—also emerged in other countries. In Germany, the Federal Institute for Migration and Refugees (BAMF) performs a role in policy-making that is very similar to that of the Dutch SCP. They play a key role by producing data that help to legitimize national policies, promote policy learning, and monitor and identify areas for policy intervention at the national, regional, and local levels. Similarly, in Denmark the Ministry of Refugees, Immigration and Integration Affairs has developed in-house research facilities, bringing together knowledge and information that are important for policy coordination (see Bak Jørgensen 2011).

One case that clearly defies the hypothesis on politicization and de-institutionalization of research–policy dialogues is that of the EU, which is distinctive for two reasons. The first reason concerns timing: the EU entered this policy area rather late, at a moment when politicization of the issue was thriving in much of Europe. In this respect, it resembles the situation in Poland, where the emergence of a policy could not lead to any form of de-institutionalization for the simple reason that no relevant institutions had yet been set up. A second reason is that the EU's position is completely different from that of national governments. In the absence of direct competencies in the field of migrant integration, mobilizing research has proved to be one of the few strategies the EU possesses to influence policies in this domain. A selective mobilization of research has provided a tool for the soft-governance of migrant integration in a European setting (see Geddes and Scholten 2014). In particular, this has led to a number of comparative studies of migrant integration policies aiming to facilitate 'horizontal policy learning' between European countries. It has also led to more systematic efforts to measure integration policies so as to monitor compliance with EU policy frameworks (for example, the Migrant Integration Policy Index, MIPEX).

What stands out in the national cases in terms of dialogue structures is the central role of ad hoc and, often, government-sponsored commissions at critical junctures in the policy process. In Germany, Italy, the UK, and the Netherlands, such commissions were put in place in the aftermath of focusing events in order to create a temporary platform for research–policy dialogues. Such commissions, however, are often highly selective in opening up to researchers and in their knowledge claims (cf. Chapters 7 and 9 in this volume). This suggests that creating ad hoc commissions should be seen as a political reflex in the face of immediate and intractable policy controversies, rather than as an effort to engage in critical reflection based on research. Furthermore, although their public profile was often high, the policy impact of the work of these commissions was not always very direct. In fact, commissions in the UK (for example, the Community Cohesion Review Team, led by Ted Cantle), the Netherlands (the Temporary Parliamentary Investigative Commission on Integration Policy, led by Stef Blok) and, to a lesser degree, also Germany (the Commission on Immigration, led by Rita Süssmuth) show how easily the knowledge claims selected by these commissions can lead to public controversy and to contestation of the commissions' authority.

Towards a More Symbolic Knowledge Utilization?

Our comparative analysis provides strong support for the second hypothesis on the increasingly symbolic character of knowledge utilization. It shows that politicization does not impede knowledge utilization but, rather, changes its nature. All national cases show that the use of knowledge became increasingly symbolic in the 2000s. This includes forms of substantiating knowledge utilization, where research is used to support policy choices that have already been decided, as well as forms of legitimizing use, where research is used to boost the authority of specific policy actors.

Some of the cases, such as the British case in the 1950s and the Dutch case in the 1980s, do indeed show how research initially provided a direct stimulus for policy development, thus accounting for instrumental forms of knowledge utilization. This was also the case in Sweden, which, however, was not included as a case study in DIAMINT (Hammar 2004). The other countries studied do not provide such clear evidence: generally, we have found only incidental cases where individual academics may have had an impact on policy development at key moments, as did the Vesselbo report in Denmark.

Most of the cases examined reveal intriguing examples of symbolic knowledge utilization. In the originally more instrumental cases of the Netherlands and the UK, the use of knowledge claims clearly became more selective around the year 2000, aimed at substantiating policies formulated in the political arena. In the UK, for example, research was utilized (at least partly) to substantiate the Community Cohesion frame that emerged in politics after the 'mill town riots' of 2001. In the Netherlands, research–policy dialogues virtually came to a halt after a largely unforeseen rise of populism (Pim Fortuyn, and later Geert Wilders) in the 2000s, with government only selectively using outcomes of carefully commissioned research for purposes of policy monitoring. Similarly, in Austria, there is broad consensus over the selective use of knowledge, mainly driven by the development of in-house research facilities at the Ministry of the Interior. In Denmark, the state supported the Academy for Immigration Studies (AMID), thus legitimizing its policy position. However, it hardly ever drew on the findings and recommendations of AMID studies.

In some cases, politicization has also contributed to a growing contestation of research at large. This applies in particular to the case of Italy, traditionally characterized by a certain distrust of social-scientific knowledge. To some extent, it also applies to the Dutch case, where the credibility of migration scholars involved in policy-making in the 1980s and 1990s was openly put on the line in the 2000s; they were blamed for introducing a multiculturalist bias into Dutch policies. This reinforced a mode of 'articulation politics' characterized by clear political primacy, an orientation towards popular—if not populist—views and distrust, especially of research on a conceptual level (Caponio et al. 2014).

Knowledge Production: Beyond National Models of Integration

Our third hypothesis, on the diversification of knowledge claims and the rise of knowledge conflicts, finds partial support in our comparative analysis. We observe a decreasing relevance for researchers of so-called national models of integration in the various cases that have been examined. However, this seems to be related not just to politicization and changing research–policy dialogues in these national settings, but also to broader developments, such as the growing involvement of both the EU and local authorities, and the internationalization of the migrant integration research community.

Whereas research in Austria, Germany, and Italy was fragmented even before the issue had become more politicized, the Dutch and British cases show a more gradual fragmentation. Before politicization, migration scholarship in these countries was characterized by a relative consensus within their respective national contexts, leading to distinct 'national models of integration': the Dutch Ethnic Minorities model and the British Race Relations model. Following politicization, which occurred much earlier in the UK than elsewhere, these models became fragmented and contested. Both the UK and the Netherlands also reveal many instances of knowledge conflicts amongst scholars. In other countries—for example, in Germany—migration scholarship has always been more fragmented, possibly even because of the absence of an institutional relationship to policy that could have sustained a single national model of integration. However, it is fair to say that in Germany, but also in other countries—such as Austria and Italy—knowledge claims have meanwhile become even more diversified, also along disciplinary lines. The EU case, again, appears to be different, due to its recent genesis: there was simply no pre-existing unity against which a possible fragmentation could have taken place. Research initiated and supported by the EU has always had a special, comparative character.

Conclusions

Our analysis has revealed profound changes in the *dialogue structures* associated with the research–policy nexus in the domain of migrant integration, rather than a clear de-institutionalization of these dialogues, as we had initially expected. On the one hand, we have found that dialogue structures have become more ad hoc, often established in response to distinct political events or to specific problems. On the other hand, we have also found that politicization has not thwarted all efforts to develop more institutionalized structures of dialogue between producers and users of knowledge. 'Going technical' or mobilizing specific types of research should not always be seen as a tactic of depoliticization; it can also represent a strategy of 'politics by different means'.

Additionally, we have found that, in all the countries studied in the DIAMINT project, research–policy dialogues have gradually become more open. Although it is difficult to establish a clear relationship with politicization here, we can speak of a gradual evolution from 'research–policy dialogues' to broader 'science–society dialogues'. In all the countries analysed, several new actors have emerged as participants in these dialogues. In the British case, this can be illustrated by comparing the composition of three independent commissions created to advise the government at different moments since the 2000s. The membership of these commissions not only consisted of academics, but also included expert practitioners in areas such as law, health, local government, education, and journalism (Boswell and Hunter 2014). In the Netherlands, the role of 'public intellectuals' in research–policy dialogues has increased notice-ably; relevant names here are Paul Scheffer and (the late) Jaap Dronkers. From the Italian case, it becomes apparent how important (primarily faith-based) NGOs can be in providing knowledge to policy-makers. The Austrian case study documents a central role for social partners alongside the very dominant Ministry of the Interior. In Austria, NGOs have been largely excluded from research–policy dialogues. In Germany, by contrast, civil society initiatives, such as the Academies, have been very open to diverse actors, playing an important stabilizing role in research–policy dialogues on issues such as nation-ality legislation and Islam. In all cases, the DIAMINT project has shown that the media should be conceptualized both as a platform for research–policy dia-logues and as an important participant in such dialogues.

In the rational model of governance, *knowledge utilization* has traditionally been assumed as being direct and instrumental. Our analysis provides clear evidence that more symbolic forms of knowledge utilization prevail in almost all cases. Knowledge is being used primarily not in an instrumental manner but, rather, to legitimize government institutions or to substantiate govern-ment policies. Generally speaking, this has become more visible as migrant integration has been more politicized.

Finally, our analysis has revealed a sharp increase in both the quantity and diversity of *knowledge production* and knowledge dissemination over the past two to three decades in all cases examined. This makes it more complicated than in the past to identify or to construct a distinct research–policy nexus. Nowadays, many centres for knowledge production exist. This has facilitated a more selective use of knowledge claims within specific policy settings. It also signals, however, the maturing of migrant integration as a research area, in which room has developed both for more policy-oriented and for more theory-oriented schools. Migrant integration has come of age as an academic field of study.

Lessons from DIAMINT

At first glance, the volume of which this chapter is part uses an approach that is somewhat different from what we did in the DIAMINT project. Like DIAMINT, it deals with the interface between scientific research and policy-making or, as we called it, knowledge production and knowledge utilization.

This volume, however, seems to leave more space than we did for the role of public debates in affecting and shaping the dialogue. The interface in DIAMINT was defined more narrowly, since it was limited to 'dialogue structures', at least initially. As DIAMINT progressed, however, we found that this approach was too narrow. In reality, many more ways of communicating exist, both formal and informal. With the rise of migrant integration on the public and the political agenda, which has gone hand in hand with the politicization of the issue, such alternative ways have become much more apparent.

In DIAMINT, we came to the conclusion that our original approach of 'research–policy dialogues' had been broadened gradually to what we then labelled 'science-society dialogues': a diversification of methods of mutual influencing. We have noticed a clear increase in contestation of evidence-based research outcomes in the public debate. Donald Trump's presidency of the United States has familiarized us all with 'alternative facts' and 'post-truths' but, in fact, many older examples exist—also in the field of immigrant integration—of scientifically based knowledge being publicly contested, and therefore not taken seriously by politicians. There is a link between this phenomenon and the recent rise of populism in several European countries. It is not without reason that many populist movements and political parties give immigration a prominent place in their manifestoes.

In DIAMINT we also found that the media can play an effective role when the gap between researchers and policy-makers widens. They enable researchers to reach out to policy-makers and politicians, particularly when more direct opportunities for contact do not—or no longer—exist. The media also influence the public debate, a phenomenon that policy-makers are equally aware of, of course, and which they also use themselves. As a consequence, the debate on a sensitive issue such as migrant integration has broadened and no longer takes place in closed-shop settings, as was often the case in the early years of immigration. A similar role can be attributed to NGOs. DIAMINT has shown that, throughout Europe, NGOs play a much more prominent role than in the early days when it comes to providing policy advice. Sometimes, such advice is based on scientific research: NGOs also carry out research themselves, or may commission research to academic experts. Advice, however, may also be based on different considerations, such as the interests of specific communities, or political or ideological views. With the rise in prominence of migrant integration, it is only natural that such interests have gained more influence on policy-making. Facts and opinions are not always separated in the arena of the public debate; this is how democracy works. Scientists will have to live with this; however, they should never lose sight of their own responsibilities, which is to produce evidence-based facts and insights that help us understand how society really works.

Notes

1. IMISCOE began as an EU-funded Network of Excellence (2004–2009) and has continued since then as an independent consortium of research institutes in Europe, which in 2018 number forty (see www.imiscoe.org).
2. The full report of the study was published as Scholten et al. (2015).
3. All findings mentioned in the following sections can be traced back to Scholten et al. (2015), unless otherwise stated.

References

Bak Jørgensen, M. 2011. Understanding the research–policy nexus in Denmark and Sweden: The field of migration and integration. *British Journal of Politics & International Relations* 13(1): 93–109.

Bommes, M., and Morawska, E. T. 2005. *International Migration Research: Constructions, Omissions, and the Promises of Interdisciplinarity*. Aldershot: Ashgate.

Boswell, C. 2009. *The Political Uses of Expert Knowledge: Immigration Policy and Social Research*. Cambridge: Cambridge University Press.

Boswell, C., and Hunter, A. 2014. The political functions of independent commissions: Comparing UK commissions on migrant integration and cohesion. *Journal of Comparative Policy Analysis* 17(1): 10–25.

Caponio, T., Hunter, A., and Verbeek, S. 2014. (De)constructing expertise: Comparing knowledge utilisation in the migrant integration 'crisis'. *Journal of Comparative Policy Analysis* 17(1): 26–40.

Entzinger, H., and Scholten, P. 2014. The interplay of knowledge production and policymaking: A comparative analysis of research and policymaking on migrant integration in Germany and the Netherlands. *Journal of Comparative Policy Analysis* 17(1): 60–74.

Favell, A. 2003. Integration nations: The nation-state and research on immigrants in Western Europe. *Comparative Social Research* 22: 13–42.

Florence, E., and Martiniello, M. 2005. The links between academic research and public policies in the field of migration and ethnic relations: Selected national case studies—Thematic introduction. *International Journal on Multicultural Societies* 7(1): 3–10.

Geddes, A. 2005. Migration research and European integration: The construction and institutionalisation of problems of Europe. In *International Migration Research: Constructions, Omissions and Promises of Interdisciplinarity*, eds M. Bommes and E. Morawska. Aldershot: Ashgate, 265–80.

Geddes, A., and Scholten, P. 2014. Policy Analysis and Europeanization: An Analysis of EU Migrant Integration Policymaking. *Journal of Comparative Policy Analysis* 17(1): 41–59.

Hammar, T. 2004. Research and Politics in Swedish Immigration Management. In *Towards a Multilateral Migration Regime: Special Anniversary Edition Dedicated to Jonas*

Widgren, eds M. Jandl and I. Stacher. Vienna: International Centre for Migration Policy Development, 11–34.

Hoppe, R. 2005. Rethinking the Science–Policy Dialogue Structure: From Knowledge Utilization and Science Technology Studies to Types of Boundary Arrangements. *Poiesis & Praxis: International Journal of Technology Assessment and Ethics of Science* 3(3): 199–215.

Jasanoff, S. 2005. *States of Knowledge: The Co-production of Science and the Social Order*. London: Routledge.

Penninx, R. 1988. *Wie betaalt, bepaalt? De ontwikkeling en programmering van onderzoek naar migranten, etnische minderheden en woonwagenbewoners 1955–1985*. Amsterdam: SGI-reeks, Universiteit van Amsterdam.

Penninx, R. 2005. Bridges between research and policy? The case of post-war immigration and integration policies in the Netherlands. *International Journal on Multicultural Societies* 7(1): 33–48.

Scholten, P. 2011. *Framing Immigrant Integration: Dutch Research–Policy Dialogues in Comparative Perspective*. Amsterdam: Amsterdam University Press.

Scholten, P., and Timmermans, A. 2010. Setting the immigrant policy agenda: Expertise and politics in France, the UK and the Netherlands. *Journal of Comparative Policy Analysis* 12(5): 527–43.

Scholten, P., and Verbeek, S. 2014. Politicization and expertise: Changing research–policy dialogues on migrant integration in Europe. *Science and Public Policy* 42(2): 188–200.

Scholten, P., Entzinger, H., Penninx, R., and Verbeek, S. (eds). 2015. *Integrating Immigrants in Europe: Research–Policy Dialogues*. Heidelberg: Springer.

Thränhardt, D., and Bommes, M. (eds). 2010. *National Paradigms of Migration Research*. Göttingen: Vandenhoeck & Ruprecht.

Vasta, E., and Vuddamalay, V. (eds). 2006. *International Migration and the Social Sciences: Confronting National Experiences in Australia, France and Germany*. Basingstoke: Palgrave Macmillan.

Wimmer, A., and Glick Schiller, N. 2002. Methodological nationalism and beyond: National-state building, migration and the social sciences. *Global Networks* 2(4): 301–34.

4

Informing Realities

Research, Public Opinion, and Media Reports on Migration and Integration

William Allen, Scott Blinder, and Robert McNeil

Research on migration often aims to influence not only relatively specialized research communities, but also broader society including political institutions, policy processes, and media and public debates. Whether motivated by the intrinsic value of relating their work to the wider world, or prodded by shifting financial and professional incentives, academic researchers increasingly find themselves being asked to demonstrate how their work has impact beyond universities—especially when that research is publicly funded. Yet, defining and generating that impact is often elusive. Public debate and major policy decisions often seem to fly in the face of the evidence base accumulated by researchers in the academy, civil society, and even in government agencies themselves. Despite escalating pressure to produce impactful research, evidence-based public debate seems as far off as ever—particularly on the issue of immigration, where public discussion is often polarized, emotive, and based on perceptions rather than reality (Duffy 2014).

In this chapter, we explore the relationships between research and public debate, two aspects of the tripartite model proposed in the Introduction to this volume.[1] We argue that the idea of 'research impact' is often based on a naive model of one-way effects that does not reflect the multifaceted relationships between research and elements of public debate. The pathway from research evidence to public debate is not only uncertain, it is also inevitably bi-directional: media and public discussions affect research as well as being affected by it. As academics aim to have impact on public debate, they should acknowledge even further how their research—comprising the questions they ask, the methods they employ, and the modes and venues in which they present their findings—relates to the contours of public debate. Therefore, despite growing expectations that research can and should influence public debate, the implicit model of impact underlying such expectations is misleading and simplistic.

Public Debate about Migration: Media Coverage Informing Public Perceptions

For the purposes of this chapter, we view 'public debate' as referring to discussions among members of the general public that both reflect and shape attitudes toward migration and perceptions of migrants.[2] Media coverage also constitutes an aspect of these debates. This includes not only opinion pieces that directly and literally debate policy options, but also news articles that help set the terms for policy debates by shaping the way members of the public and even policy-makers think about migrants and migration.

Across many immigrant-receiving countries, members of the public tend to view migrants in negative terms, and/or express preferences for increased restrictions on immigration. For example, global surveys find that pluralities— if not outright majorities—in a variety of traditionally migrant-receiving countries favour reducing immigration, or at least keeping levels the same, although this varies along lines of age and education levels (IOM 2015). Sometimes, this preference is associated with a perception that there are simply too many migrants in the country (Transatlantic Trends 2014), or that immigrants cause problems for the economy and society (Hainmueller and Hopkins 2014). Although direct experiences with social and economic changes linked to immigration may play a role in shaping these perceptions, information gained through second-hand sources also contributes to what people think about migration (Sides and Citrin 2007). Media, notably news media and social media, are particularly visible sources of information about migration and migrants for many people. Stories, images, narratives: media coverage, whether explicitly focusing on migration or tangentially relating to the issue, provides a variety of raw materials from which people generate their own ideas and thoughts about who immigrants are and what they do (Blinder and Allen 2016).

What is the nature of these raw materials? The picture of how media cover migration is mixed. To be sure, in higher-income and traditionally 'destination' countries, media coverage of immigrants, asylum seekers, and refugees tends to be negative and focused on the threats—economic, socio-cultural, security—these groups pose towards 'host' publics (McAuliffe et al. 2015). Examples include the 'Latino Threat narrative' in the United States (Chavez 2013), casting Romanian migrants to the UK as criminals in British newspapers (Vicol and Allen 2014) and discussions about the fiscal impacts of migrant workers in European press sources (Caviedes 2015). But these kinds of portrayals are neither universally observed nor completely negative. Newspapers in New Zealand, for example, became more sympathetic towards migrants after 2000 (Spoonley and Butcher 2009), while Canadian newspapers have tended to display more positive sentiment, especially since 2004 (Lawlor 2015). One type of sympathetic coverage depicts refugees, asylum seekers, or other types of migrants as victims in need of humanitarian assistance (Thorbjørnsrud 2015), as shown in studies of media in France (Benson 2013), the Netherlands (Lecheler et al. 2015), and South Korea (Park 2014). Media in migrant-sending countries, including Vietnam, have recently produced more positive content about migrants—although, overall, coverage remains mostly negative (McAuliffe et al. 2015). Also, thanks to social media, migrants can create and promote their own content, highlighting positive and personalized aspects of their migration experiences (The Observers 2017).

Media coverage contributes to public opinion and perceptions in several ways. First, negative coverage is associated with negative attitudes toward migration. At the level of individual choice, people who read a newspaper that takes a negative line towards immigration are more likely to share that negative view. Of course, this correlation may stem, at least in part, from selection: people choose media sources that confirm their prior opinions. However, research using controlled experiments or advanced statistical techniques supports the claim that media coverage plays a part in causing these negative views as well (Abrajano and Singh 2009; Boomgaarden and Vliegenthart 2009; van Klingeren et al. 2015). Second, coverage that emphasizes particular aspects of immigration can shape public understandings of what immigration is and who immigrants are. For example, by highlighting the scale of migration in numerical terms, media may raise levels of concern by feeding into a tendency the public has to overestimate the actual sizes of minority groups and base their perceptions on this information (Herda 2010). Indeed, several studies in Europe and the United States show that members of the public become more opposed to immigration when they believe there are large numbers of migrants in their country (Strabac 2011; Hooghe and de Vroome 2015). These effects are in keeping with a well-established set of research findings on the ability of media to influence 'what people think about', known as 'agenda-setting' and 'priming' effects in the empirical literature (Iyengar and Kinder 1987; McCombs 2014).

Research, Media, and Public Perceptions: The Naïve 'Impact' Model

As set out in the Introduction, 'research' refers to a broad set of knowledge including theories, concepts, data and datasets, and empirical findings.

Research may influence public opinion and public debate in several ways. Researchers often presume or wish for a model of influence in which researchers conduct inquiries, report on their results and inject research-based evidence into public debate. We characterize this desired model of research impact as involving a simple, one-directional flow: information originating with researchers influences the public (or a specified subset, such as a targeted audience). A slightly more nuanced version acknowledges how much of the public does not consume research directly but, rather, relies on mass media for information, as discussed in the previous section. In this case, evidence-based research needs to attract media coverage in order subsequently to inform public perceptions. We represent these two pathways in Figure 4.1.

At first glance, this model resonates with some findings from studies that considered how information influences what people think. Presenting 'facts' or definitive statistics can sometimes correct prior biases or misperceptions to move them closer to reality. For example, majorities of residents in immigrant-receiving countries overestimate the number of immigrants in their country. Providing people with correct information about the foreign-born proportion of their country's population has been shown, at times, to change attitudes, generating a shift towards more favourable opinions of migration (Transatlantic Trends 2014). Further experiments in the United States indicate that this positive effect can last up to one month after encountering

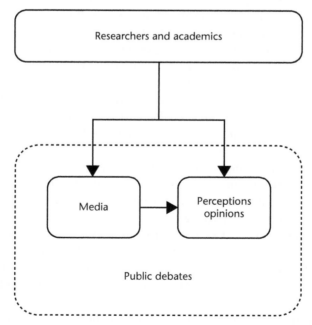

Figure 4.1 Naïve model of research impact on public debates

53

the statistical information (Grigorieff et al. 2016). This phenomenon may extend beyond numerical statements to include qualitative claims about who migrants are: in one study, British people presented with a media headline about highly-skilled migrants became less likely to think of asylum seekers and 'illegal' immigrants when thinking about who immigrates to Britain (Blinder and Jeannet 2018).

Shifts in available information—a type of 'head'-oriented intervention that prioritizes facts, numbers, and rational thinking—are not the only channel through which information is connected to public perceptions. Rather, 'heart'-oriented approaches that account for emotions and story-based techniques also matter, and, in light of motivated reasoning accounts, these may be more effective. Negative feelings, particularly anxiety, mediate the impact of media content on perceptions (Brader et al. 2008). Anxiety can create self-reinforcing feedback as well: anxious people seek out information that reinforces their pre-existing beliefs that migrants constitute a threat, adding further to their anxiety (Albertson and Gadarian 2015).

While 'head'- or 'heart'-based appeals may play a role in the effectiveness of research-based interventions in public debate, these effects are conditional on trust in the messenger. Generally, information has greater impact when coming from a source or messenger that is seen as credible (Druckman 2001). Credibility, whether curated and implicitly signalled over time as part of reputation, or explicitly claimed in a particular moment of communication, is an important heuristic by which individuals evaluate messengers (Mackiewicz 2010).

Therefore, research-based evidence will vary in its impact on public debate, depending on public views of universities (and other sources of research). For example, university researchers enjoy a relatively high degree of public trust in Britain: 81 per cent of the British public place either a fair amount or great deal of trust in academics, compared to 45 per cent who trust the UK government and 25 per cent who trust politicians (ComRes and Research Councils UK 2017). But this is not the case across all country contexts. In the United States, recent public opinion research shows a wide partisan divide in views of universities, with Republican partisans rating professors more coldly and increasingly seeing universities as a negative influence on American society (Fingerhut 2017).

Therefore, by highlighting their generally credible status, researchers may gain some traction in impacting public perceptions, especially among less ideologically motivated citizens. However, this credibility varies across countries, as well as across different segments of the public within a country. Of course, relatively high levels of credibility may not matter anyway if researchers are not prominent in migration media coverage, compared to politicians and other 'official' government representatives (Allen 2016).

Research can also contribute to public debate more subtly by delimiting the terms available for discussion. For example, public opinion surveys implicitly shape the nature of public debate by choosing which questions to ask and which topics to ignore (Lewis 2001). As a result, pollsters and survey researchers provide informative, yet inevitably selective, portraits of what 'the public' thinks about immigration, which, in turn, feeds back into public and policy debates. In the case of Britain, pollsters' and academics' survey questions have been consistently framed around quantities of migration (i.e. whether there are 'too many' migrants, or whether the number of arrivals should be reduced). This frame, in turn, soared to prominence in media coverage: recent policy debate has often focused on quantitative goals for immigration (Allen and Blinder 2018).

Furthermore, this quantitative frame for debate and policy draws on another essential form of research-based evidence: government-collected data on migration stocks and flows. Government-collected data often forms the raw material for the construction of research evidence on the economic and social impacts of migration, which, in turn, can be referenced in media stories. For example, US and UK estimates of unauthorized migrant populations are based on data on foreign-born populations from government-conducted censuses (Woodbridge 2005; Warren and Warren 2013). It is easy to miss these subtler forms of influence by focusing on the narrower—although more enticing—question of whether research influences public attitudes and media coverage. However, these forms of research and data, such as polling results, are often the basis of media reports on migration trends.

Thus, research may shape public perceptions by generating new knowledge for practitioners about audience receptivity to different approaches to the presentation of data and evidence. Provision of new information may be more effective for some audiences when packaged in narratives that appeal to emotions, or in visual ways that enable both exploration of the data and explanation of key trends or outliers (Kennedy et al. 2016; Kirk 2016). But misperceptions may also exist for mundane reasons: people may lack the time, interest, or resources to seek out relevant information independently, or to question the information they are presented with by the sources they use. Regardless of their provenance, misperceptions place public debate on shaky foundations. Therefore, providing and publicizing correct statistical information—using empirically evaluated approaches to presenting data—remains a useful pathway through which evidence can reshape public debate.

Moving Beyond a Naïve Model of Impact

However, a working model of impact that only focuses on the ways that information flows into public debates—whether through direct engagement between researchers and publics, or through mediated channels—greatly oversimplifies the realities that confront researchers. Two critiques are especially relevant here: first, the public should not be conceived as passive recipients of information, whether from researchers or media; and second, public opinion and media environments—as well as developments in the wider 'real world'—also influence the practice and communication of research.

Addressing Mutual Influence between Media and Perceptions

Media influence is not a one-way street. Public perceptions and popular opinion can also influence what kinds of media content are produced. In market-driven media systems typical of Anglo-American democracies, media organizations create 'products' that they try to sell to audiences (Croteau and Hoynes 2006). This requires a keen sense of who their audiences are, what they think and what kinds of stories will motivate customers to access whatever product is being offered—a physical newspaper, digital subscription, or other kinds of content—and, nowadays, also share it with their networks via word of mouth or social media. Content that matches audiences' pre-existing beliefs and worldviews is more likely to be seen as interesting and, as a result, purchased or shared (Winter et al. 2016). Moreover, media exist within contexts that vary widely in terms of their institutional freedom, or links with states and political parties (Hallin and Mancini 2011; Freedom House, 2017). This can be seen in media ties to political parties in the 'polarized pluralist' model typical of Southern Europe, or in media connections with major elements of civil society in the Northern European 'democratic corporatist' model (Hallin and Mancini 2004). These media systems are less market-based than the Anglo-American model, but retain feedback loops in which elements of the public can also shape media content.

Besides shaping media outputs through demand, members of the public also push back against media by resisting new information that conflicts with pre-existing political beliefs or values. Public opinion scholars call this tendency 'motivated reasoning' (Kunda 1990) or 'motivated scepticism' (Taber and Lodge 2006), and see it as one of the biggest obstacles for creating a better-informed public on migration or any other issue (Druckman 2012). The difficulty, then, is not with the existence or even the dissemination of accurate evidence; rather, it is in the lack of effect on members of the public. Someone with strongly held negative views about immigration might be unlikely to accept or trust research showing, for example, that migrants have a positive impact on the economy. Instead, the motivation to defend one's own political convictions and personal values takes priority over alternative motivations (such as a desire to hold accurate beliefs), resulting in a dismissal of counter-attitudinal evidence. As a result, in politically polarized times, people may trust research only when it confirms their political orientations—or trust in research itself may become politicized as seen in the recent March for Science in the United States (*Financial Times* 2017). Therefore, in contexts where migration is a salient issue and firmly held opinions are common, motivated reasoning would be expected to dampen the impact of evidence on public opinion and public discussion, regardless of the quality or relevance of the evidence.

How Public Debates Influence Research Outputs and Practice

Meanwhile, the relationship between the worlds of research and public debate is not unidirectional, either. For example, engagement with users can shape the kinds of questions researchers ask in the first place. On the one hand, some migration scholars express concern about the extent to which policy-makers, or any user for that matter, exert influence over the definitions, categories, and topics that researchers pursue (Bakewell 2008). In a polarized political environment around migration, and where a variety of organizations (called 'intermediaries') connect university researchers with media and other public users, there are many opportunities for evidence-generating and reporting processes to be led by popular and institutional politics. When a campaigning organization is facing a fast-moving issue of high strategic importance, it may commission research for which it already knows the conclusions (Allen 2017b). In this case, the research serves a legitimizing function that confers political benefit, rather than scientific understanding, to the body that commissioned it (see also Chapter 2 in this book). On a more routine level, existing data and research can become relevant for media when real world conditions change, as was the case with quarterly migration figures produced by the UK's Office for National Statistics. As levels of 'net migration' (the difference between the number of immigrants entering the country and those who were leaving) continued rising to record heights during 2013–2015, the British press began demanding and using these statistical packages to report on the government's performance (Allen and Blinder 2018).

On the other hand, engaging with public users may actually generate more refined understandings of problems without imposing pre-determined solutions (Spencer 2017). Researchers and users can learn from each other in processes of 'knowledge exchange' (Kitagawa and Lightowler 2013), possibly improving both the quality of the academic outputs as well as fostering trust with key stakeholder groups. These kinds of personal relationships and feelings of goodwill, notwithstanding research quality and credibility, also facilitate the successful use of evidence (Contandriopoulos et al. 2010; Ward et al. 2012).

A Multidirectional Model of Impact

Our brief survey of media coverage, public perceptions, and research on migration aimed to highlight how these elements relate to each other. Sometimes, this is exemplified through specific mechanisms such as agenda-setting, information effects, or motivated reasoning. At other times, these relationships are either more diffuse, as in assumptions which drive survey development, or event-specific. A clear implication arising from this synthesis is that 'effectively' communicating research for public impact involves much more than presenting facts and figures. Instead, it involves being aware of both the conditions and the contexts in which researchers supply information, as well as the ways that media and members of the public generate demand for certain kinds of research or data.

Critically, researchers and users of research should no longer think in terms of the simple model depicted in Figure 4.1, in which research findings simply flow downstream to the public through media or other intermediaries. This model omits reciprocal relationships and points of resistance to new information, possibly leading to misdirected effort and missed entry points where evidence may inform public debate in less direct ways. Rather than the unidirectional model, we suggest that the relationships between public debate (itself comprising links among media and public perceptions) and research look more like a complex web with potential influence between participants running in both directions, as seen in Figure 4.2. Moreover, these interrelations sit within wider social, political, and economic contexts that may favour some possibilities over others.

Research-based evidence can enter into public debate but, equally, public perceptions and the media environment create demand for certain types of evidence that shape researchers' activities. This includes which topics to investigate, and also how to design, execute, and disseminate research in order to have an 'impact' on these elements of public debate. Migration research may help set the agenda for public debate, but the public, media, and policy environments have their own agendas which exert their own force on researchers' activities. What is more, the goal of public 'impact' actually magnifies the reciprocal impact of public, media, and policy communities on research activity itself. When impact is an explicit or implicit goal, researchers must focus on topics or questions that are meaningful to broader audiences instead of, or in addition to, research communities. Data and methods must be legible to non-specialists, or at least able to be translated into more accessible forms.

Thus, successfully impacting public debate through research—whether by changing what people think about migration directly or through media coverage—involves navigating a complex world of reciprocal relationships.

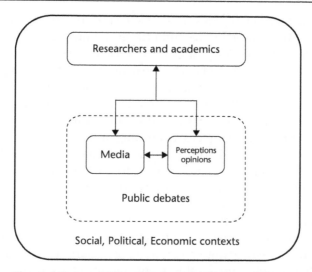

Figure 4.2 A multidirectional model of research impact

That complex world leaves open the very real possibility that, even when information can find its way into media coverage, it will encounter citizens who are inclined to seek media coverage that confirms their prior beliefs, and dismiss or discount information that challenges those beliefs.

Conclusions and Extensions

What our synthesis does not explicitly deal with are the normative questions surrounding media, public perceptions, and research. How should media cover migration issues? To what extent, and through what means, should academics seek to introduce 'correct' viewpoints about migration, its impacts, or determinants? Instead, what we have aimed to do is paint a picture of complex interrelationships—a feature that becomes more apparent when we include policy-making, as discussed in Chapter 2 in this book. Debates and concepts originating in policy, for example, can stimulate media to focus on particular aspects of migration, which, in turn, generates further public discussions. The natures and compositions of these interactions are changing, as well as the conditions in which they are occurring.

One way this is happening is evidenced by the rise of 'fake news' in popular discussion, even if the phenomenon itself is not new: producing false, or at least questionable, information to achieve political ends is a standard propaganda technique (Bernays 1947). Moreover, fraudulent assertions about migrants and minorities have been part of policy and press narratives throughout history, often as justifications for the control of human mobility (Anderson 2013). Examples range from the grotesque pictorial representation of Jews in thirteenth-century England (Menache 1985), to *The Sun*'s 2003 article 'Swan Bake', which told a fabricated story of Eastern European asylum seekers killing and eating the Queen's swans in British parks (Medic 2004). More recently, in the United States, senior Republican Party officials produced fraudulent stories in the early stages of the Trump administration, including a terrorist incident allegedly undertaken by migrants—the 'Bowling Green massacre'. This event was used both to argue that mainstream media were not properly reporting on immigration threats to the United States and to justify severe restrictions on migration to the United States from a number of Muslim majority countries (Kendzior 2017).

In this context, research potentially plays two critical roles. First, it can enable informed public debates about migration by providing a solid foundation of evidence on which both media and policy narratives can be built. 'Fake news' is actually not a single object but, rather, many objects with many purposes: from information that may unintentionally mislead, to material deliberately constructed to deceive, to ideas with which we strongly disagree (Beckett 2017). As a result, the phenomenon may be forcing people to reassess their use of media, and move back towards 'respected' and trusted media, or to fact-checking organizations and other sources of research evidence (Graves and Cherubini 2016). Second, in the digital age, research is providing new routes for wider public scrutiny of those narratives. Large-scale analysis of large amounts of text and digital content, ranging from news to tweets to forums, can reveal connections, patterns, or relationships that previously were not possible to identify (Hardaker 2010; Allen 2017a).

But, we also see that research outputs, and researchers themselves, are often under-exploited in debates about migration. Also, merely making research available does not guarantee its successful use, access, or understanding (Easton-Calabria and Allen 2015). The challenges facing those wanting to promote evidence uptake in global migration debates, such as those exemplified in this volume, are manifold. Addressing those challenges in responsible, thoughtful, and effective ways is the task ahead.

Notes

1. 'Perceptions' and 'opinions' are different: opinions refer to specific evaluations of attitude objects, while perceptions refer to more general awareness of an object and, possibly, its characteristics. In this chapter, we use both terms as indicative of 'what people think' about migration, though see Fiske and Taylor (2016) for more information.

2. Public debate can, of course, also refer explicitly to policy debate, which can take place within governmental institutions or between government officials and organizations seeking to influence policy decisions. This form of public debate is addressed in detail in Chapter 2 of this book.

References

Abrajano, M., and Singh, S. 2009. Examining the link between issue attitudes and news source: The case of Latinos and immigration reform. *Political Behavior* 31(1): 1–30. DOI: 10.1007/s11109-008-9067-8

Albertson, B., and Gadarian, S. K. 2015. *Anxious Politics: Democratic Citizenship in a Threatening World*. Cambridge: Cambridge University Press.

Allen, W. L. 2016. *A Decade of Migration in the British Press*. Migration Observatory Report. Oxford: COMPAS, University of Oxford. Available at: www.migrationobservatory.ox. ac.uk/wp-content/uploads/2016/11/Report-Decade_Immigration_British_Press-1.pdf

Allen, W. L. 2017a. Making corpus data visible: Visualising text with research intermediaries. *Corpora* 12(3): 459–82. DOI: 10.3366/cor.2017.0128

Allen, W. L. 2017b. Factors that impact how civil society intermediaries perceive evidence. *Evidence & Policy: A Journal of Research, Debate and Practice* 13(2): 183–200. DOI: 10.1332/174426416X14538259555968

Allen, W. L., and Blinder, S. 2018. Media independence through routine press–state relations: Immigration and government statistics in the British press. *The International Journal of Press/Politics* 23(2): 202–26. DOI: 10.1177/1940161218771897

Anderson, B. 2013. *Us and Them? The Dangerous Politics of Immigration Control*. Oxford: Oxford University Press.

Bakewell, O. 2008. Research beyond the categories: The importance of policy irrelevant research into forced migration. *Journal of Refugee Studies* 21(4): 432–53.

Beckett, C. 2017. 'Fake news': The best thing that's happened to journalism. In *Polis: Journalism and Society at the LSE*. Available at: http://blogs.lse.ac.uk/polis/2017/03/11/fake-news-the-best-thing-thats-happened-to-journalism/(Accessed 27 March 2017).

Benson, R. 2013. *Shaping Immigration News: A French–American Comparison*. Cambridge: Cambridge University Press.

Bernays, E. L. 1947. The engineering of consent. *The Annals of the American Academy of Political and Social Science* 250(1): 113–20.

Blinder, S., and Allen, W. L. 2016. Constructing immigrants: Portrayals of migrant groups in British national newspapers, 2010–2012. *International Migration Review* 50(1): 3–40. DOI: 10.1111/imre.12206

Blinder, S., and Jeannet, A.-M. 2018. Numbers and waves, the illegal and the skilled: The effects of media portrayals of immigrants on public opinion in Britain. *Journal of Ethnic and Migration Studies* 44(9): 1444–62.

Boomgaarden, H. G., and Vliegenthart, R. 2009. How news content influences anti-immigration attitudes: Germany, 1993–2005. *European Journal of Political Research* 48(4): 516–42. DOI: 10.1111/j.1475-6765.2009.01831.x

Brader, T., Valentino, N. A., and Suhay, E. 2008. What triggers public opposition to immigration? Anxiety, group cues, and immigration threat. *American Journal of Political Science* 52(4): 959–78. DOI: 10.1111/j.1540–5907.2008.00353.x

Caviedes, A. 2015. An emerging 'European' news portrayal of immigration? *Journal of Ethnic and Migration Studies* 41(6): 897–917. DOI: 10.1080/1369183X.2014.1002199

Chavez, L. 2013. *The Latino Threat: Constructing Immigrants, Citizens, and the Nation.* 2nd edn. Stanford: Stanford University Press.

ComRes and Research Councils UK. 2017. *Research Councils UK: Public Insight Research.* London: ComRes. Available at: www.rcuk.ac.uk/documents/publica tions/rcukpublicinsightproject-pdf/?utm_content=buffer0b1a6&utm_medium= social&utm_source=twitter.com&utm_campaign=buffer.

Contandriopoulos, D., Lemire, M., Denis, J.-L., and Tremblay, E. 2010. Knowledge exchange processes in organizations and policy arenas: A narrative systematic review of the literature. *Milbank Quarterly* 88(4): 444–83. DOI: 10.1111/ j.1468–0009.2010.00608.x

Croteau, D., and Hoynes, W. 2006. *The Business of Media: Corporate Media and the Public Interest.* Newbury Park, CA: Pine Forge Press.

Druckman, J. N. 2001. On the limits of framing effects: Who can frame? *Journal of Politics* 63(4): 1041–66. DOI: 10.1111/0022-3816.00100

Druckman, J. N. 2012. The politics of motivation. *Critical Review* 24(2): 199–216. DOI: 10.1080/08913811.2012.711022

Duffy, B. 2014. Perceptions and reality: Ten things we should know about attitudes to immigration in the UK. *Political Quarterly* 85(3): 259–66. DOI: 10.1111/1467-923X.12096

Easton-Calabria, E., and Allen, W. L. 2015. Developing ethical approaches to data and civil society: From availability to accessibility. *Innovation: The European Journal of Social Science Research* 28(1): 52–62. DOI: 10.1080/13511610.2014.985193

Financial Times. 2017. Thousands join March for Science in US cities. 22 April. Available at: http://on.ft.com/2q2jd5N

Fingerhut, H. 2017. Republicans much 'colder' than Democrats in views of professors. Available at: www.pewresearch.org/fact-tank/2017/09/13/republicans-much-colder-than-democrats-in-views-of-professors/ (Accessed 1 November 2017).

Fiske, S. T., and Taylor, S. E. 2016. *Social Cognition: From Brains to Culture.* 3rd edn. London: Sage Publications.

Freedom House. 2017. *Freedom of the Press 2017: Press Freedom's Dark Horizon.* Available at: https://freedomhouse.org/sites/default/files/FOTP_2017_booklet_FINAL_April28. pdf

Graves, L., and Cherubini, F. 2016. *The Rise of Fact-checking Sites in Europe.* Oxford: Reuters Institute for the Study of Journalism. Available at: http://reutersinstitute. politics.ox.ac.uk/sites/default/files/The%20Rise%20of%20Fact-Checking%20Sites% 20in%20Europe.pdf

Grigorieff, A., Roth, C., and Ubfal, D. 2016. Does information change attitudes towards immigration? Representative evidence from survey experiments. IZA Discussion Paper No. 10419. SSRN. Available at: https://ssrn.com/abstract=2889665.

Hainmueller, J., and Hopkins, D. J. 2014. Public attitudes toward immigration. *Annual Review of Political Science* 17(1): 225–49. DOI: 10.1146/annurev-polisci-102512-194818

Hallin, D. C., and Mancini, P. 2004. *Comparing Media Systems: Three Models of Media and Politics*. Cambridge: Cambridge University Press.

Hallin, D. C., and Mancini, P. (eds). 2011. *Comparing Media Systems beyond the Western World*. Cambridge: Cambridge University Press.

Hardaker, C. 2010. Trolling in asynchronous computer-mediated communication: From user discussions to academic definitions. *Journal of Politeness Research* 6(2): 215–42.

Herda, D. 2010. How many immigrants?: Foreign-born population innumeracy in Europe. *Public Opinion Quarterly* 74(4): 674–95.

Hooghe, M., and de Vroome, T. 2015. The perception of ethnic diversity and anti-immigrant sentiments: A multilevel analysis of local communities in Belgium. *Ethnic and Racial Studies* 38(1): 38–56. DOI: 10.1080/01419870.2013.800572

IOM. 2015. *How the World Views Migration*. Geneva, Switzerland: International Organization for Migration. Available at: http://publications.iom.int/system/files/pdf/how_the_world_gallup.pdf.

Iyengar, S., and Kinder, D. 1987. News that matters: Television and public opinion. Chicago: University of Chicago Press.

Kendzior, S. 2017. From Andijon to Bowling Green: Fabricated terrorism in Uzbekistan and the United States. *World Policy Journal* 34(1): 9–12.

Kennedy, H., Hill, R. L., Allen, W., and Kirk, A. 2016. Engaging with (big) data visualizations: Factors that affect engagement and resulting new definitions of effectiveness. *First Monday* 21(11). DOI: 10.5210/fm.v21i11.6389

Kirk, A. 2016. *Data Visualisation: A Handbook for Data Driven Design*. London: SAGE.

Kitagawa, F., and Lightowler, C. 2013. Knowledge exchange: A comparison of policies, strategies, and funding incentives in English and Scottish higher education. *Research Evaluation* 22(1): 1–14. DOI: 10.1093/reseval/rvs035

Kunda, Z. 1990. The case for motivated reasoning. *Psychological Bulletin* 108(3): 480–98.

Lawlor, A. 2015. Framing immigration in the Canadian and British news media. *Canadian Journal of Political Science—Revue Canadienne De Science Politique* 48(2): 329–55. DOI: 10.1017/S0008423915000499

Lecheler, S., Bos, L., and Vliegenthart, R. 2015. The mediating role of emotions: News framing effects on opinions about immigration. *Journalism & Mass Communication Quarterly* 92(4): 812–38.

Lewis, J. 2001. *Constructing Public Opinion: How Political Elites Do What They Like and Why We Seem to Go Along with It*. New York: Columbia University Press.

McAuliffe, M., Weeks, W., and Koser, K. 2015. *Media and Migration: Comparative Analysis of Print and Online Media Reporting on Migrants and Migration in Selected Countries (Phase II)*. Occasional Paper Series 17/2015. Belconnen, ACT: Department of Immigration and Border Protection. Available at: www.border.gov.au/ReportsandPublications/Documents/research/mcauliffe-weeks-koser.pdf

McCombs, M. E. 2014. *Setting the Agenda: The Mass Media and Public Opinion*. 2nd edn. Cambridge, UK: Polity Press.

Mackiewicz, J. 2010. The co-construction of credibility in online product reviews. *Technical Communication Quarterly* 19(4): 403–426. DOI: 10.1080/10572252.2010.502091

Medic, N. 2004. How I took on The Sun—and lost. *The Telegraph*, 15 July. London. Available at: www.telegraph.co.uk/news/uknews/1467073/How-I-took-on-The-Sun-and-lost.html

Menache, S. 1985. Faith, myth, and politics: The stereotype of the Jews and their expulsion from England and France. *The Jewish Quarterly Review* 75(4): 351–74. DOI: 10.2307/1454402

Park, K. 2014. Foreigners or multicultural citizens? Press media's construction of immigrants in South Korea. *Ethnic and Racial Studies* 37(9): 1565–86. DOI: 10.1080/01419870.2012.758860

Sides, J., and Citrin, J. 2007. European opinion about immigration: The role of identities, interests and information. *British Journal of Political Science* 37(3): 477–504. DOI: 10.1017/S0007123407000257

Spencer, S. 2017. *The Global Exchange Approach to Knowledge-exchange*. Global Exchange on Migration & Diversity Research Paper. Oxford: COMPAS, University of Oxford. Available at: www.compas.ox.ac.uk/media/GEM-approach-to-knowledge-exchange-paper-030417-1.pdf

Spoonley, P., and Butcher, A. (2009). Reporting superdiversity. The mass media and immigration in New Zealand. *Journal of Intercultural Studies* 30(4): 355–72. DOI: 10.1080/07256860903213638

Strabac, Z. 2011. It is the eyes and not the size that matters: The real and the perceived size of immigrant populations and anti-immigrant prejudice in Western Europe. *European Societies* 13(4): 559–82. DOI: 10.1080/14616696.2010.550631

Taber, C. S., and Lodge, M. 2006. Motivated skepticism in the evaluation of political beliefs. *American Journal of Political Science* 50(3): 755–69. DOI: 10.1111/j.1540-5907.2006.00214.x

The Observers. 2017. Facebook group unites Syrian refugees around recipes from home. Available at: http://observers.france24.com/en/20170602-facebook-group-uniting-syria-refugees-around-recipes-exiles-kitchen

Thorbjørnsrud, K. 2015. Framing irregular immigration in Western media. *American Behavioral Scientist* 59(7): 771–82. DOI: 10.1177/0002764215573255

Transatlantic Trends. 2014. *Transatlantic Trends: Mobility, Migration and Integration*. German Marshall Fund of the United States. Available at: http://trends.gmfus.org/files/2014/09/Trends_Immigration_2014_web.pdf (Accessed 12 March 2016).

van Klingeren, M., Boomgaarden, H. G., Vliegenthart, R., and de Vreese, C. H. 2015. Real world is not enough: The media as an additional source of negative attitudes toward immigration, comparing Denmark and the Netherlands. *European Sociological Review* 31(3): 268–83. DOI: 10.1093/esr/jcu089

Vicol, D.-O., and Allen, W. 2014. *Bulgarians and Romanians in the British National Press: 1 December 2012–1 December 2013*. Migration Observatory Report. University of Oxford: COMPAS.

Ward, V., Smith, S., House, A., and Hamer, S. 2012. Exploring knowledge exchange: A useful framework for practice and policy. *Social Science & Medicine* 74(3): 297–304. DOI: 10.1016/j.socscimed.2011.09.021

Warren, R., and Warren, J. R. 2013. Unauthorized immigration to the United States: Annual estimates and components of change, by state, 1990 to 2010. *International Migration Review* 47(2): 296–329. DOI: 10.1111/imre.12022

Winter, S., Metzger, M. J., and Flanagin, A. J. 2016. Selective use of news cues: A multiple-motive perspective on information selection in social media environments. *Journal of Communication* 66(4): 669–93. DOI: 10.1111/jcom.12241

Woodbridge, J. 2005. *Sizing the Unauthorised (Illegal) Migrant Population in the United Kingdom in 2001*. Home Office Online Report 29/05. London: Home Office.

Part II
National Experiences

5

'Independent Experts' and Immigration Policies in the UK

Lessons from the Migration Advisory Committee and the Migration Observatory

Martin Ruhs

This chapter discusses the experiences of the Migration Advisory Committee (MAC)[1] and the Migration Observatory (MigObs)[2] in providing independent analysis to inform immigration debates and policy-making in the UK. The MAC was established by the UK government in 2007 and MigObs was launched as an 'impact project' by the University of Oxford in 2009. I provide critical reflections and personal assessments based on my role as one of five members of the MAC during 2007–2014 and as the first Director of MigObs during 2009–2012.

The chapter begins with a brief overview of the changing scale, public opinion, and politics of immigration in the UK since the mid-1990s. It then discusses the origins and goals of the MAC and MigObs, their approaches and strategies, as well as effects and experiences. My assessment of the MAC and MigObs is necessarily selective and focuses on what I think have been the most important issues and experiences. I conclude with a few implications and suggestions for 'research impact initiatives' and researchers who aim to bridge the gaps between research, public debates, and policy-making on migration.

Migration to the UK: Rising Numbers, Public Opinion, and Changing Politics

The size of the foreign-born population in the UK increased from about 3.8 million (7 per cent of the population) in 1993 to over 8.7 million (13.5 per cent of the population) in 2015 (Rienzo and Vargas-Silva 2017). This rise in the number of migrants in the UK is the result of considerable increases in net migration flows (i.e. immigration minus emigration) since the mid-1990s (see Vargas-Silva and Markaki 2017). Net migration increased sharply in the late 1990s, after 2004 (the year of EU enlargement), and in 2013 (when the UK economy was recovering from economic downturn following the financial crisis that began in 2008). In 2015, annual net migration reached a record high of 332,000 but it fell sharply to 248,000 in 2016, the year when the UK voted to leave the European Union. This decrease was primarily the result of a decline in EU net migration which was the consequence of a fall in immigration and an increase in emigration of EU citizens to and from the UK (Migration Observatory 2017).

Since 2004, a large part of the growth of the number of migrants in the UK has been driven by immigration from the EU. Together with Ireland and Sweden, the UK was in a minority of EU15 countries that opened its labour markets to workers from the new member states immediately upon EU enlargement on 1 May 2004. Following this decision (and subsequent rounds of enlargement that included Romania and Bulgaria in 2007[3] and Croatia in 2013), the number of EU-born migrants in the UK tripled from about 1.2 million in 2003 to over 3.5 million in 2016. EU migrants now constitute over one-third of all foreign-born persons in the UK. Poland has recently replaced India as the most common country of birth and citizenship among the migrant population in the UK (Rienzo and Vargas-Silva 2017).

The rise in migration since the mid-1990s has been accompanied by an increase in the salience of immigration as an issue of concern to the British public (Blinder and Allen 2016). During most of the 1990s, fewer than 5 per cent of the British public considered immigration as one of the 'most important issues facing the UK'. Since the early 2000s, immigration has consistently ranked among the five most important issues. In most of 2015, immigration was the biggest issue of concern to the British public, more important than the economy and the National Health Service.[4] Notably, following the 2016 UK referendum vote to leave the UK, the salience of immigration in public opinion in the UK declined markedly. By April 2018, immigration had dropped to the fourth most important issue among the British public (Ipsos MORI 2018).

Opinion polls in recent years show that a majority of the British public would like to see immigration reduced. Over 56 per cent of respondents to the British Social Attitudes Survey 2013 said that immigration should be 'reduced a lot', while 77 per cent chose either 'reduced a lot' or 'reduced a little' (Blinder and Allen 2016). While public opinion data are not always comparable over time, the evidence suggests that public attitudes have been in favour of reductions in immigration for a long time, even when the actual number of migrants and the salience of immigration as an issue of concern were much lower than today. Since the early 1960s, a majority of the British public has said that there were 'too many immigrants' in the UK (Blinder and Allen 2016).

The rise in the scale of immigration and its salience in public opinion have been accompanied by considerable changes in the domestic politics of migration in the UK. The Labour government that came to power in the late 1990s strongly believed in the economic benefits of immigration. It implemented a number of 'managed migration' policies, such as expanding the UK's work permit programme for employing skilled non-EU workers and encouraging foreign students to enrol at British universities. The government's decision not to impose any transitional controls on the employment of A8 workers at the time of EU enlargement in May 2004 was fully in line with its goal of expanding migration to fill vacancies in skilled and, especially, in low-skilled occupations, where employers found it difficult to employ migrants legally before EU enlargement (because the work permit system focused on admitting skilled non-EU workers only).

The increase in EU immigration in the UK after enlargement in 2004 turned out much larger than the government had anticipated, fuelling a popular impression that immigration was 'out of control'. With public opinion hardening against immigration, the Labour government decided to reform its immigration policy. In 2008, the government introduced a 'points-based system', which comprised three tiers for admitting migrant workers from outside the European Economic Area (EEA). According to the UK Home Office: Tier 1 was for 'highly skilled individuals to contribute to growth and productivity'; Tier 2 for 'skilled workers with a job offer to fill gaps in the UK labour force'; and Tier 3 (which has never been opened) could facilitate the admission of 'limited numbers of low skilled workers needed to fill specific temporary labour shortages'. The UK's points-based system was designed to make policy simpler and more 'rational'. Increased selection and regulation of admission by skill, with higher-skilled migrants facing fewer restrictions than lower-skilled migrants, was at the heart of the new policy. Importantly, while the new points-based system aimed to increase the 'selectivity' of the admissions policy, it did not include a limit on the number of migrants coming to the UK.

After coming to power in May 2010, the Conservative–Liberal Democrat Coalition government, led by David Cameron, essentially maintained the structure of the existing points-based system but added an explicit annual migration target. The overriding objective of the UK's immigration policies since 2010 has been to reduce net migration to the 'tens of thousands' (i.e. to less than 100,000). The target has never been achieved but, nevertheless, remains, at the time of writing this chapter (mid 2018), at the heart of the government's immigration policies. The desire to reduce net migration to the tens of thousands was affirmed after the Conservatives won a majority in 2015 and it has remained a key goal for the current Conservative government under Theresa May. Few people believe that the target can ever be achieved, yet in early 2018 it remains a stated policy goal while Britain is negotiating its exit from the European Union. Concern about immigration has been a major factor, and some argue the most important issue, in explaining Britain's referendum vote to leave the European Union (Goodwin and Milazzo 2017).

The Migration Advisory Committee (2007–)

Aims and Rationale

Set up by the then Labour government in 2007, the MAC is an independent body[5] of five academic economists and migration experts tasked to 'provide transparent, independent and evidence-based advice to the government on migration issues'. The MAC is sponsored and funded by the UK's Home Office. The work of the MAC is supported by a secretariat comprising civil servants (researchers and policy experts) from within the UK's Home Office. Appointments to the MAC are made in line with guidance by the Office of the Commissioner for Public Appointments; that is, it is an open and competitive recruitment process. Members of the MAC are usually appointed for three years. Re-appointment is possible for another limited period of time (typically a further three years). The Committee usually meets once a month.

The establishment of the MAC was part of the process of introducing the new points-based system for regulating non-EU immigration in 2008. The MAC was set up with the specific (and narrowly defined) mandate of recommending which occupations should be on the 'shortage occupation list' within Tier 2 of the points-based system. Tier 2 (for admitting skilled migrant workers with job offers) includes three sub-channels: one admits migrants to fill jobs in 'shortage occupations' (the 'shortage occupation route'); a second admits migrants after employers try and fail to find 'local workers', including British workers or workers from other EEA countries (the 'resident labour market test route'); and a third admits 'intra-company transfers' employed by multinational companies; that is, workers who are employed by a multinational abroad and are transferred to an office of the same company in the UK.

Employers wishing to recruit migrants from outside the EU have a keen interest in their vacancies being on the shortage occupation list because there are relatively fewer obstacles to admission. Employers thus frequently lobby the government to include specific occupations on the list. Before 2007, the shortage occupation list was drawn up by civil servants. The pre-MAC process of deciding which occupations should be included and excluded from the list was once described to me as 'analytically inelegant'. The initial rationale for establishing the MAC was to make the shortage occupation list more evidence-based.

The mandate of the MAC has expanded over the years to cover a wide range of migration policy issues. Since 2007, the MAC has produced over forty reports and advised on most—although not all—major changes in UK immigration policies, including, most recently, the development of a post-Brexit immigration policy.[6] To understand why the MAC was established and why its remit expanded over time, it is important to understand two key features of the MAC's processes and work. First, the MAC only advises in response to specific questions asked by the government. The MAC normally responds to government queries within three to six months, issuing a public report (usually launched at a press conference) that lays out the questions posed by the government, the analysis, and its recommendations. The fact that the MAC cannot independently launch an inquiry with a published report and recommendations means that the government remains in control of the issues and questions analysed by the MAC.

Second, the MAC provides advice but does not directly make policy. In other words, the MAC's recommendations are non-binding, which means that the government can accept or reject the MAC's advice. The fact that the MAC's advice is public can make it hard, but not impossible, for the government to reject MAC recommendations without good reason or further evidence. Since 2007, the government has accepted the great majority of the MAC's recommendations but, as discussed further later in this chapter, not all of them.

Approach and Strategies

All of the MAC's analysis has been based on a combination of 'top-down' and 'bottom-up' approaches. Top-down analysis refers to analysis of existing large-scale data such as labour force survey data on earnings, employment, and other characteristics of the labour market. Bottom-up analysis includes consideration of qualitative data and information, as well as extensive engagement with all the relevant stakeholders including employers, trade unions, government departments, civil society, and so on. Whenever the MAC launches a new inquiry, it issues a public 'call for evidence' inviting any interested party to make written submissions. In addition to soliciting written evidence, MAC members and the secretariat also meet a large number of people and organizations including through site visits at major companies, schools, hospitals, and the like. This extensive engagement with stakeholders has been a key aspect of the work of the MAC, adding to its transparency and credibility. The MAC has always tried to avoid working and being seen as a body of experts who advise on policy without engaging the relevant affected people and organizations. In many cases, the government's questions to the MAC cannot be answered without engaging at the micro-level because relevant top-down data simply do not exist. For example, when the government asked the MAC to investigate claims about a shortage of mathematics teachers, the MAC's analysis had to rely heavily on bottom-up information as the top-down (labour force survey) data were not detailed enough to capture mathematics teachers.

A second important feature of the MAC's approach has been to be clear about subjective normative judgements that are inevitable when providing policy advice. Immigration generates uneven benefits, and migration policy-making ultimately requires a balancing of competing interests. For example, deciding whether the optimal response to labour shortage is the admission of migrant workers, higher wages, or some other option is an inherently normative and political decision. Independent expert commissions such as the MAC can make the trade-offs between these options and their consequences clearer, but they cannot, and should not, replace an explicit political debate about how to balance and prioritize competing policy objectives. The MAC's approach has thus been to highlight trade-offs and different policy options. As an advisory body, the MAC makes specific policy recommendations but they are usually based on an explicit discussion of the relevant trade-offs and normative judgements made.

Impacts and Experiences

Following its establishment by a Labour government in 2007, the MAC was retained by the subsequent Conservative–Liberal Democrat Coalition government (2010–2015) and Conservative governments (2015–). In my view, its principal benefit has been to improve the quality of policy debates on migration and related public policy issues in the UK. Not all stakeholders agree with the specific policy recommendations made by the MAC but there has generally been widespread agreement about the data and evidence presented by the MAC as part of its analysis of the questions asked by the government. On a wide range of migration policy questions, the MAC's reports and analysis have become the accepted starting point and evidence base for debate.

Another key benefit of the MAC has been to highlight and trigger debates about the important interconnections between migration and a wide range of public policies, such as labour market policies, welfare policies, education, and training policies, housing policies, enforcement policies, and so on. A key problem with immigration debates is that they are often conducted in isolation from other public policies that not only directly impact on, but can also be directly affected by, immigration. For example, in its analysis of alleged shortages of social care assistants, the MAC highlighted the important links between public funding for social care and the demand for migrant care assistants. London is one of the world's most expensive cities, and two-thirds of the caregivers in London who look after the elderly and disabled in their homes or in nursing homes were born outside the UK. Caregivers are often employed by private firms and non-governmental organizations that have contracts with the local authorities (i.e. local government) that pay for social care (Ruhs and Anderson 2010). Public underinvestment in the care sector has kept caregivers' wages low, while the desire to provide good care means that caregivers must have credentials that require training. British workers with credentials can earn more outside the publicly funded care sector, so training more British workers—a common suggestion to curb labour shortages—would not help in this case. The MAC's analysis highlighted the trade-off between taxes and caregiver wages. It concluded that care 'budgets need to be larger, or at least better targeted toward those parts of the sector suffering from labour shortage, so that those workers can be paid more'. The MAC recommended that only the highest skilled care workers be added to the shortage occupation list to avoid 'institutionalising low pay in the care sector' (Migration Advisory Committee 2009: 96).

Based on my experience as a member of the MAC during 2007–2014, I would highlight four key limitations and problems. First, the fact that the government decides the questions for MAC analysis means that there can be important questions that the MAC does not analyse for political reasons. For example, the Labour government in power until 2010 never asked the MAC to advise on limits to immigration despite the fact that the pros and cons of numerical targets were key issues in public debates on migration at the time. Similarly, subsequent Conservative-led governments were, until recently, unwilling to ask the MAC to advise on the immigration of students despite huge public controversies about whether student immigration should be restricted, and whether students should be taken out of the net migration target. In late 2017, after sustained pressure about this issue for many years, the government finally asked the MAC to advise on the impacts of international students in the UK. To be clear, the fact that the MAC cannot independently start inquiries on issues of its choosing is a limitation—but it is also a key reason why the MAC exists and has found continued political support. By choosing the questions, the government can clearly control the scope of the work and recommendations of the MAC.

A second limitation—which is not accidental—stems from the composition of the MAC in terms of the disciplinary backgrounds of its independent academic members. The MAC was conceived as a body of economists. When the MAC was established, the government also created the Migration Impacts Forum (MIF) which was meant to advise the government on social issues related to immigration (with the MAC focusing on economic concerns). However, the government did not provide the MIF with a secretariat and its work was, therefore, extremely limited. It never really got off the ground and ceased to exist after a couple of years. As a consequence, the MAC became the key advisory body dealing with a range of migration issues, primarily but not always economic in nature.

A third key issue that has affected the impacts of the MAC relates to the implementation of the MAC's recommendations. The government has formally and publicly accepted the great majority of the MAC's recommendations since the late 2000s but it has not implemented all the recommendations it accepted. At times, the government claimed that it had made policy changes that were 'in the spirit' of the MAC's recommendations without really doing at all what the MAC had recommended. To the best of my knowledge, nobody has ever analysed how and to what degree UK governments have actually implemented the numerous recommendations by the MAC that have been formally accepted. In my view, this would be an important piece of work.

Fourth, given the set-up of the MAC, and especially the government's ability to decide on the questions, there is clearly the danger that the 'independent' MAC is used to provide 'evidence' and 'objective analysis' that ends up being used to support a particular policy in a way with which the MAC would not necessarily agree. As a former member of the MAC, and speaking for myself only, I think this was the case with the MAC's inquiry and report on the minimum threshold for admitting family migrants (Migration Advisory Committee 2011). The government had asked the MAC to advise on the following question:

> What should the minimum income threshold be for sponsoring spouses/partners and dependants in order to ensure that the sponsor can support his/her spouse or civil or other partner and any dependants independently without them becoming a burden on the State? (MAC 2011: 6)

The context and motivation for this question was that the government felt that the existing minimum threshold was too low. At the time, a UK-based sponsor (UK national or foreign national with indefinite leave to remain) required a post-tax income of £105.95 per week (£5,500 per year), excluding housing costs, to apply to bring a spouse or partner into the UK. This figure was determined by the Home Office following an Immigration Appeal Tribunal ruling in 2006 that the sponsor's income must be at least equal to what the family would receive on income support.

The MAC's conclusion and recommendation was as follows:

> The MAC recognises that family migration regulations are not determined by economic factors alone. But it is an economic issue—required family income— that we have been asked to address. On this basis, the present income stipulation is too low. The MAC suggests, instead, a minimum gross income figure to support a two-adult family of between £18,600 and £25,700.   (MAC 2011: 1)

Based on the MAC's analysis and advice, the government decided to change the income threshold to £18,600. Importantly, the Home Office decided that the immigrating partner's income could not count towards the threshold (this was also made known to the MAC during its inquiry). As a consequence, a large number of British citizens (e.g. about 40 per cent of British citizens working as employees in 2015) were no longer able to sponsor a family migrant (e.g. spouse or partner) from outside the EEA. Young people and women are less likely to meet the threshold because of their relatively lower earnings in the labour market (Sumption and Vargas-Silva 2016).

Unsurprisingly, the new threshold led to a series of court cases that concluded with a Supreme Court Judgment in early 2017. As explained in more detail in Sumption and Vargas-Silva (2016), in July 2013 the High Court ruled that the family income requirement was not unlawful in itself and that the aims of the policy were legitimate. However, the whole set of requirements— including the level at which the threshold was set and the exclusion of spouses' future income—was deemed disproportionate and unlawful (High Court 2013). This decision was overturned in July 2014 by the Court of Appeal, which ruled that the Home Secretary had 'discharged the burden of demonstrating that the interference was both the minimum necessary and strikes a fair balance between the interests of the groups concerned and the community in general' (Court of Appeal 2014). The case was then heard by the Supreme Court in February 2017. The Supreme Court decided not to overturn the new income threshold.

During the various court cases, the MAC's report played an important role. The government argued that it presented an objective evidence-base that could be used to justify the new threshold. The government thus used the MAC to support its position in court cases about a new and higher threshold (which the government would have surely tried to implement with or without the MAC's advice). This example shows how the government was able— through its power to decide on the scope and wording of the question, as well as the exclusion of the partner's current or future income—to shape and influence the MAC's analysis and its impacts on debates and policies.

The Migration Observatory (2009–)

Aims and Rationale

Based at the Centre on Migration, Policy, and Society (COMPAS) at the University of Oxford, MigObs is an 'impact project' set up in 2009. It aims to provide impartial, independent, and evidence-based analysis of data on migration and migrants in the UK in order to inform media, and public and policy debates, and to generate high-quality research on international migration and public policy issues. Comprising a core team of four to six staff, the Observatory's analysis involves a large number of experts from a wide range of disciplines and departments at the University of Oxford and beyond.

The rationale for establishing MigObs was to inform debate with 'neutral' reviews of existing data and research, as well as discussions of the trade-offs associated with different policy options. With immigration rarely out of the news and high on the policy agenda, we felt that there was an opportunity and need to provide journalists, policy-makers, civil society, and the general public with an accessible 'one-stop' website with easily downloadable data, information, and analysis on migration in the UK, set in an international context. A key aim has been to enable media and participants in the UK's migration debate to use MigObs materials to make more evidence-based arguments about migration.

MigObs was initially funded by a consortium of three charitable foundations (Unbound Philanthropy, the Barrow Cadbury Trust, and the Diana, Princess of Wales Memorial Fund) that were concerned to see a less polarized debate on migration and migrants in the UK. Over the years, MigObs managed to expand and diversify its funding sources, which now include a wide range of different organizations including various academic funding bodies.

The work of COMPAS, the umbrella research centre where MigObs is based, has always included extensive public engagement activities. The establishment of MigObs was regarded by COMPAS as an additional 'impact initiative' which would further facilitate linkages between research, public debates, and policy-making. It also served the purpose of generating policy-oriented research and an 'impact case study' that could be submitted to the UK's Research Excellence Framework (REF) which plays an important role in the allocation of public funds to different universities and university departments.[7] Such research evaluations take place every four to five years.

Approach and Strategies

The recruitment and make-up of the initial core team of MigObs was an important strategic decision. The initial MigObs team included three post-doctoral researchers (two economists and one political scientist) all of whom were actively pursuing research agendas on issues related to migration and public policy. Given our aim to present migration data and research in an authoritative and credible way, we felt it was important to recruit researchers with recognized academic expertise and publications. Perhaps somewhat unusually for a project based at a university, we also recruited a senior Head of Media and Communications (a former journalist with several years of work experience in the UK and United States) and a web developer (who was with us full-time for one year, and part-time subsequently). Given the characteristics of the British media landscape, we felt it was critical to recruit an experienced media expert who could help us researchers 'navigate' the British (and international) media. The full-time web developer was needed because the MigObs website was going to be one of the principal ways of disseminating our work.

I remember sitting down with the newly recruited team in 2008 to discuss how to develop the project for launch in early 2009 (we were given a one-year development period). We faced two major challenges. First, how should we balance 'neutral', evidence-based, and potentially 'dry' presentations of the data and available research with our aims to be relevant, up-to-date, and 'interesting' to media, policy-makers, civil society, and other participants in the UK's highly polarized migration debate? Second, given the relatively small size of the core team, how could we generate data and materials that remain up-to-date and relevant to current debates?

We decided to structure the MigObs outputs and website in four sections:

- *Briefings*: Overviews of key migration issues, supported with data, analysis, and explanations of the nature of the evidence and its limitations. The MigObs website now includes in excess of forty briefings of about 3,000 words each, updated annually.

- *News and commentary*: Analysis of migration issues in the news and newsworthy elements of migration research, press releases, and a space for links to media coverage featuring the MigObs. MigObs usually publishes one or two commentaries per month.

- *Data and resources*: Key charts, maps, tables, and other data—including a facility to create your own charts based on specific datasets.

- *Policy primers*: In depth expert discussions considering the complexities, challenges, and trade-offs associated with particular migration issues. The primers included submissions from MigObs staff and other experts on migration issues from COMPAS and from other Oxford University centres and departments.

A third important decision that was taken during the early stages of the development of MigObs was to pursue a strategy of pro-active engagement with a wide range of stakeholders and potential users of MigObs materials. This included organizations and individuals who were known for their arguments in favour of and against immigration (such as the Institute for Public Policy Research, a 'left-leaning' think tank and Migration Watch, a well-known pressure group), as well as a wide range of different media outlets including tabloids, broadsheets, television, radio, and online presence.

Impacts and Experiences

Since 2009, the MigObs has become widely recognized as a major source of independent and evidence-based commentary and analysis of key migration policy issues in the UK. The Observatory's work has been heavily used and cited in senior policy circles (including by various government ministers), among a wide range of civil society organizations, as well as all major news outlets in the UK. I focus my following comments on three interrelated challenges with which MigObs has had to deal since its inception (and mainly during my time as Director in 2009–2012), relating to 'independence', 'credibility', and 'visibility'.

Somewhat predictably, but perhaps still earlier than we had expected, soon after its public launch the independence of MigObs came 'under attack' by the *Daily Mail* and Frank Field, a Labour MP, alleging a 'left-wing bias' in our work.[8] Critics asked how MigObs could be independent given that its funders were charitable organizations with a broad interest in 'improving migration debates' and helping bring about more just societies? Part of the MigObs response was to argue that, while our charitable funders did have their own normative goal and arguments, they funded MigObs specifically for the purpose of providing non-partisan analysis.[9] To the extent possible, MigObs also continued to engage proactively with organizations and people who were sceptical about its 'independence'. Over the years, claims of political or other bias in MigObs analysis have notably declined. Still, it is clear that, for some people, the characteristics of MigObs funders, together with the fact that the project is based at a university, remain reasons for questioning the neutrality of MigObs analysis and commentaries.

A second key challenge has been to establish and maintain the credibility of MigObs as an authoritative source of data and analysis in highly polarized debates and contested policy environments. Being based at Oxford University has clearly been a great help in establishing credibility in terms of the quality of MigObs research and analysis. MigObs has had access to a large number and wide range of academic researchers with considerable expertise in migration and related public policy issues. Some of the researchers who contributed to

MigObs hold strong and well-known normative and policy views. So, where briefings and analysis have been prepared by 'outside researchers', a key challenge for the editorial process has been to ensure that the presentation remains neutral and in line with the aims of MigObs. Our policy has always been that, while we respect individual researchers' personal views, all work that is part of MigObs needs to be conducted and presented in a neutral and strictly evidence-based manner.

Media and public debates often (although not always) seek out commentators with opposing viewpoints; that is, one commentator speaking in favour of immigration and the other 'against'. This can create challenges for organizations that explicitly do not 'take a line'. It can become particularly problematic when MigObs is invited to discuss migration with one other 'expert' who takes a strong view. MigObs strategy has been to avoid most of such interviews and discussions.

A third challenge relates to the aim of maintaining visibility in media and public policy debates. In the context of a highly polarized debate, organizations that focus on explaining insights and limitations of existing data and research without advocating for a particular policy position can easily find themselves crowded out by other 'experts' with stronger views, 'more clarity', and 'less uncertainty'. As a *Daily Mail* journalist once told us, 'the *Daily Mail* reader does not like uncertainty'. While this has been a challenge in the early years of MigObs, more recently it appears to have become a strength. Given the increasing polarization of the debate, there seems to be an increasing demand for commentators who present analysis (e.g. about numbers and impacts) without suggesting what the policy conclusions should be.

Conclusion

The MAC and MigObs have undoubtedly played important roles in linking data and research to public debates and policy-making on immigration in the UK. Comparing the constraints and impacts of the two organizations illustrates the obvious but important point that the 'institutional design' of an impact initiative such as MigObs, or of an expert advisory body such as the MAC, has important implications for its credibility and political acceptability, and thus long-term impacts on debates and policy-making. While national migration debates and policy-making processes differ across countries, evidence-based and transparent analytical approaches that generate public but non-binding policy recommendations are likely to be important characteristics of successful impact initiatives in a range of different countries.

It is also important to recognize and emphasize, as MAC and MigObs have done repeatedly, that it is neither feasible nor desirable to 'take the politics out' of migration debates and policies. Policy-makers sometimes present and justify expert advisory bodies in terms of their alleged function of 'de-politicizing' migration debates and policy decisions. In my view, this impression should be avoided and resisted by the experts involved whenever possible. Ultimately, all policy decisions are inherently normative, in the sense that a decision needs to be made about whose interests to prioritize and how to evaluate the inevitable trade-offs. Experts can advise and suggest policy options but they cannot, and should not, identify the one 'optimal' policy solution that, for most questions, does not exist.

Linking research to media debates and policy-making processes carries 'risks' for all sides—for the researchers, journalists, and policy-makers. Understanding and appreciating the different actors' objectives, constraints, and perceived risks is critical to constructive engagement. For researchers who wish to inform public debates and policies, this means that trying to understand the 'politics' of immigration, as well as the characteristics of policy-making processes and media debates, is of fundamental importance. As Christina Boswell, in Chapter 2, and other contributors to this book have pointed out, research and researchers can have various different 'functions' in public debates and policy-making processes, some of which may go against the researchers' personal views and motivations for engagement. This is a clear risk that, in my view, can never be avoided. More evidence and analysis can lead to better-informed migration debates and policy-making processes but this is, of course, not necessarily the same thing as 'better policies'.

Notes

1. See www.gov.uk/government/organisations/migration-advisory-committee
2. See www.migrationobservatory.ox.ac.uk
3. In contrast to its policy of granting A8 nationals immediate unrestricted access to the UK labour market in 2004, the UK government decided, in 2007, to impose transitional controls on the employment of A2 workers in the UK, primarily due to the larger than expected inflows of A8 workers during 2004–2007.
4. Until 2015, the 'most important issue' coding scheme combined 'race relations' with 'immigration' and 'immigrants'.
5. Formally, the MAC was set up as a 'non-departmental, non-time limited public body'.
6. In July 2017, the government commissioned the MAC 'to advise on the economic and social impacts of the UK's exit from the European Union and also on how the UK's immigration system should be aligned with a modern industrial strategy'.
7. See www.ref.ac.uk

8. See, for example, www.dailymail.co.uk/debate/article-2033155/QUENTIN-LETTS-Is-best-way-honour-Diana.html
9. See www.migrationobservatory.ox.ac.uk/resources/commentaries/migration-observatory-independent-and-evidence-based/ and http://www.migrationobservatory.ox.ac.uk/about/more/independence-means-us/

References

Blinder, S., and Allen, W. 2016. UK public opinion toward immigration: Overall attitudes and level of concern. Migration Observatory briefing, COMPAS, University of Oxford.

Court of Appeal. 2014. *MM & Ors, R (On the Application Of) v Secretary of State for the Home Department* (Rev 1) EWCA Civ 985, 11 July 2014.

Goodwin, M., and Milazzo, C. 2017. Taking back control? Investigating the role of immigration in the 2016 vote for Brexit. *The British Journal of Politics and International Relations* 19: 450–64.

High Court. 2013. *MM, R (On the Application Of) v The Secretary of State for the Home Department*. EWHC 1900 (Admin), 5 July 2013.

Ipsos MORI. 2018. April 2018. Ipsos MORI Issues Index. London.

Migration Advisory Committee. 2009. *Skilled, Shortage, Sensible. First Review of the Recommended Shortage Occupation Lists for the UK and Scotland: Spring 2009*. London: MAC.

Migration Advisory Committee. 2011. *Review of the Minimum Income Requirement for Sponsorship under the Family Migration Route*. London: MAC.

Migration Observatory. 2017. Brexodus? Migration and uncertainty after the EU referendum, Migration Observatory commentary, University of Oxford.

Rienzo, C., and Vargas-Silva, C. 2017. *Migrants in the UK: An overview*. Migration Observatory briefing, COMPAS, University of Oxford.

Ruhs, M., and Anderson, B. 2010. *Who Needs Migrant Workers? Labour Shortages, Immigration, and Public Policy*. Oxford: Oxford University Press.

Sumption, M., and Vargas-Silva, C. 2016. The minimum income requirement for non-EEA family members in the UK. Migration Observatory report, COMPAS, University of Oxford.

Vargas-Silva, C., and Markaki, Y. 2017. Long-term international migration flows to and from the UK. Migration Observatory briefing, COMPAS, University of Oxford.

6

The Changing Relationships between Research, Society, and Policy in the Netherlands

Reflections on the WRR 'Máxima Report'

Monique Kremer

Introduction

'Unscientific', 'political', 'naive', 'leftist', 'cosmopolitan', 'out of touch with the people', but also 'courageous'—these were among the many different, but overwhelmingly critical, reactions towards the Netherlands Scientific Council for Government Policy (*Wetenschappelijke Raad voor het Regeringsbeleid*—WRR) on the publication of its 2007 report *Identificatie met Nederland* (*Identification with the Netherlands*). In the report, the WRR, one of the Dutch government's leading scientific think tanks, advised against an immigrant integration policy that promotes 'the [Dutch] national identity' in favour of a strategy focusing on processes of identification in education, in the labour market, and in the community. The message incensed many, among them politicians, scientists, and royalists.

The heated reception of *Identification with the Netherlands* (WRR 2007)—rechristened the Máxima report after a speech by the then Crown Princess became a lightning rod for criticism—marked a turning point in the provision of scientific advice on migration and integration issues in the Netherlands. The WRR had been a key advisory body in this field since the late 1970s and, although some of its reports had sustained criticism, many went on to influence the course of subsequent policy. In the wake of the Máxima report, the status of the WRR's advice was no longer so self-evident.

This chapter considers the case of the Máxima report—not its content but its heated reception—which shows that scientifically informed policy advice must increasingly address two interrelated developments that are visible in many societal domains but are particularly pronounced in the field of migration and integration: the growing significance of public opinion and the changing relationship between science, policy, and politics. We also consider how scientists can better advise policy-makers in this new reality. But, before turning to the lessons contained in the reception of *Identification with the Netherlands*, we describe the role of the Scientific Council for Government Policy in Dutch policy-making.

The WRR and the Policy Advisory System in the Netherlands

The WRR is an independent scientific think tank subsidized by the national government. Its role is to advise—and, where necessary, criticize—the government. Established in 1975 alongside other policy assessment agencies including the Netherlands Bureau for Economic Policy Analysis (for economic issues) and the Netherlands Institute for Social Research (for social and cultural issues), the WRR operates within its own statutory framework and reports directly to the Ministry of General Affairs, the ministry headed by the prime minister.

The WRR's statutory responsibility is to 'furnish scientifically sound information on trends and developments that may influence society in the longer term. It is the Council's duty to draw timely attention to anomalies and anticipated bottlenecks and to focus on identifying problems associated with major policy issues, and to propose policy alternatives.' The WRR is independent and—unlike many think tanks in other countries—has no political affiliation. While it offers both solicited and unsolicited advice, the emphasis is on the latter. The WRR draws up its own work programme and decides which issues appear on its agenda. The act establishing the WRR also states that the government must comment on its reports. These comments are usually discussed in the House of Representatives. While the government is not required to comment on the WRR's other publications, foresight studies and policy briefs, it has in recent years done so on a growing number of occasions, in part because the media tend to report on most WRR publications.

The WRR produces its advice by combining its scientific expertise with its knowledge of policy-making. It gathers scientific evidence by asking university-based researchers to contribute to its studies by having its staff conduct academic literature and policy studies, and, in some cases, by performing statistical analyses of data provided by Statistics Netherlands, the national statistics office. Advising policy-makers based on scientific evidence is a specialized endeavour that involves building bridges between science and policy. In recent decades, the WRR has come to see its role as that of what Pielke (2003) calls the 'honest broker': a body that integrates scientific knowledge in order to arrive at policy alternatives (Den Hoed and Keizer 2007).

The WRR in the Field of Immigration

In his dissertation 'Constructing Immigrant Policies', Peter Scholten (2008) describes how the WRR, from its founding until the turn of the millennium, functioned at the intersections of science and policy. In his view, it had a 'solid reputation' (Scholten 2008: 203) in the domain of immigration and integration. In 1979, a WRR report laid the foundations for the government's subsequent minorities policy, focusing on disadvantaged minorities and emphasizing socio-economic integration *and* cultural emancipation; for example, by teaching minority languages and culture. In 1989, another WRR report, *Allochtonenbeleid* (*Immigrant Policy*), informed the transition to a new minorities policy that focused on socio-economic integration, rather than ethno-cultural origins. It introduced the term *allochtoon* (while difficult to translate precisely, this infers an 'alien' or 'foreigner') as a uniquely Dutch policy concept, referring to 'all those who have migrated to the Netherlands plus their descendants up to the third generation, insofar as the latter wish to regard themselves as non-indigenous'.

Since the turn of the millennium, the WRR's impact on policy-making in the domain of immigration and integration has dwindled. When its third report, *Nederland als immigratiesamenleving* (*The Netherlands as an Immigration Society*), appeared in 2001, it was overshadowed by the events and aftermath of the terrorist attacks in the United States on 11 September (WRR 2001). For the first time, a WRR report on integration had little influence on the direction of policy. The scientific council had seemingly gone too far by calling the Netherlands an 'immigration society'. The same period saw a motion introduced in parliament asserting that Dutch integration policy had failed. The WRR's report was criticized but otherwise largely ignored by the press and politicians.

This encouraged the WRR to embark on another project that eventually led to *Identification with the Netherlands*. The report addressed the theme of 'national identity', which was then omnipresent within public debate. To some extent, the Netherlands' concern with national identity can be traced to Paul Scheffer's essay 'Het Multiculturele Drama' (The Multicultural Drama), published in one of the country's leading newspapers in 2000. In it, Scheffer argued that a whole generation of *allochtonen* was lagging behind in the education system, as well as on the labour market. Immigrants had also brought with them values incompatible with the liberal foundations of Dutch society. 'Indifferent multiculturalism'—one that preserved minority identities rather than emphasizing integration into Dutch society—had given rise to a new social question. He concluded that if 'the Dutch' were better able to define and communicate the boundaries of their national identity—especially for their own language, history, and culture—immigrants would know better what they were integrating into.

Although scholars disagree on the extent to which the Netherlands ever truly embraced multiculturalism (Duyvendak et al. 2016), most agree that 'national identity' has become central within public debate, as well as in policy-making. For example, Dutch lawmakers in 2004 enacted legislation severely restricting dual citizenship, with prohibitions unique to the Netherlands and a few other countries. National identity was to be espoused in education through the introduction of a canon for Dutch history and through an envisioned 'museum of national identity'. Sociologists have labelled this shift from previous policy the 'culturalization of citizenship' (Duyvendak et al. 2016)—that is, citizenship becoming less a formal matter of legal rights and obligations, and more a subjective state of mind, of belonging. More concretely, it means that newcomers must prove their cultural integration into Dutch society. For instance, they must pass a mandatory language and culture test within five years lest they be fined and disqualified for permanent settlement. The test includes questions on what to do when one's neighbour has given birth to a child.

Identification with the Netherlands was critical of such rigid, ancestry-based interpretations of national identity which allow scant space for multiple identities. Emphasizing the fluidity of national identity, the report advised the government to look to the future, rather than to the past, and to adopt a more dynamic, pluralistic approach to belonging. Rather than offering a blueprint for Dutch national identity, it espoused the idea that there can be multiple routes towards identification with the Netherlands. In particular, the report distinguished between three processes of identification: emotional (feelings of belonging), normative (shared norms), and functional (when people meet not as a member of an ethnic group but rather as an individual with numerous functional relationships at work, in the community, and so on). The authors of the report further argued that functional identification could lead to emotional and normative bonding, and eventually to a new 'we'.[1]

Two Responses to the Máxima Report

In September 2007, the WRR presented *Identification with the Netherlands* to the then Minister of the Interior and Justice, Ernst Hirsch Ballin (a Christian Democrat), and Crown Princess (now Queen) Máxima, herself an *allochtoon*—she had come from Argentina to marry Crown Prince Willem Alexander. In her speech at the report's unveiling, the popular Crown Princess said that she had been searching for the Dutch identity for quite some time and had so far failed to find it. 'The typical Dutch person doesn't exist', were her words. She also made other comments: that the typical Argentinean also didn't exist; that Dutch identity could not be summed up in clichés; and that it was not a good idea, even for newcomers, to think in terms of stereotypes. But these other comments were largely ignored by the media. In her speech, which had been vetted by the responsible ministers and read by the WRR, Crown Princess Máxima focused mainly on the importance of diversity and less on the report's other message: the importance of functional identification (shared experiences such as attending school, going to work, and being active in the community) in promoting normative identification (shared values) and emotional identification (a sense of belonging). She said: 'So I find it very interesting that the title of the WRR's report is not "the Dutch identity" but "Identification with the Netherlands". That allows space for evolution. And for diversity' (Koninklijk Huis 2007).

Upon its release, the report received considerable media coverage: interviews with its main authors in the leading national (quality) newspapers and a slot on the televised evening news. While, at first, the reporting was mostly neutral, this changed quickly when *De Telegraaf*—the country's largest circulation daily newspaper billing itself as the newspaper of 'Wide-awake Netherlands'—ran an interview with Michiel Zonnevylle, the chairman of the *Oranjevereniging* (Association of Royalists). Zonnevylle was outraged by Crown Princess Máxima's statement that 'the typical Dutch person doesn't exist' as it denied there was such a thing as a Dutch identity. 'The princess is a classic example of a young, upper-class cosmopolitan who works and lives all over the world. Her description of our culture is simply not representative of the ordinary man' (*Telegraaf* 2007). It later became clear just how many people shared Zonnevylle's views, with many venting their feelings in the newspapers, on TV, and at public meetings. How dare these academics suggest that we 'Dutch' don't have an identity? Paul Scheffer, author of 'The Multicultural Drama', stated in a television interview that the Crown Princess's comments were irresponsible and implicitly rejected all those voters who valued their Dutch identity and who had voted for right-wing nationalists such as Geert Wilders and Rita Verdonk or for the Dutch Socialist Party.

The WRR was accused of being 'alienated from the world' and 'out of touch with society'—particularly with the 'majority' of society. Some people nevertheless praised the WRR for its courage. Minister of Justice Ernst Hirsch Ballin, when he accepted the report, called the WRR brave for going against the general consensus. Many later journal articles and academic treatises referred to the report as 'brave' and 'courageous'. While immigrant groups also generally welcomed *Identification with the Netherlands*, this only encouraged the perception that the WRR was out of touch with the majority of society.

Politicians also reacted to the report. The right-wing anti-Islam member of Parliament Geert Wilders denounced it as 'politically correct tittle-tattle'; the WRR was 'a club of naive people. Get rid of it.' 'The WRR has completely missed the mark,' said member of Parliament Halbe Zijlstra of the People's Party for Freedom and Democracy (VVD). 'They want to keep harping on that multicultural drivel. They're about fifteen years behind the times. In this way the WRR is gradually calling its own *raison d'être* into question' (*Volkskrant* 2007).

Zijlstra's statement represents a second prominent way in which the report was framed: as the product of politics, not of science. More specifically, it was the product of a particular kind of politics—that of 'politically correct multiculturalists'. The WRR was assigned to the camp of 'multiculti' leftists, migration advocates, problem-deniers, migrant-huggers, and bleeding-heart liberals, while the opposite camp was populated by realists, those who loved the Netherlands, who called a spade a spade and valued a firm hand. Although the authors of *Identification with the Netherlands* had addressed precisely this division and maintained that they were following a 'third way', the WRR was conflated with one side in the debate.

Some politicians were more positive about the report. The Minister of Integration and Housing, Ella Vogelaar of the Labour Party, pointed to its scientific merits; she considered *Identification with the Netherlands* 'well-researched and valuable'. Alexander Pechtold of the progressive-liberal Democrats' 66 also defended the WRR, stating that 'I was already very happy with the previous report and the tone of this one is even more to my liking. I'm a big fan of these researchers' (*Volkskrant* 2007). But, by emphasizing his appreciation of the report's tone, he also turned it into a political missive.

A few days later, the report drew sharp criticism from several well-established professors—the most effective fault-finders for a scientific council such as the WRR—commenting in the major newspapers. In his article in the national broadsheet *NRC*, sociologist Ruud Koopmans (2007) criticized the report's 'unscientific nature'; choices had been made that were not dictated by scientific motives, the report lacked empirical underpinnings and did not advance any scientific facts. Koopmans felt that it painted an all-too-frivolous picture of dual identities and asserted that there was not enough evidence that being critical of immigrants affected their behaviour. 'By allowing itself to stray from its scientific bedrock, the WRR is jeopardizing its own legitimacy and may also be eroding its credibility precisely in subject areas about which it undeniably has sensible things to say—for example, when it argues against segregation in education and in favour of banning the term *allochtoon*.' Historian Frank Ankersmit (2007) fanned the flames further. In his article 'This is politics, not science', he criticized the report for being murky in its definitions and for lacking long-term statistical analyses, insinuating that it was a pet project: 'It will not do to crown the private political opinions of a few ladies and gentlemen in the WRR with the halo of scientific dispassion. The WRR should either be scientifically respectable or throw in the towel altogether.'

Identification with the Netherlands ultimately had little direct impact on policy. Although the government came out in support of the report's main conclusions in its (compulsory) comments—that national identity should not be the overriding concept in integration policy and that dual citizenship is unrelated to loyalty—it ignored all of the report's policy recommendations. Until the present day, and in contrast to most countries of the world, dual citizenship remains problematic under Dutch law. Many politicians continue to portray Dutch citizenship as an achievement, something that is granted to an individual on the basis of successful integration (Groenendijk 2011); as Dutch nationality is a precious gift, people with other nationalities must first renounce them. Neither has much changed in the realms of education and labour market segregation. The hardening of political discourse, which the report also addressed, has only continued.

While the museum celebrating Dutch national identity never materialized, this was largely due to financial reasons and mismanagement. Funding for all sorts of ethnicity-based public participation bodies was cancelled without new forms of public participation to replace them, as the report recommended. In 2016, the WRR—this time acting in concert with the Netherlands Institute for Social Research and Statistics Netherlands, and at the explicit request of the Minister of Social Affairs (Lodewijk Asscher of the Labour Party)—suggested an alternative for the politically charged and inappropriate term *allochtoon*. The Máxima report may have, almost a decade earlier, planted the seeds for this long overdue change in terminology.

When asked on television about the critical reception of *Identification with the Netherlands*, WRR chairman Wim van de Donk replied: 'Don't worry, our head will grow back' (*Buitenhof* 2007). The WRR has often encountered pushback before; for example, against its 1989 report *Allochtonenbeleid*. It can be years before ideas and insights take hold and usher in change. Impact is never immediate, let alone quantifiable. Nevertheless, the critical response to the Máxima report, I argue, points to broader challenges in the provision of scientifically informed policy advice: the growing importance of public opinion and the changing relationship between science and policy. What do these developments mean in practice?

The Growing Weight of Public Opinion

The charge that the WRR was 'alienated from the majority of citizens' illustrates the growing importance of public opinion within political debate. While some lauded the WRR as 'courageous' for largely ignoring public opinion, others said it was 'naive' for disregarding the feelings of 'the Dutch people'. Both viewpoints share the premise that the study was not in line with (majority) feelings in society. Although the report did discuss tensions within communities, crime, uneasiness about Europeanization and globalization, and the importance of a sense of belonging for native Dutch people also, the report—and especially Crown Princess Máxima's speech—did not emphasize these dimensions.[2] To what extent was the message, indeed, not in line with 'the public'?

It is too reductionist to argue that Dutch public opinion has turned against immigrants and immigration, and that the WRR is therefore out of touch with society. There was, and still is, no overwhelming Dutch majority against immigration; neither is there any clear upward trend in negative feelings. When the report was published in 2007, a minority—40 per cent—said that the Netherlands would be a better place with fewer foreigners. This was *less* than in 2000, when more than 50 per cent said the same thing (SCP 2012). In fact, negative feelings towards immigration decreased from 2001 until the more recent arrival of refugees in the Netherlands (SCP 2016).

That said, the issue of national identity goes much deeper than opinions about immigration. Although *Identification with the Netherlands* acknowledged the importance of a sense of belonging—including for Dutch 'natives'—the WRR at the time may have underestimated the importance of feelings of national identity for many people, who interpreted the phrase 'The typical Dutch person doesn't exist' as a denial of national identity. Survey research in the ensuing years indeed revealed that the majority of the Dutch population (52 per cent) said that the Netherlands' open borders were 'placing Dutch national identity at risk' (SCP 2012). National surveys in the ensuing years confirmed national identity to be among citizens' major worries (SCP 2015).

This suggests that scientifically informed policy advice must be more aware of deeper public worries and emotions, without of course being captured by public opinion. It is also important to relate to various 'publics' (plural). The populist politician Geert Wilders often states that he represents the average Dutchman—'Henk and Ingrid' who are fed up with immigration. Although 'Henk and Ingrid' do exist, so do many other citizens who are less vocal in their opinions. The opinions and feelings of the Dutch population do not fall into two oppositional 'black and white' camps. This can be seen in more recent surveys of public opinion (SCP 2016) concerning the arrival of refugees, where a small minority was explicitly and unconditionally in favour of welcoming refugees, a small minority was explicitly against this, and the majority held much more nuanced views (SCP 2016). All this suggests that criticisms of 'not being in touch with society' build on the mistaken premise that there is such a thing as a singular 'public opinion'.

Nevertheless, to be effective, scientifically informed policy advice must be aware of attitudes and feelings across the host society. When *Identification in the Netherlands* was written in the mid-2000s, there was only fragmented scientific data about native Dutch citizens' feelings towards immigrants and immigration—an important gap in our knowledge. More recently, there has been much more scientific attention to analysing and explaining citizen discontent (e.g. for the USA, Hochschild 2016; for the UK, Goodhart 2017; for the Netherlands, Sniderman and Hagendoorn 2007; Van der Waal and Houtman 2011; Van der Waal et al. 2017; see also: Larsen 2013)—a trend that will most likely intensify in the wake of Brexit and President Trump's election. In addition, we also need to know more about the feelings of first- and second-generation immigrants, who should also be considered as part of the host society.

The criticism that the WRR is 'out of touch with society' does not acknowledge the diversity and the roots of opinions, feelings, and interests in the country. 'Society' or 'the public' consists of groups with different, often ambiguous feelings towards issues surrounding immigration and national identity. Acknowledging this is crucial since 'publics' are increasingly important audiences of scientifically informed policy advice, especially as immigration policy becomes politicized—the subject of the next section.

Changing Relationships between Policy, Politics, and Science

A prominent response to *Identification in the Netherlands* was that 'science has gone political'—a slogan that captures the changing relationships between policy, politics, and science. Peter Scholten (2008)—who, in his dissertation, examined the evolution of the relationship between policy and science in the Netherlands—argues that a 'technocratic symbiosis' held sway in the 1970s, with academic researchers deeply involved in and influential in policy-making, especially through their relationships with bureaucrats. The 1979 WRR report, in which the WRR worked closely with the Institute for Migration and Ethnic Studies at the University of Amsterdam, directly informed the government's subsequent minorities policy. In the 1980s, a new 'enlightenment model' emerged in which researchers often advocated 'paradigm shifts' to existing policy; here, a report was deemed successful if the government initially distanced itself from it. The year 2000 saw the dawn of a new phase of political primacy; under what Scholten terms the 'engineering model', the role of research was now to support politics. Put more negatively, politicians can shop around for truths that suit their views (Den Hoed and Keizer 2007). One could argue that the WRR was naive in its belief that, with the Máxima report, one could still press for a paradigm shift as in the 1990s—hence its conclusion: from national identity to pathways of identification. The WRR may have been insufficiently aware that times had changed; presenting an alternative view was now more easily considered as being political—that is, not being neutral.

This was certainly the case in the highly politicized domain of immigration and integration. Since the rise of Pim Fortuyn in the first years of this century, anti-Islam and anti-immigration politicians have dominated political discourse. Although they never broke through at the ballot box—Pim Fortuyn's LPF party won 17 per cent of the vote in 2002 and Geert Wilder's PVV 13 per cent in 2017—other political parties, in particular the VVD (the right-wing liberal party, now the biggest political party in the Netherlands) have adopted some of their viewpoints and themes, as well as tone.[3] Prins (2002) argues that Dutch opinion leaders since the 1990s have embraced a new political genre—'new realism'—that emphasizes 'facing the truth', being the 'voice of the (ordinary, native-born, ethnically Dutch) people', and the desire to bring down 'leftist' progressives, the politically correct 'libtards'. Under this 'new realism', scientists are often said to 'cover up' the facts and are quickly deemed to be 'political'.

This is the primacy of politics that scientists and evidence-informed policy advice must deal with in the twenty-first century. Academic advisers have little direct influence on politics and policy-making, except through the media or through citizens. Communicating directly through the media has become necessary, as Dutch politicians tend to set their agendas and ask parliamentary questions on the basis of media coverage (Vliegenthart 2007). This, however, is no easy task as the logic of science often collides with a media logic in which images are more important than words and issues are often portrayed in black and white—migration is either 'good' or 'bad' (see Chapter 4 in this volume). We also need to communicate directly to citizens—for instance, through public meetings and social media—not only because this may generate media attention, but also because citizens are voters and crucial stakeholders in the public debate on immigration and integration.

At the same time, science no longer has the authority it once enjoyed (Scholten 2008), although in the Dutch context it is an exaggeration to speak of 'science in crisis' or 'the death of expertise'—as, for instance, Nichols (2017) does. Public opinion research shows that people trust science more than government, parliament, newspapers, trade unions, and courts (Tiemeijer and De Jonge 2013). Then again, many people place high trust in democracy but are distrustful of politicians, an analogy that may apply here as well: people trust science but not necessarily all scientists. Science is not self-evidently credible. As Jasanoff (2012: 14) puts it: 'At the turn of the twenty-first century, many things that seemed self-evident about science even fifty years back no longer seem so. In particular, the image of an impersonal science, standing apart from human interest and values, and sternly committed to the delivery of truths, has given way to an awareness that science is frequently commissioned to serve political ends, is constrained by the limits of human imagination and capability, and, through its very ambition, extends the horizons of uncertainty while producing new knowledge.'

Moreover, science pursued at universities can be out of touch with social and policy issues. Science is growing more specialized and more focused on publications in academic journals. 'Impact' often means impact on other scientists as measured by the h-index (an author-level metric based on a researcher's most cited papers and citations in other academic publications) and not impact on policy. There is little funding for provocative research which may or may not produce useful findings (Dijstelbloem et al. 2013). This 'narrowing of science' has made it all the more necessary for the WRR to act as an honest broker, a role that has become harder to perform at a time when politicians can shop around for truths and the media logic often differs from that of research.

In the Wake of the Máxima Report: Lessons for Scientific Policy Advice

What can scientifically informed policy advice learn from the response to the WWR report *Identification with the Netherlands*? Given the changing (power) balance between science, policy, and politics, scientific policy advisers must learn to cultivate greater modesty; Jasanoff (2012) speaks about a shift from 'technologies of hubris' to 'technologies of humility'. Indeed, the 1990s buzzword 'paradigm shift' is scarcely heard in the WRR's offices today. Those who, like the WRR, are charged with 'producing long-range views and policy alternatives' would do better to acknowledge that scientific research is *always* subject to bias in its choices and that uncertainty is intrinsic to science. Scientifically informed policy advice needs to go beyond the simple model of 'speaking truth to power'.

The provision of scientific policy advice today also requires greater collaboration and stakeholder involvement. If science has less authority than it once had and politicians can 'shop around for convenient truths', researchers and academics cannot always operate on their own to advise government; knowledge coalitions matter. For example, the WRR in recent years has collaborated more often with other Dutch research and public knowledge organ-izations working in the domain of migration and integration, including the Netherlands Institute for Social Research and Statistics Netherlands (e.g. Engbersen et al. 2015) as well as with international scientists (e.g. Holtslag et al. 2012). Although it is crucial to stress that academic research rarely produces consensus, it is possible to come up with composite views on specific themes. Some truths are more plausible than others. Moreover, different stakeholders are now more likely to be drawn into the process of producing WRR reports and foresight studies, consisting both of a variety of academics (including critics of the WRR), policy-makers, and civil society organizations such as employers' associations and trade unions. This consultation and participation process hardly existed in the early 2000s when *Identification with the Netherlands* was written. At the WRR today, there is a greater emphasis on the role of the 'honest broker'.

Academic think tanks such as the WRR depend on extant research and scientific knowledge. This is a strength, but also a vulnerability. To do justice to their role as honest brokers, science must be diverse and funding must be made available for research that roams beyond the beaten paths and whose conclusions are not known in advance. Although scientific conclusions seldom lead directly to policy alternatives, it is crucial that social scientists look beyond academia. They must be willing and allowed to play a public role.

To fulfil its role as honest broker, scientific policy advice in the domain of immigration and integration must be aware of the breadth of academic and other stakeholder opinion; the research should be varied and focus on the host society, as well as on immigrants. This does not mean that researchers should bow to societal majorities. On the contrary, one must at times be brave, as one of the ministers stressed at the launch of the Máxima report. Nevertheless, without a deeper understanding of the impact of immigration across the breadth of society, policy recommendations will often miss their mark. For instance, the WRR may have underestimated the various feelings of the citizenry towards the idea of national identity. Better understanding of the breadth of feelings and experiences in society is necessary in an age when reaching out to the publics—often via media—appears as the most effective route to impact on politicians and policy-making.

Notes

1. The report was supported by two background studies: *In debat over Nederland* (Sleegers 2007) and *Nationale identiteit en meervoudig verleden* (Grever and Ribbens 2007). The WRR also staged a creative intervention in the public debate by

commissioning a documentary film-maker from the Dutch public broadcasting association VPRO to produce a film on immigrants in the Dutch army and their (at times strained) feelings of loyalty. The documentary was broadcast a few days prior to the report's publication.

2. According to the WRR's internal evaluation, the report's message was not always univocal, in places too multi-layered and ambiguous to communicate clearly.

3. Political scientists debate whether political parties mainly express the feelings of 'the people' or whether they are also catalysts of resistance to immigration. For Koopmans and Muis (2009), who refer to a 'spiral of discursive escalation', it is the latter. Others, such as Van der Meer (2017), argue that democracy is doing a good job as new parties arise giving voice to otherwise hidden feelings and voices.

References

Ankersmit, F. 2007. Dit is politiek, geen wetenschap. *Trouw*, 29 September.

Buitenhof. 2007. Wim van de Donk en Ruud Koopmans, 1 October (TV programme).

Den Hoed, P., and Keizer, A. G. (eds). 2007. *Op steenworp afstand. WRR 35 jaar*. The Hague: WRR.

Dijstelbloem, H., Huisman, F., Miedema, F., and Mijnhardt, W. 2013. *Science in Transition. Waarom de wetenschap niet werkt zoals moet, en wat daaraan te doen is*. http://scienceintransition.nl/wp-content/uploads/2013/10/Sience-in-Transition-Position-paper-versie-2.pdf

Duyvendak, J. W., Geschiere, P., and Tonkens, E. (eds). 2016. *The Culturalization of Citizenship: Belonging and Polarization in a Globalizing World*. London: Palgrave.

Engbersen, G., Dagevos, J., Jennissen, R., Bakker, L., and Leerkes, A. 2015. *Geen tijd verliezen. Van opvang naar integratie van asielmigranten*. Policy Brief 4. The Hague: WRR. Also published as: *No Time to Lose*. The Hague: WRR.

Goodhart, D. 2017. *The Road to Somewhere: The Populist Revolt and the Future of Politics*. London: C. Hurst & Co.

Grever, M., and Ribbens, K. 2007. *Nationale identiteit en meervoudig verleden*. The Hague: WRR.

Groenendijk, K. 2011. *From Assisting to Requiring Integration: Selective Citizenship Policies in the Netherlands. Naturalization: A Passport for the Better Integration of Immigrants?* Paris: OECD.

Hochschild, A. R. 2016. *Strangers in Their Own Land: Anger and Mourning on the American Right*. New York: The New Press.

Holtslag, J. W., Kremer, M., and Schrijvers, E. (eds). 2012. *In betere banen: de toekomst van arbeidsmigratie in de Europese Unie*. The Hague: WRR. Also published as: *Making Migration Work*. The Hague: WRR.

Jasanoff, S. 2012. *Science and Public Reason*. London and New York: Routledge.

Koninklijk Huis. 2007. Toespraak van prinses Maxima. www.koninklijkhuis.nl/documenten/toespraken/2007/09/24/toespraak-van-prinses-maxima-24-september-2007

Koopmans, R. 2007. Identiteiten is niet altijd complimentair. *NRC*, 26 September.

Koopmans, R., and Muis, J. 2009. The rise of right-wing populist Pim Fortuyn in the Netherlands: A discursive opportunity approach. *European Journal of Political Research* 48: 642–64.

Larsen, C. A. 2013. *The Rise and Fall of Social Cohesion: The Construction and Deconstruction of Social Trust in the US, UK, Sweden, and Denmark*. Oxford: Oxford University Press.

Nichols, T. 2017. *The Death of Expertise. The Campaign against Established Knowledge and Why It Matters*. Oxford: Oxford University Press.

Pielke, R. A. 2003. *The Honest Broker*. Cambridge: Cambridge University Press.

Prins, B. 2002. The nerve to break taboos: New realism in the Dutch discourse on multiculturalism. *Journal of International Migration and Integration* 3(3–4): 363–79.

Scheffer, P. 2000. Het multiculturele drama. *NRC*, 29 January.

Scholten, P. 2008. Constructing Immigrant Policies: Research–Policy Relations and Immigrant Integration in the Netherlands (1970–2004). PhD dissertation, University of Twente.

SCP. 2012. *Continu onderzoek burgerperspectieven*. Kwartaalbericht 1. The Hague: Sociaal en Cultureel Planbureau.

SCP. 2015. *Continu onderzoek burgerperspectieven*. Kwartaalbericht 4. The Hague: Sociaal en Cultureel Planbureau.

SCP. 2016. *Continu onderzoek burgerperspectieven*. Kwartaalbericht 2. The Hague: Sociaal en Cultureel Planbureau.

Sleegers, F. 2007. *In debat over Nederland*. The Hague: WRR.

Sniderman, P. M., and Hagendoorn, L. 2007. *When Ways of Life Collide: Multiculturalism and Its Discontents in the Netherlands*. Princeton, NJ: Princeton University Press.

Telegraaf. 2007. Máxima vervreemd van gewone mensen. 6 October.

Tiemeijer, W., and de Jonge, J. 2013. *Hoeveel vertrouwen hebben Nederlanders in wetenschap?* The Hague: Rathenau Instituut.

Van der Meer, T. 2017. *Niet de kiezer is gek*. Houten: Unieboeks/het Spectrum.

Van der Waal, J., and Houtman, D. 2011. 'Tolerance in the postindustrial city: Assessing the ethnocentrism of less educated natives in 22 Dutch cities'. *Urban Affairs Review* 47(5): 642–71.

Van der Waal, J., de Koster, W., and van Noord, J. 2017. Opleidingsverschillen in maatschappelijk onbehagen en wantrouwen in de politiek in Nederland, 1970–2012. In *De val de middenklasse? Het stabiele en kwetsbare midden*, eds G. Engbersen, E. Snel, and M. Kremer. The Hague: WRR.

Vliegenthart, R. 2007. Framing Immigration and Integration: Facts, Parliament, Media and Anti-Immigrant Support in The Netherlands. PhD dissertation, Free University Amsterdam.

Volkskrant. 2007. WRR zet integratiedebat op scherp. 25 September.

WRR (Wetenschappelijke Raad voor het Regeringsbeleid). 1989. *Allochtonenbeleid*. The Hague: WRR.

WRR (Wetenschappelijke Raad voor het Regeringsbeleid). 2001. *Nederland als immigratiesamenleving*. The Hague: WRR.

WRR (Wetenschappelijke Raad voor het Regeringsbeleid). 2007. *Identificatie met Nederland*. Amsterdam: Amsterdam University Press.

7

Investigating Immigration and the Sustainability of the Norwegian Welfare State

The Role of Government Commissions

Grete Brochmann

Research based policy-making has held a prominent position in the Norwegian polity—particularly since the Second World War. The development of the comprehensive welfare model, the basis of which was established *before* the War, required intensive expertise. Economics, in particular, served as a 'master-profession' in the formative years of the Norwegian post-war political economy. Economists—within and without government—played a prominent role in policy-making, as 'doers' and as 'premise providers' (Slagstad 1998; Sejersted 2011). Following completion of the basic structure of the welfare model in the late 1960s, other academic professions also entered the arena, contributing to the unremitting task of 'social engineering' that characterized post-war policy-making in Norway.

In 1972, the contribution by experts to policy-making processes was formalized through a new institution—the Norwegian Official Commissions (*Norges offentlige utredninger NOU*). The Official Commissions have since played a significant role in policy-making in Norway,[1] arguably representing a core factor of the consensual Norwegian governance (see also Chapter 9 in this volume; Christensen and Holst 2017).

The composition and content of the NOUs have changed somewhat over the years; it can also be argued that the NOU genre covers different *kinds* of consideration under the general heading. This variation can be related to the importance of the subject under scrutiny; committees directly responsible for preparing legislation have their own rationales, and there has been a quite significant difference between clear-cut expert committees and more corporative committees, where social partners, members from the civil services and other relevant organizations are represented. But, by and large, they represent ad hoc advisory commissions, appointed by the government (sometimes a ministry), led by a chairman and supported by a secretariat. Having been assigned to investigate a specifically defined policy problem, the commissions are expected to come up with appropriate policy advice after having conducted a thorough examination in accordance with their terms of reference. Usually, the advice contributes to the policy-making process before concrete proposals are handed over to parliament. These commissions usually last for approximately one year, sometimes longer, depending on the scope of the task and—quite often—the urgency of the problem for the government. The commission reports are often 'state-of-the-art' in character due to the commission synthesizing existing research, in addition to commissioning new studies and, occasionally, undertaking its own. Over the years, the level of academic representation on these commissions has risen substantially. Over recent decades, the leaders of commissions have increasingly recruited from academia, to the extent that criticism has been raised to the effect that a 'scientization' is taking place in this democratic institution (Christensen and Holst 2017).

Since the 1970s, many researchers have been prepared to serve in such functions, although social/political scientists may have felt less than comfortable with regard to engagement with government—this was more so during the 1970s and 1980s than is the case today. The critical voices have been prevalent throughout; however, ultimately, many—and perhaps most—social and political researchers would make themselves available when called upon by the Norwegian Welfare State. Even during the radical 1970s, when the modern Norwegian immigration policy was formulated, researchers possessed the field knowledge; thus, they were used extensively as advisors to the state administration. State officials often sympathized politically with the radical researchers and, together, they could influence government to some degree in what they considered the right direction (Brochmann and Kjeldstadli 2008). Regarding the Official Commissions, the understanding among academics has on the whole been that, even though the terms of reference are formulated by the government, one can usually maintain academic integrity and independence throughout the process, and one may dissent from majority conclusions if necessary. Besides, being a member of a commission is interesting and rewarding in terms of access to information and influence.

Thus, the NOUs have had a high level of legitimacy generally speaking, to the degree that a popular weekly Norwegian newspaper hailed the NOU institution as 'the prose that builds the country; the intellectual footprint on policy-making' (Lien and Gundersen 2014). This assertion should nevertheless be nuanced by the fact that NOUs not only sometimes trigger vast debates, but may also be highly controversial.

Norwegian academics working on an issue may also serve as a 'bridge' between research and policy-making outside of the NOU institute. Norwegian social science has a long tradition in dealing with policy relevant issues and, in fact, a large part of Norwegian research is 'commissioned'—that is, ordered and financed by the authorities in order to feed policy-making processes. An unrelenting discussion on the pitfalls of commissioned research has taken place over the years, in which the question of academic freedom has been a core issue.

In this chapter, I will concentrate on the NOU institute and use my experience from a number of such commissions to describe and analyse preconditions for bridging some of the gaps between academic knowledge and policy-making in the Norwegian context. As cases, I will draw on my experience with two commissions on the relationship between international migration and the sustainability of the Norwegian welfare state (NOU 2011:7 and NOU 2017:2). Since I served as head of both endeavours, I had direct access to all the investigation processes; also, to a certain extent, I had access to the preparatory phases, as well as the important dissemination periods afterwards. Yet, when it comes to the appraisal of impact, my opinion will necessarily be subjective. It is possible to trace the influence of these commissions on policy changes—concrete reforms, as well as references in the press and in research documents—but, in my view, the most interesting impact has been in terms of the change of public discourse. In assessing this, I rely on my own impressions, as neither I nor anyone else—yet—systematically evaluated this specific part of the impact of the work of these two commissions.

Context: Challenges to the Welfare Model

Before discussing the two commissions, it is important to understand the broader socio-economic and political context. As in the other Scandinavian countries, the welfare state in Norway has had an outstanding political position—'Scandinavia's holiest cow', as it was labelled in the Danish periodical *Weekendavisen* in April 2007. No political party would challenge this major institution in a basic sense. The welfare model has represented a fine-tuned institutional set-up: a small, open-market economy relying on an interplay between stability oriented macro-economic policies, an organized working life with coordinated wage setting and a comprehensive public, tax-based welfare system. Based on a regulated labour market governed by social partners, its key traits are: pooling of risks through extensive social insurance, public services, corporatist coordination, and low inequality.

Today, the welfare model is challenged by multiple forces, many of which are related to globalization. The most central fiscal challenges are represented by demographic changes—an ageing population—and the decline in oil revenues. Yet, a growing worry has developed as to the potential fiscal and structural challenge of immigration. The universally oriented Norwegian welfare model—in which legal residency in principle is the only qualifier[2] for basic access to benefits and services—is particularly vulnerable to a large increase in the number of low-skilled persons. The compressed wage structure in combination with the equal treatment policy implies that newcomers with low productivity tend to become reliant on welfare. Challenges with enduring underemployment in significant parts of the immigrant population have come to the fore politically speaking, particularly at the beginning of the twenty-first century.

Before 2004, these challenges were associated with people coming from the global South (refugees and family members). Lacking education, they typically experienced problems in a highly paid labour market that required good skills, thus imposing a challenge to systemic inclusion. After 2004, when the enlargement of the European Union (EU) eastward resulted in the largest influx ever of semi-skilled and low-skilled labour migrants in Norway, different challenges occurred. By and large, the inflow of new migrants from Eastern Europe has served the Norwegian economy well, yet there have been concerns about low wage competition and 'social dumping' which, arguably, could disturb the fine-tuned labour–welfare nexus in the longer run. What is at stake is general social protection by means of the balancing mechanism of the welfare model: having an income from work is a fundamental pillar of the expensive, tax-based welfare system in Norway. If the wage level is pressured downwards through low wage competition, the level of welfare benefits will also come under downward pressure to maintain the incentives to work.

The First Commission: 2009–2011

Even though concerns about underemployment among (some) immigrant groups, value conflicts, and social marginalization had grown among the Norwegian public, the impact of immigration on the Norwegian welfare system was still highly contentious at the beginning of the twenty-first century. The only party in parliament to have addressed this issue earlier was the Progress Party, which was not only critical of immigration, but had also, during the 1990s, called for a large-scale cost–benefit analysis of immigration to Norway. None of the other parties wanted to touch the issue at the time.

It was consequently a significant event when the Centre-Left government[3] of Jens Stoltenberg appointed the first Official Commission on Migration and the sustainability of the Norwegian welfare model in 2009. The assignment came after a period of public debates about the future of the welfare state. Opposing fronts were asserting either that immigration was the largest threat to the sustainability of the welfare state or, conversely, that immigration was a central factor in securing labour supply and finances for the economy, which was confronted with the demographic challenge of an ageing population. The government thus wanted a thorough investigation and analysis based on as many reliable facts and as much robust evidence as possible. The time was seen to be politically right for such an undertaking.

The Commission was given comprehensive terms of reference, asking for both economic analyses, and more substantial descriptions and evaluations of the existing integration regime. The aim of the report was 'to raise the level of knowledge on how the Norwegian welfare model functions in a time of increased migration; to identify mechanisms that impact the interplay between working life and welfare in light of this development and to propose a direction for future policy and some strategies to deal with the challenges' (NOU 2011:7, 1). Three main themes were analysed: economic sustainability; relevance of existing policies; and the political legitimacy of the regime. Three policy areas were singled out as most relevant: welfare policy; policies on working life; and integration policy. Immigration policy—although an important parameter—did not form part of the terms of reference. The Commission was given a two-year period of operation and a large secretariat that included eleven persons. The Committee itself consisted of seven members, predominantly professors and researchers, but also two members from the state administration. Economists were in the majority although, as the leader of the Commission, I was a sociologist.

The main conclusions of the Commission were, in the main, in line with ongoing reform processes in the Norwegian model: better education, vocational qualification, activation, grading of benefits, inclusive working life, and the defence of high standards and equal income distribution in working life were all important components. The central elements suggested by the Commission's report were a public cost–benefit analysis of public finances, including certain economic prospects for the future (based on a new model generated in the National Bureau of Statistics); overarching advice as to mechanisms to be applied to improve integration; and a number of concrete policy recommendations, based on an analysis of the existing regime.

The findings of the Commission were not dramatic but nonetheless provided a basis for concern. Improving labour market inclusion for marginalized groups was seen as essential, as were the efforts to keep up the orderly labour market regime. Even though the task was to evaluate the effects of 'immigration' as such, the major part of public attention after publication of the Commission's report was concerned with EU labour immigration, and—not least—the potential for the export of welfare benefits to countries of origin. This focus came as a surprise to us in the Commission, having expected a greater emphasis on refugees and their welfare dependency rates. The main explanation for this is most likely the novelty of the labour migration issues, combined with the volume of the influx at the time. The issue of exporting welfare benefits highlighted an important discussion on the potential threat to the generous benefit levels, considering new pressure on the sustainability of the welfare model with increasing internationalization.

Public attention was extensive after the publication of the report. The combination of the contentious nature of the issue and the great demand for data and reliable information probably explains the extraordinary level of public interest taken in the report. As the leader of the Commission, I had expected heated discussion and attacks, particularly from the immigration-friendly political Left. To a certain extent, this materialized. Some journalists and representatives of non-governmental organizations reiterated arguments that were present before the assignment, addressing the legitimacy of the whole operation. To investigate the relationship between immigration and the sustainability of the welfare model was, in itself, seen as illegitimate—potentially discriminatory, if not racist. Even though very few of these voices questioned the substance of the analysis, for these critics the research and report produced by the NOU represented 'unwanted knowledge'.

There was heated discussion along these lines in social media and, occasionally, also in the print media. However, the main impression I was left with, once the dust had settled, was an immensely and surprisingly positive response, both among party politicians and, generally, among the public. There could be many and combined reasons for this. The government minister in charge of the NOU belonged to the Socialist Left Party, which may have soothed the critical reactions in that camp; the political Right—conservatives and liberals—found the analysis accommodating many of their concerns as well; and the general public were presented with allegedly more reliable and systematized data. Importantly, since the dominating discussion was occupied with *labour* immigration more than refugees, some of the most emotionally sensitive issues were under-communicated in the debates. Clearly, there existed milieus that continued to be in opposition to the whole undertaking, yet a new consensus had been established that these issues were important for all residents of Norway—both the majority and minorities—and, consequently, that open debates about these issues should be welcomed.

In the years following the finalization of the Commissions' report and recommendations, the economic and sociological analyses of the NOU became standard reference in public debates on issues related to immigration and the Norwegian model. The legacy of the report was, by and large, a constructive, scientifically based approach, largely occupied with the improvement of labour market integration and adjustments of the Norwegian welfare system, in order to make it more robust towards different kinds of immigration. Immigration, as such, was appraised as a social fact.

As to concrete *impact*, I believe this has been twofold. First, the NOU contributed to creating a new frame of understanding of the relationship between immigration and the welfare system, primarily through increasing the knowledge basis in the public. Since the content and the analysis were basically received as solid and reliable, it created legitimacy for the discussions on prospects and concerns in this area of policy-making. Second, the report has influenced a series of reform processes, predominantly through a new and more systematized thinking in terms of integrating immigration perspectives into *general* policy reform processes. It can therefore be difficult to 'measure' its direct impact. Reforms of welfare institutions are slow and complicated processes, and many critics have complained that only a few of the NOU's recommendations have actually materialized in new policy-making. I believe this is only partly true, as 'the immigration perspective' has become a standard concern in reform endeavours after the NOU, yet the interconnectedness of general reforms with integration policy changes makes it difficult to claim unequivocal 'ownership' of this impact. It is, nevertheless, possible to trace the effects on family policy, on educational policy, welfare and integration policies, activation policies, and approaches related to EU immigration.[4] The attention paid to the export of welfare benefits, 'social dumping', and low wage competitions has increased markedly following the NOU.

The Second Commission: 2015–2017

The high number of asylum seekers and refugees arriving in the summer and autumn of 2015 placed severe pressures on the Norwegian immigration regime. The number of asylum applications reached its highest level ever, and the magnitude of the international refugee crises indicated that this pressure was likely to persist. When viewed in relation to population, Norway was among the European countries that accommodated the highest proportion of asylum seekers and refugees during this period, with more than 31,000 asylum seekers arriving in 2015.

As a result of this development, emergency measures were implemented, much in line with other major receiving countries in the EU and the European Economic Area, with the support of a broad political coalition in parliament. Border controls were re-established, the prompt return of failed asylum applicants was intensified, temporary protection was reinstated and retrenchments of various rights for asylum seekers were proposed to legislative bodies.

Faced with this extraordinary situation, the government also appointed an Official Commission to investigate the 'long-term consequences of high immigration'. The Commission was asked to examine the consequences of this development for the national economy, the capacity to integrate newcomers, and for the continued development of trust and unity in society. Neither the immigration-policy nor the asylum-policy in Norway was to be reassessed, and the term 'high immigration' was not further specified.

The Commission chose to interpret this as meaning *a level of immigration of sufficient scope to subject the vital institutions, in their present form, to significant pressure*. This interpretation is intentionally not precise with regard to the number of immigrants. This approach was chosen because it is a dynamic issue. National institutions are being changed and adapted continuously, and increased immigration is only one reason for this. The 'pressure' on the system will always be dependent on the broader context, and it will also vary over time. The pace of change in the wake of the refugee crisis in 2015 is illustrative of this. Swift action at many levels, both internationally and nationally, contributed to the number of arrivals being drastically reduced from December 2015 onwards.

Therefore, the situation that motivated the appointment of the Commission in 2015 had already changed in 2016 and 2017. The mandate nevertheless called for a full assessment of continued high immigration in the coming years. Even though the pressure on the authorities and the tone of the public debate had waned due to the unusually low number of asylum seekers in 2016, there was little reason to believe that this would be a permanent situation. The conflicts that caused the refugee crisis in 2015 had not been resolved and new, serious conflicts in other regions were erupting. The Commission considered it important to look ahead and analyse how the Norwegian labour market and welfare system could be made more robust in order to cope with high pressure from immigration in the future.

There has been a significant increase in immigration to Norway in the past twenty years, particularly since the EU enlargements in 2004 and 2007. Net immigration of foreign citizens reached a peak of approximately 48,000 per year in 2011–2012. By the end of 2015, almost 850,000 people in Norway had an immigrant background—triple the number in 2000. Just over half of these immigrants were from countries in Africa, Asia, and Latin-America. Among countries of the Organisation for Economic Co-operation and Development (OECD), Norway has had one of the highest rates of immigration in relation to the size of its overall population in the past decade and the national demographic picture has—within a short period of time—changed significantly as a result of this development.[5]

Again, to understand the work and impact of the new Commission, it is important to understand its background and context. Even though the motivating setting was one of alarm and crisis, the terms of reference were in many ways similar to those of the first Commission. Both commissions focused on 'the sustainability of the Norwegian Welfare Model' as the central issue. What could be done to make it stronger in the face of large inflows of immigrants? The second Commission explicitly asked for an investigation based on the analysis of the first Commission. This is interesting considering the fact that the second Commission was assigned by a Conservative–Right coalition government, even with the Progress Party, a party critical of immigration, in charge. More than anything, this underlines the extraordinary standing of the Norwegian welfare model throughout the political landscape. The second Commission was, however, asked to put a specific emphasis on the inclusion of refugees. In addition, a brand-new issue was included in the mandate; namely, an evaluation of preconditions for maintaining unity and trust in Norwegian society in light of persistent, high immigration. Increasing *inequality*—economic, cultural, and social—was asserted as being an important factor for the analysis of the potential for diminishing trust and for polarization and conflict.

The composition of the group of people appointed to serve on the Commission was different the second time. Even though researchers were still in the majority, the representation of persons from government authorities and think tanks was stronger. A broader representation was obviously of concern for the government, and a total of eleven persons were appointed. The fact that I myself was asked to be leader of both endeavours, can be interpreted as the government wanting an independent academic direction for the overall task. It can also be interpreted as indicating a growing consensus in Norwegian politics on issues related to immigration and the welfare state.

The second Commission was also provided with a total of eleven persons in the secretariat; however, this time the working period was only one year. The limited time frame, the different composition of the Commission and, not least, the new theme to be analysed—preconditions for trust and unity—made the second undertaking much more demanding in terms of leadership.

The NOUs that are considered 'expert committees', with their academic robustness, hold a nimbus of 'independence' and 'evidence basis'. Yet, when a commission is asked to enter a field where such evidence is hard to come by, and where the contentiousness is at its highest, researchers' different normative platforms come to the fore. Researchers will disagree on how to approach the field of study, which factors to emphasize or omit, as well as how to interpret the findings. And such disagreements often spring out of normative cleavages. The issue of 'trust and unity' triggered intense discussions, ending with four notes of dissent from three different members of the Committee.

The disagreements basically related to an analysis of *national culture*—the degree to which it is (and should be) changing as a result of immigration—and to the question of the conduciveness of *governance* in relation to newcomers' cultural affiliation and practices. What could be done to facilitate a greater overlap in and shared experiences in everyday life? What kind of roles would be feasible for public bodies in facilitating interaction in order to promote social cohesion? What responsibilities should be placed on individuals versus institutions?

The essence of the overall NOU 2017:2 analysis was that the Norwegian welfare society is facing a period of structural upheaval. An increased burden of dependency and increased uncertainty surrounding the returns from the Government Pension Fund of Norway (formerly known as the Government Petroleum Fund) will require the reprioritization of economic and welfare policies. High levels of immigration, including people with little ability to provide for themselves, will represent an additional challenge and increase the pressure on public finances. The Norwegian welfare model is both a resource and a problem when considered in relation to the integration of immigrants and their descendants. The model is vulnerable to the immigration of a high number of adults with low qualifications. At the same time, low economic inequality and solid educational institutions contribute to a high level of mobility among descendants of immigrants. Thus far, Norway has not been sufficiently successful in integrating refugees into the labour market. The Committee's analyses showed that there is potential for improvement in Norway's existing integration policies, and also outlined alternative strategies for application in the event that the results continue to be inadequate, or if there is a significant decline in the economic framework conditions. If Norwegian society does not improve its ability to integrate immigrants and refugees from countries outside Europe, there is a risk that increasing economic inequality in conjunction with cultural differences could weaken the foundation of unity and trust and the legitimacy of the social model.

The Commission report was handed over to the government on 1 February 2017. It is consequently too early to evaluate the political impact of the investigations and recommendations. I will nevertheless conclude with some comparative reflections on the two varying receptions of the first and second Commissions.

Conclusion

Since the turn of the millennium, public discourse in Norway has been quite polarized, not least in relation to refugee issues—one of the most emotionally charged immigration issues debated in the public sphere. Yet, the public tenor has changed during this period, becoming more critical of immigration: spelling out frustrations over immigration and inadequate integration has gained more legitimacy. At the same time, immigrant voices have become much more prevalent, revealing a variety of positions among the 'immigrant population', thus contributing to the playing down of stereotypes and prejudices in the majority population. The first Commission contributed to this ongoing process by emphasizing strongly the diversity *among* immigrants. The fact that labour migration became the major concern may have paved the way for a more open and direct tone in the debate.

The summer and autumn of the refugee crisis in 2015 stirred up the old schism again in the Norwegian public; the divide between the people for whom refugee protection was the overriding concern and those who emphasized the limited capacity of the Norwegian reception system, as well as the sustainability of the welfare state. The climate of the discussion was quite harsh, and it was not until the inflow was seen as out of control by the larger public that a broad political coalition emerged to curtail the inflow.

The second Commission that sprang out of this crisis situation could have been expected to induce *more* commotion than was the case with the first Commission, not least since refugee issues were now at the centre of the debate. Now, as time has passed since its dissemination, it seems safe to conclude that this has not been the case. An important reason for this is most likely the extraordinary low influx of refugees after 2015, which has strongly reduced the heat in the public debate. Besides, the NOU's terms of reference did not include the most contentious immigration issue—the immigration policy proper; that is, how to control or possibly reduce the inflow. Thus, the report basically dealt with the 'soft side' of the issue—how to include people more constructively and productively in the Norwegian welfare society.

The reception of the second Commission has been largely positive. All the major newspapers (liberal, conservative, and Left) welcomed the report and praised it for being nuanced, analytical, and trustworthy. The critical voices from the first round—those that emphasized the illegitimacy of the operation, as such—were close to non-existent.

The relatively limited criticism that appeared argued either that there was 'nothing new' in the Commission's analysis, or that it was too weak with regard to future prospects. The latter criticism came from sources on the political Right that were critical regarding immigration. This was in contrast to the major line of criticism in 2011, which came from the political Left.

Two issues, nevertheless, caused quite intense discussions in the press: certain technicalities concerning the calculations of future costs for the welfare state but, first and foremost, questions related to *trust and social cohesion.*

The trigger of the debate was a couple of dissenting notes from one of the Commission members,[6] rather than the analysis of the Commission, as such. By and large, the Commission had recommended an institutional approach to integration and cultural adaptation, emphasizing the importance of the long-term processes of inclusion and socialization through the educational system and the labour market. The dissenting notes underlined the need for an active assimilation policy. One of the notes also underscored that 'ethnic Norwegians' would become a minority in a few decades—a fact that this member felt had been omitted from the Commission's analysis.

It remains to be seen what direct policy impacts will come out of the report of the second Commission but the public reception so far reflects a *zeitgeist* in which policy-making based on research and facts has become almost common sense in Norway in the field of immigrant integration. This *zeitgeist* has come about over a number of years. The contentious interrelationship between immigration and the sustainability of the Norwegian welfare model gradually gained attention and credibility as a public issue. In the late 2000s, sufficient apprehension had accumulated both in the public debate and in policy-making circles to warrant the appointment of a research-based operation in the form of an Official Commission. *Timing* is of central importance in this regard. 'Legitimacy' is clearly an essential matter when judging the impact of endeavours such as these. Inappropriate timing could have adversely affected the Commission's efforts, regardless of the solidity of the investigation. The systemic worries and the public attention—the tenor of the debate— had gradually surfaced during the 1990s and the 2000s to the extent that immigration and welfare state issues had been (partly) decoupled from the ownership of the populist right-wing Progress Party. On the one hand, the Progress Party had succeeded in pushing concerns about immigration into mainstream politics. On the other hand, the Party—through its ambitions to enter government—had had to tone down their rhetoric in relation to immigration issues. These parallel processes may have made Norway a special case when it comes to a *more* pragmatic, matter-of-fact-approach to the contentious issues of immigration and the sustainability of the welfare state than may be the case in some other European contexts. This is, however, not to argue that Norway's immigration debates are generally more evidence-based and considered than in other countries.

In the aftermath of the two Commissions, it is also possible to trace causalities from both sides. The first Commission definitely moved public discourse in the direction of accepting more open discussion on the impact of immigration on the essential labour–welfare nexus of the welfare model, thus also preparing the ground for more conscious policy-making in the institutional field of immigrant integration. The high standing of the research-based NOU institution—with its facts, figures, and clear-cut analyses—has most likely contributed to a reduction in the emotional charge of the Norwegian public on issues related to immigration and the welfare state.

Notes

1. Sweden and Denmark have, by and large, the same polity-tradition (Christensen and Holst 2017).
2. EU migrants need to have been employed (sometimes only for one day) to obtain access to welfare benefits.
3. Consisting of the Labour Party (by far the largest), the Center Party (rural; rather conservative as to values) and the Socialist Left Party (to the left of the Labour Party; very immigration friendly).
4. For example, several NOUs after 2011 have built on or referred to the Commission report (e.g. NOU 2012:2 Europautredningen; NOU 2017:6 Barnefamilieutvalget). A White Paper to parliament came as a direct result of the Commission (Meld. St. 6 (2012–2013) En helhetlig integreringspolitikk). Currently, a new NOU committee on employment policies uses the Commission report as a central premise (Sysselsettingsutvalget).
5. For figures, see NOU 2017:2.
6. One of the remarks was signed by two commission members, yet only one of them was targeted in the subsequent debates. Dissenting notes are published as addendums to the NOU.

References

Brochmann, G. and Kjeldstadli, K. 2008. *A History of Immigration. The Case of Norway 900–2000*. Oslo: Universitetsforlaget.

Christensen, J. and Holst, C. 2017. Advisory commissions, academic expertise and democratic legitimacy: The case of Norway. *Science and Public Policy* 44(6): 821–33.

Lien, M., and Gunderson, H. 2014. Heia NORGE! *Morgenbladet*, 16 May.

NOU 2011:7. *Velferd og migrasjon: Den norske modellens framtid*. Oslo.

NOU 2012:2. *Utenfor og innenfor—Norges avtaler med EU*. Oslo.

NOU 2017:2. *Integrasjon og tillit: Langsiktige konsekvenser av høy innvandring*. Oslo.

NOU 2017:6. *Offentlig støtte til barnefamiliene*. Oslo.

Sejersted, F. 2011. *The Age of Social Democracy. Norway and Sweden in the Twentieth Century*. Princeton, NJ: Princeton University Press.

Slagstad, R. 1998. *De nasjonale strateger*. Oslo: Pax.

8

Gaps and Challenges of Migration Policy Advice

The German Experience

Klaus F. Zimmermann

Introduction

The gap between scientific insights and societal perception of international migration is large. It stems, at least in part, from the complexity of the matter and the unspecific fears the unknown raises. This chapter reflects upon these issues against the background of post-World War II migration and migration policy in Germany. Providing robust evidence is not sufficient for a policy adviser to succeed. In my experience, patience, persistent argumentation, and the propagation of successful migrant role models seem to be the key to influencing public debates and policy-making on migration and integration. A 'jobs approach' that integrates both migrants and refugees into the labour force early could make a difference. Germany, while stumbling slowly on its path, still has a chance to find a proper balance between observing humanitarian migration and following economic needs.

Since the end of World War II, Germany has experienced large migratory movements: war refugees and resettlements after 1945; guest worker recruitments, mostly in the 1960s until an abrupt ban in 1973 in face of the oil crisis; the unification and integration of East Germany after 1990; integration of European labour markets, including the Eastern enlargement of the European Union (EU) in the mid-2000s; and, most recently, the so-called European 'refugee crisis' in 2015 and thereafter. Although only recently and slowly recognized and accepted, Germany has long been a country of immigration. However, this status is not yet fully accepted by German society and, even more importantly, not sufficiently considered to react flexibly and success-fully to the major challenges of our time. Such challenges include the ageing and shrinking of the population, the rising and increasingly unsatisfied demand for skilled workers, the rising use of robots, the humanitarian and economic challenges raised by the inflows of refugees, and—more generally—the search for a proper balance of economic rationales and human concerns in public policies on migration and integration.[1]

Facing these developments, Germany has struggled and stumbled on its way to a balanced strategy towards migration phenomena. A key question and challenge on this path has been how to deal with the rising gap between scientific evidence on migration and integration, and the many myths that often dominate public perceptions of the issue, as outlined in this book by Martin Ruhs, Kristof Tamas, and Joakim Palme (Chapters 1 and 15). The question has to be understood in the context of the use of expert knowledge in policy-making as discussed, for instance, by Zimmermann (2004), Boswell (2012) and Davies (2012).

This chapter intends to describe and understand Germany's evolving policy challenges and developments, from the perspective of a scientific observer and academic policy advisor over a period of several decades. For over thirty years, I have been intensively involved in migration research and policy advice. As Programme Director of the Centre for European Policy Research (CEPR), Founding and Acting Director of the Institute for the Study of Labor (IZA), and President of the German Institute for Economic Research (DIW), Berlin—the largest German think tank in economics—I was concerned among other issues with the creation of research on migration and related topics in Europe and, in particular, in Germany. I was also deeply involved in the dissemin-ation process of research to policy-making.

I will outline the major migration policy debates and developments since World War II in Germany, and discuss the difficulties encountered in convey-ing messages to society and politics which are widely accepted by the research community. The core issues of concern have been about:

- accepting the status of Germany as an immigration country;
- the struggle of creating an immigration law allowing for skilled migration with Schröder's 'Green Card' and its cessation after the terrorist attack on 11 September 2001;
- the fight around free and unfettered labour markets in the context of EU Eastern enlargement;
- the fight against misperceptions about 'welfare migration';
- the debate about the need for internal labour mobility in Europe;
- the challenge of openness to high-skilled labour migration to Germany; and

- the 2015 refugee crisis, including the policy switch from an attempt to open up even more to economic migration, to welcoming refugees, and to hindering refugee migration in 2016–2018.

The Migration Debate in Historical Perspective

In this section, I outline and discuss the evolution of German migration and migration policy since World War II in distinct periods.[2] For a considerable time, the migration issue was characterized by substantial ignorance about empirical facts and scientific knowledge.[3] This section describes how, over time, the country has dealt with this and how it has moved closer to reality and to considering—if not always accepting—scientific facts and advice.

Over decades, the German government was unwilling to recognize that the country was, de facto, an 'immigration country'. It would have been more accurate to argue that the country did not want to be an immigration country, which was still the case in 2018. Although labour immigration has frequently been debated, Germany still has no clear legislation in place. With the exception of the 1960s, the prevalence of labour scarcity was not acknowledged, although the scarcity of skilled labour has progressively become more of an issue during the 2010s. Further, the long-term challenges of an ageing German population and the long-term needs of migrants are still not taken seriously.

Extending the analysis of previous literature (Schmidt and Zimmermann 1992; Zimmermann 1996), one can distinguish the following migration phases that have affected Germany following World War II:

- *1950–1961: War Adjustment Phase* from 1950 to 13 August 1961, the day of the building of the Berlin Wall.
- *1961–1973: Manpower Recruitment Phase* in West Germany from August 1961 to November 1973, when the guest worker regime was halted at the onset of the oil price crisis.
- *1974–1987: International Migration Consolidation Phase* in West Germany.
- *1988–2003: Transition after the Socialism Phase* including the process of German unification, the Bosnian war, and ethnic German resettlement after the end of communism.
- *1992–2003: European Labour Market Integration Phase* following the 1992 Maastricht Treaty, intensifying the EU and free labour mobility.
- *2004–2014: EU Eastern Enlargement Phase.*
- *2015–2018: European Refugee Crisis.*

In the 1990s, economic research slowly began to provide the necessary empirical evidence for policy-making (Kahanec and Zimmermann 2009, 2016; Zimmermann 2014a, 2016, among others). However, since the time of the EU Eastern enlargements, the flow of evidence seized up.[4] Schmidt and Zimmermann (1992) evaluated the West German immigration experience at that time and found that Germany has been an immigration country since the beginning of the 1950s. Adjusting for population size, Schmidt and Zimmermann found the inflow comparable to that of the United States at the beginning of the last century, when immigration there was the greatest. So, Germany was, de facto, an immigration country from early on.

What else can we learn from the various periods? Certainly, we can observe that it was possible to integrate many ethnic Germans either as war refugees or, later, as ethnic migrants, and to organize substantial labour immigration with official recruitment offices in many sending countries. So, (West) Germany always was a covert immigration country. We have also seen many guest workers returning after 1973, when labour recruiting was abruptly stopped in the middle of the first oil crisis and a recession. Similarly, many refugees from the Bosnian war left after 1995. One can generalize that while, most of the time, policy debates concentrate on the potential burden caused by the inflow of migrants, a fully realistic picture also has to take into account the large parallel outflow of people; this can typically be seen, but is ignored. The net effects are relevant, and those flows have been either positive or negative over time. It is important to observe the size of long-term net inflow, which was at an annual average of about 200,000 in Germany for many decades.

Germany also had to learn that the guest worker regime of the 1960s was not easy to terminate in reality; the 'guests' were not necessarily leaving and the country was suddenly confronted with unplanned integration challenges. In contradiction to the myth, the majority left after 1973, but there were interesting differences. As Zimmermann (2014b) has noted, numbers of migrant from countries that either were EU members or became members, and hence enjoyed free labour mobility, decreased or stagnated. In contrast, the number of Turkish nationals rose substantially, although there was no free labour mobility between Germany and Turkey. More openness correlated with lower migration, a phenomenon which was also observed with Mexican–US migration (Massey et al. 2016). This can be explained easily and is another important message for policy-making. Labour migrants come and go according to the attraction of the economic situation. If flexibility is stopped, however, workers stay even if they cannot easily find employment. They bring their family and have children. Hence, the transition of mobility-restricted populations from full employment to a much lower labour market attachment is—at least in part—associated with or caused by labour mobility restrictions. Establishing the right to return to Germany for work in the future for Turkish workers returning to Turkey after 1973 would probably have reduced the levels of Turkish migrants in Germany.

The Maastricht Treaty (1992) later imposed free labour markets for all EU member countries as a pillar of existence, although the European labour markets were, de facto, not only far from being integrated, but they are also still not fully integrated (Constant and Zimmermann 2017; Krause et al. 2017). With the creation of the euro in 2002, the need for rising internal labour mobility became transparent. To fight internal asymmetric economic shocks, labour was expected to play the role of an adjustment factor to substitute for the exchange rate flexibility that was no longer available. The labour markets have taken on this role; labour mobility in Eurozone member states has increased, but not yet sufficiently (Zimmermann 2014a; Constant and Zimmermann 2017; Jauer et al. 2018). Hence, the subsequent decades can be referred to as the European Labour Market Integration Phase (1992–2003), which overlapped the Transition after Socialism Phase (1988–2003) and was followed by the EU Eastern Enlargement Phase (2004–2014), which involved a larger number of Eastern European countries with a complex set of transition periods to free labour mobility. The EU Eastern Enlargement Phase is often seen as a 'natural experiment', a reliable model that shows that the labour market effects have largely been positive, in particular in the UK (Kahanec and Zimmermann 2009, 2016; Wadsworth et al. 2016).

Finally, we are currently in the middle of what has been called the European Refugee Crisis (2015–2018), which is more a crisis of the European political regime than of refugees, and is strongly driven by perceptions and public sentiments.[5] Later observers may call this and the Brexit decision the beginning of a *European Disintegration Phase*, a phase that also encompasses rising concerns about internal mobility—in general, and also for EU citizens—in correlation with the rise of far right-wing and populist parties. This is connected with general propagated fears that migration causes welfare take-up, creates job losses for natives, and depresses their wages—even though the facts do not support these concerns.

Behind the ups and downs in migration and migration policy across the diverse phases, one can identify a path that will lead Germany to a more open society and a better developed immigration law. I shall now analyse the elements of this process.

With the decline of non-labour migration and rising scarcity of skilled labour at the end of the 1990s, reflections about the status of Germany as an immigration country increased. The understanding was that Germany should open up more. An indication of this was the announcement by Chancellor

Gerhard Schröder, in February 2000 at the Cebit Fair in Hanover, that a *German 'Green Card'* (temporary work permit) was to be created to attract non-EU IT specialists. This initiative broke the ice in the public debate to allow labour immigration to be viewed as beneficial and to reflect Germany's status as an immigration country. Consequently, in June 2000 a high-ranked government commission began to prepare modern immigration legislation that was potentially to include a points system; the commission reported in July 2001. Germany was close to a significant change in its migration policy;[6] however, the New York terrorist attacks of 11 September 2001 caused a de facto termination of the initiative. The 'Green Card' initiative, although quite successful, faded into the shadows.

The reservations against migration in German migration policy remained strong in the following years and policy was also cautious towards the citizens of the new EU member states during the EU Enlargement Phase that began in 2004. Unlike other member states of the EU, Germany and Austria applied full labour market flexibility only after the end of the seven-year transition period. The media played a particular role, predicting large inflows of migrants in all the phases of enlargement (2004, 2011, and 2014) although scientific research at the time was suggesting that this would not be the case (Kahanec and Zimmermann 2009, 2016; Zimmermann 2014a, 2016, among others). If anything, the decision to keep Germany's labour market closed for as long as possible redirected qualified Polish and Baltic labour migrants to Ireland and the UK, where their presence was very beneficial, while Germany did not get the workers it needed but, instead, only lower-qualified and mainly black market migrants.[7] Furthermore, for over a decade, practically every year since the EU Eastern Enlargement, the media has supported rumours about welfare shopping by the citizens of the new member states'. It did not matter that these circular debates died out swiftly because the claimed evidence was, at best, anecdotal. In particular, EU2 migrants (Romanians and Bulgarians) were blamed, but mostly they found employment and did not take up welfare benefits.

Over the years and across many party lines, policy-makers began to understand that a more flexible and open labour market-oriented immigration regime was needed. However, politicians often acted in a helpless fashion and were either too defensive to fight openly for such a policy, or were overwhelmed by political pressures. Under Chancellor Angela Merkel's first grand coalition cabinet of Christian and Social Democrats (22 November 2005–27 October 2009), Germany began a double-sided migration policy that attempted to attract the skilled migrants while trying to keep out the unskilled migrants. On the one hand, the country remained closed as long as possible to the citizens of the new Eastern European member states, but, on the other hand, began to open up to worldwide high-skilled migration.

Merkel's labour minister in 2007–2009, Olaf Scholz,[8] discretely managed to liberalize high-skilled labour immigration through changes in various administrative regulations and through the preparation of the Work Migration Control Act of 2008.[9] Under this new policy and since that time, all those considered qualified (either by virtue of a university degree or a high salary) mainly needed a concrete job offer to be able to take up work in Germany. This policy continued and was refined through the next two Merkel cabinets, the last again a cabinet with the Social Democrats.

However, in the opinion of many observers, Germany's worldwide immigration image was determined by its closed-door policy towards Eastern Europe and the low-skilled world; see, for instance, Fihel et al. (2015) and SVR (2015). Hence, in spite of an ever-improving labour market and a substantial need for skilled labour, only few such workers came. This was interpreted as having been caused by the absence of a 'welcoming culture' (*Willkommenskultur*). Observing short-term pressures and expecting long-term needs, in the first half of 2015 all the major parties started debating how to update the immigration regulations into concise immigration legislation.[10]

When, in 2015, an increasing number of refugees crossed the German borders, Merkel and large parts of the German media took the chance to use the asylum seekers to promote a more open German welcoming culture. What first got the sympathy of Germans, and many in the world, was soon destroyed by the alternative media picture of refugees 'invading' Europe and Germany, which was (wrongly) portrayed in the public after Merkel solved the problem of the stranded migrants in Budapest later in 2015. It is unknown what motivated Merkel to help the Hungarians, but one could see this as a move to establish European solidarity and the introduction of a fair quota system between the EU member states. I had recommended this in various studies including Rinne and Zimmermann (2015), a paper which, indeed, was on the desk of the Chancellery. I still think that there was no alternative for Germany but to lead Europe into a solution to the refugee challenge. This issue remains valid, since there is no alternative if one wants to preserve the EU in the future.

After the events in Budapest, the paranoia about migrants exploded, fuelled the rise of right-wing populists, and ended any ongoing efforts to establish a modern and flexible labour immigration regime in Germany. The Christian Social Union in Bavaria (CSU), the Bavarian part within the German conservative movement with the Christian Democratic Union of Germany (CDU) as a partner in all other German states, insisted on a humanitarian quota which Merkel had for a long time (rightly) argued to be non-constitutional. Ultimately, all government parties saw a substantial loss of votes in the 2017 federal elections in favour of a new right-wing party, the Alternative für Deutschland (Alternative for Germany—AfD).

However, the situation is much less dramatic than some people claim. Politically, Germany has remained rather stable, although it has taken by far the greatest number of asylum applications in Europe (Constant and Zimmermann 2016). If there is a country in Europe with the right to be nervous about keeping the refugee inflow manageable, it is Germany. Nevertheless, the AfD won only 12.6 per cent of the votes. This is a relatively small number if one compares it with many other recent country elections—for instance, the Netherlands, Austria, Italy, or even the French presidential elections. It is not even necessary to weight the results with the relatively small numbers of refugees those countries received. Nevertheless, the AfD is larger than the other small parties (the Left, the Greens, and the Liberals) and hence can claim the constitutional role of opposition leadership, which gives it significant visibility.

However, the formation of a new government took six months, from 24 September 2017 (election day) to 14 March 2018, the longest in German post-World War II history. At first, the Social Democrats preferred to lead the opposition, but coalition talks between the Conservatives, the Greens, and the Liberals did not converge. Hence, after challenging negotiations, Conservatives and Social Democrats finally formed a third cabinet under Merkel. The government contract reveals a two-tier migration policy strategy. The difficult refugee issue was addressed by the agreement to seek a maximum of 200,000 refugees net (!) per year, if possible and in accordance with the German Basic Law. Largely undiscussed in the media is that the government contract clearly announces modern immigration legislation allowing for a much stronger labour market oriented immigration policy. The contract signals clear criteria which can be associated with a points system. Hence, my prediction is that Germany will soon have modern labour immigration legislation, which would be a great success for those researchers who have supported such a policy for a long time.

What can we learn from recent German migration policies? One can ignore economic or social constraints for a while, following one's own objectives or the preferences of voters. However, in the long run, one has to observe constraints such as budget deficits while, in the short run, overspending or ignoring environmental or social damage is possible. Destroying Europe and keeping migrants out can imply large welfare losses in the long run. Reality will then force policy-makers to adjust—see the recent French elections. Such a policy is sustainable, if it is clearly formulated and consequently followed.

Rethinking Policy Advice

This section reflects the failures of past migration policy-making from my perspective as a policy advisor. Optimizing the impact of policy advice on migration issues must begin with an analysis of the interests and weaknesses of the main actors—voters, politicians, media, and scientific policy advisors. The task of policy advice is challenging, since the migration topic is analytically complex and emotionally heated.

It is natural that voters follow preferences and emotions, and are not always aware of facts and constraints. Hence, scientists need to communicate facts and insights to a broader public through both traditional and social media, to act as a policy advisor by providing reports or personal face-to-face advice, or to communicate directly with the public through speeches and popular books. Too few are doing this; neither are they educated for this purpose, nor are they free of self-interest.

However, academic success is related to creating new knowledge, which can be too specialized to be helpful to policy-making processes. In my view, in their advisory role, scientists need to advocate the mainstream, not outsider positions. Scientific advisors need to respect the different time-horizons of science, which are long term, and policy-making, which is short term and often immediate. This means that the production of knowledge should be completed long before its time to be used in the political arena has come. This implies that the researcher should stand by, until the right time comes. Obviously, in 2018 it is high noon for policy advice on the migration issue. New political directives are needed, and the scientific profession is better prepared for it than ever.

In my view, the media is the most important channel for policy advice; here, both society and policy-makers can be reached informally and effectively. However, the traditional media are committed to providing balanced reporting, which leads to a bias against mainstream scientific findings. The weights given to minority findings are too great. Scientists are much less prepared for the traditional media, which focus more strongly on entertainment, than for social media. Social media are not only easier to access, they are also easier to use and communication is faster.

In my observation, policy-makers tend to use facts and scientific evidence, if this supports their own ambitions, if it is unavoidable due to constraints or the challenge has become unacceptable. A crisis is helpful to push for reforms. Hence, explaining constraints and trade-offs is an important task; for instance, outlining the existence of budget constraints, or explaining that following one objective may often hurt another. Although migration is a very complex topic, the policy-makers I have interacted with in all major parties understand it. However, since the general public has a broad misperception of the need of migrants and their economic effects, the policy-makers often only engage in low-dimensional or simplistic migration policies. Over the years, I have seen few German politicians who regard themselves capable of explaining the benefits of mobility for society to their voters. An example is that immigration can fight unemployment if migrants help to create jobs; since this is more difficult to explain, it is easier to argue that migrants are not needed if the country faces a large unemployment level. On the contrary, some take the easy way to collecting votes by following the prejudices of their voters, instead of convincing them about true insights. It is, however, the job of policy-makers to make it transparent to voters where society's long-term needs are.

It is of major importance to reach society and the voters directly—in particular, since policy-makers are caught in the political trap of short-term decision-making and muddling-through. The broad misperception in the population about the economic consequences of migration is one point that it is necessary to address. The understanding in society is often that migration causes economic problems for natives, and that migrants make excessive use of the welfare state. Others are just not aware of the large potential economic benefits mobility and migration can have (van Noort 2016). This stands against broad academic evidence that migrants are economically successful and do not take jobs but, rather, stimulate the economy and are needed in the long term—see, among many sources, Zimmermann (2005, 2014a); Kahanec and Zimmermann (2009, 2016); EU Commission (2011); Constant and Zimmermann (2013); Blau and Mackie (2016); Wadsworth et al. (2016). Migrants can reduce native unemployment if they are complements in the production of goods and services, and not substitutes for native workers. As a consequence, more employed migrants may cause a larger labour demand for natives. Besides public fears, the risk of welfare migration is also low (Giulietti and Wahba 2013; Giulietti et al. 2013).

Another point is to take the fears and concerns of people seriously and introduce them to realities that can generate positive affections: for example, to make transparent the misery of war and flight—solidarity with and responsibility for the fate of refugees can be strong incentives for acceptance and support; and informing the public about the success story of migrants in society and employment, and their usefulness for the economy demonstrated through the presentation of real-life migrant role models. As an example, the German Federal Railway recently advertised their services using the real-world example of a migrant born in Africa, who became popular as the role model for a helpful and service-oriented train conductor. Globally seen, concerns about migrants and refugees are often the largest in geographical areas where no migrants or refugees live.[11] Anecdotal evidence for Germany illustrates this. The infamous anti-migration Pegida movement (Patriotic Europeans Against the Islamisation of the West) started in Dresden, the capital of Saxony, in 2014. In the 2017 federal elections, the AfD, having won 27.0 per cent of the votes (Germany: 12.6 per cent), became the largest (!) party in that German state, while the share of foreigners in that year in Saxony was 3.9 per cent

(Germany: 10.5 per cent). Integration policies and practices in companies need to take this as a starting point to expose role models in society and in workplaces, and to mobilize and involve ethnic networks or diaspora.

Simply teaching facts about migration does not help. It is also important that migration policy is consistent, persistent, and transparent (Zimmermann 2017). Points systems in immigration laws, for instance, provide transparency for migrants and the host country. They have been effective in screening and guiding mobility for regular migrants. This enables a government to base the selection criteria on integration indicators such as education, language proficiency, job characteristics, the professions needed and social activities. This transparency is not only good for the migrant for guidance and orientation; it also helps natives to understand that the newcomers are of value for the receiving society. Using the labour market as a filter for the selection of non-humanitarian migrants ensures that the inflow focuses on people who are likely to have a job, are able to finance their own life, and are useful for society. Research has shown that countries that have clear labour immigration policies exhibit less negative attitudes to foreigners (Bauer et al. 2000). Following the public German migration debate, it seems that these insights have been understood by major policy-makers. Therefore, Germany is expected to improve its immigration law in the near future as has been announced in the coalition contract of the new government.

Similarly, access to employment needs to be discussed in the context of forced migration (Constant and Zimmermann 2016; Zimmermann 2017). First, one has to respect and accept that all refugees and asylum seekers also have economic needs—they need an income source to maintain their lives. Early access to the labour market is essential for this; poor immigration regulations at entry into the host country are often partly responsible for a slow rise in labour market performance when recognized later. Germany already allows asylum seekers to work soon after filing a refugee application. It tries to profile them upon entry to understand the abilities and qualifications requirements for educational interventions and placement services. Providing language classes is important, and the quality of the courses in Germany needs to be improved. Access to the labour market is not only an integration policy, it also becomes a development policy if the asylum seeker is not recognized later as a refugee or, if recognized, the migrant moves back home or further on. Forced migrants should also have the option to transfer to a regular labour immigration scheme if they qualify.

This all suggests that, and describes how, humanitarian and work-related migration can be integrated in one immigration concept where forced migrants are given the right early on to accept jobs temporarily and enter channels to regular immigration if they meet the requested criteria. Of course, asylum seekers have to leave the country when not recognized. Guided by research starting with Bauer et al. (2000), I expect that this labour market orientation could also raise the social acceptance of humanitarian migration.

Conclusion

The virtue of open markets and free labour mobility is not easily understood in society. A recent trend towards evidence-free policy-making and a rising mistrust about globalization is strengthening this. Against this background, this chapter has studied Germany's long path towards being a well-managed immigration country. Despite broad academic evidence of positive effects, resistance against migration remains strong in society—witnessed by the many recent election results; for instance, in Germany, Austria, France, and Italy. To reduce the gap between facts and misperceptions, the combined promotion of knowledge about the effects of migration that have been mentioned and the social identity of successful migrant workers ('role models') is suggested. How can the image of migrants be associated with being construction workers, artists, lawyers, and soccer players, for instance? This means confronting prejudices about migrants with job performances demonstrating that they are respected members of society.

Driven by questions raised about the economic consequences of migration, the research community has provided a number of insights which are important for policy-making. Among those are that Germany has long been a country of immigration and could do so much better by means of improved management through well-considered immigration legislation. Public debates often focus on the inflow of people and ignore the large outflow of migrants. Effective flexibility of labour increases the output of the economy and the welfare of people. Restricting free labour mobility may force people to stay and bring family members, which is against what policies were intended to achieve. More migrants in jobs can increase the employment of natives when they act as complements and not as substitutes. There is also no convincing evidence that migrants overly exploit the welfare state. Hiring economic migrants and finding jobs for asylum seekers help to reduce tensions in the native population and strengthen the chances for successful economic integration.

Nowadays, German policy-makers have understood that the country is an immigration country; it benefits from open labour markets and needs more migrant workers in the future, particularly skilled migrant workers. The aim therefore is to modernize the country's immigration legislation to allow for selective labour immigration policies oriented towards short-term labour market needs and long-term requirements. The refugee challenge needs to be approached in a framework of European solidarity, which could start with the early access of refugees to the labour market. Researchers need to understand that they should be ready with evidence when the right opportunity appears. Until such time, it is important to communicate evidence repeatedly through traditional and social media in order to prepare the background for change. The time for evidence-based policy-making will probably return when political realities clash with economic constraints.

Notes

1. This broader issue has been globally studied and forcefully reflected by Ruhs (2013).
2. Reviews of German migration history and policy can be found in Schmidt and Zimmermann (1992) and Zimmermann (1996), among others.
3. Germany was therefore always a model case for the gap between facts and perceptions on migration and integration—described by Ruhs, Tamas, and Palme in their introductory chapter to this book—long before the situation became globally even more challenging in many countries around the world. This is very different from labour market policies, where evidence-based policy-making played quite an important role, at least for some time (Rinne and Zimmermann 2013).
4. For instance, see Kahanec and Zimmermann (2009, 2016) for the evaluation of the consequences of EU Eastern Enlargement.
5. The refugee issue is a crucial topic for handling the migration issue in society. It can only be approached successfully in a European or even worldwide context. This has been analysed by Hatton (2013), Hinte et al. (2015), Rinne and Zimmermann (2015), OECD (2016), and Zimmermann (2016). While of great importance, it can only be a side topic in this chapter.
6. The book by Zimmermann et al. (2007) is based on analysis undertaken for the Migration Commission and has been further developed propagating a modern immigration law with a points system.
7. These and other consequences of the German closed-door policy were revealed in the studies by Brenke et al. (2009) and Elsner and Zimmermann (2016). For more details on the consequences of EU enlargements, see the various research contributions in Kahanec and Zimmermann (2009, 2016).
8. Being the First Mayor and head of the city state of Hamburg for many years, he became the new Finance Minister and Vice Chancellor in the new and third cabinet of the Christian and Social Democrats in March 2018.
9. Arbeitsmigrationssteuergesetz, 20 December 2008 archived at: https://perma.cc/2AF6-F72R. A more detailed analysis can be found in BAMF (2010: 97–101). The cabinet had discussed the new high-skilled labour immigration strategy in August 2007 and July 2008. Law and administrative regulations came into effect on 1 January 2009.
10. Various influential groups in the Conservative and Social Democratic parties had, at the time, invited me to explain what form new work-oriented immigration

legislation could take following an outline provided by my research paper 'Punkte machen?! Warum Deutschland ein aktives Auswahlsystem für ausländische Fachkräfte braucht und wie ein solches System aussehen kann' (Hinte et al. 2016).

11. Esipova et al. (2015: 14), based on interviews with over 183,000 adults across more than 140 countries between 2012 and 2014 surveyed in Gallup's World Poll, find: 'Countries where migrants constitute 10 per cent or more of the population are the most likely to have an opinion about immigration levels, and they are more likely to be positive (a combined 51 per cent favour keeping levels the same or increasing them) than negative (43 per cent favour decreasing levels). One explanation for this could be that in countries with higher percentages of migrants, the population has a greater chance to interact with migrants and this might promote greater acceptance.'

References

BAMF. 2010. Bundesministerium des Innern, Bundesamt für Migration und Flüchtlinge. *Migrationsbericht 2008*, Berlin.

Bauer, T. K., Lofstrom, M., and Zimmermann, K. F. 2000. Immigration policy, assimilation of immigrants, and natives' sentiments towards immigrants: Evidence from 12 OECD countries. *Swedish Economic Policy Review* 7: 11–53.

Blau, F. D., and Mackie, C. (eds). 2016. *The Economic and Fiscal Consequences of Immigration*, A Report of the National Academies, Washington, DC.

Boswell, C. 2012. *The Political Uses of Expert Knowledge*. Cambridge: Cambridge University Press.

Brenke, K., Yuksel, M., and Zimmermann, K. F. 2009. EU enlargement under continued mobility restrictions: Consequences for the German Labor Market. In *EU Labor Markets after Post-Enlargement Migration*, eds M. Kahanec and K. F. Zimmermann. Berlin: Springer Verlag, 111–29.

Constant, A. F., and Zimmermann, K. F. (eds). 2013. *International Handbook on the Economics of Migration*. Cheltenham: Edward Elgar.

Constant, A. F. and Zimmermann, K. F. 2016. Towards a new European refugee policy that works. *CESifo DICE Report—Journal of International Comparisons* 4: 3–8.

Constant, A. F., and Zimmermann, K. F. 2017. Le défi des migrations: quelles options pour L'Europe? *Revue Economie Financiere* 125: 195–207.

Davies, P. 2012. The state of evidence-based policy evaluation and its role in policy formation. *National Institute Economic Review* 219(1): R41–R52.

Elsner, B., and Zimmermann, K. F. 2016. Migration 10 years after: EU enlargement, closed borders, and migration to Germany. In *Labor Migration, EU Enlargement, and the Great Recession*, eds M. Kahanec and K. F. Zimmermann. Berlin: SpringerVerlag, 85–101.

Esipova, N., Ray, J., Pugliese, A., and Tsabutashvili, D. 2015. *How the World Views Migration*. Geneva: International Organization for Migration (IOM).

EU Commission. 2011. *Frequently asked Questions: The End of Transitional Arrangements for the Free Movement of Workers on 30 April 2011*. http://europa.eu/rapid/press-release_MEMO-11-259_en.htm

Fihel, A., Janicka, A., Kaczmarczyk, P., and Nestorowicz, J. 2015. *Free Movement of Workers and Transitional Arrangements: Lessons from the 2004 and 2007 Enlargements*, Centre of Migration Research, University of Warsaw.

Giulietti, C., and Wahba, J. 2013. Welfare Migration. In *International Handbook on the Economics of Migration*, eds A. F. Constant and K. F. Zimmermann. Cheltenham: Edward Elgar, 489–504.

Giulietti, C., Guzi, M., Kahanec, M., and Zimmermann, K. F. 2013. Unemployment benefits and immigration: Evidence from the EU. *International Journal of Manpower* 34(1): 24–38.

Hatton, T. J. 2013. Refugee and asylum migration. In *International Handbook on the Economics of Migration*, eds A. F. Constant and K. F. Zimmermann. Cheltenham: Edward Elgar, 453–69.

Hinte, H., Rinne, U., and Zimmermann, K. F. 2015. Flüchtlinge in Deutschland: Herausforderungen und Chancen. *Wirtschaftsdienst* 95: 744–51.

Hinte, H., Rinne, U. and Zimmermann, K. F. 2016. Punkte machen?! Warum Deutschland ein aktives Auswahlsystem für ausländische Fachkräfte braucht und wie ein solches System aussehen kann. *Perspektiven der Wirtschaftspolitik*, 17: 68–87.

Jauer, J., Liebig, T., Martin, J. P., and Puhani, P. A. 2018. *Migration as an Adjustment Mechanism in the Crisis? A Comparison of Europe and the United States 2006–2016*, Essen: GLO Discussion Paper 178.

Kahanec, M., and Zimmermann, K. F. (eds). 2009. *EU Labor Markets after Post-Enlargement Migration*. Berlin: Springer Verlag.

Kahanec, M., and Zimmermann, K. F. (eds). 2016. *Labor Migration, EU Enlargement, and the Great Recession*. Berlin: Springer Verlag.

Krause, A., Rinne, U., and Zimmermann, K. F. 2017. European labor market integration: What the experts think. *International Journal of Manpower* 38(7): 954–74.

Massey, D. S., Durand, J., and Pren, K. A. 2016. Why border enforcement backfired. *American Journal of Sociology* 121: 1157–600.

OECD. 2016. *How Are Refugees Faring on the Labour Market in Europe? A First Evaluation Based on the 2014 EU Labour Force Survey ad hoc Module*. Paris: Working Paper 1/2016W.

Rinne, U., and Zimmermann, K. F. 2013. Is Germany the North Star of Labor Market Policy? *IMF Economic Review* 61: 702–29.

Rinne, U., and Zimmermann, K. F. 2015. Zutritt zur Festung Europa? Anforderungen an eine moderne Asyl- und Flüchtlingspolitik. *Wirtschaftsdienst* 95: 114–20.

Ruhs, M. 2013. *The Price of Rights: Regulating International Labor Migration*. Princeton, NJ: Princeton University Press.

Schmidt, C. M., and Zimmermann, K. F. 1992. Migration pressure in Germany: Past and future. In *Migration and Economic Development*, ed. K. F. Zimmermann. Berlin: Springer, 201–30.

SVR (The Expert Council of German Foundations on Integration and Migration). (2015). *Immigration Countries: Germany in an International Comparison*. Annual Report, Berlin.

van Noort, S. 2016. *The Paradox of the Immigration Debate: Distorted Perceptions of the Influence of Immigrants on the Economy*, mimeo. Amsterdam.

Wadsworth, J., Dhingra, S., Ottaviano, G., and Van Reenen, J. 2016. *Brexit and the Impact of Immigration on the UK*. London: LSE, Centre for Economic Performance. http://cep.lse.ac.uk/pubs/download/brexit05.pdf

Zimmermann, K. F. 1996. European migration: Push and pull. Proceedings volume of the World Bank Annual Conference on Development Economics 1994, Supplement to *The World Bank Economic Review and The World Bank Research Observer* 10 (1995): 313–342. Reprinted in *International Regional Science Review* 19 (1996): 95–128.

Zimmermann, K. F. 2004. Advising policymakers through the media. *Journal of Economic Education* 35(4): 395–405.

Zimmermann, K. F. (ed.) 2005. *European Migration: What Do We Know?* Oxford and New York: Oxford University Press.

Zimmermann, K. F. 2014a. Migration, jobs and integration in Europe. *Migration Policy Practice* 4(4): 4–16.

Zimmermann, K. F. 2014b. Circular migration. *IZA World of Labor* 1. https://wol.iza.org/articles/circular-migration/long

Zimmermann, K. F. 2016. Migrationspolitik im Mediensturm. *Wirtschaftspolitische Blätter* 63: 497–508.

Zimmermann, K. F. 2017. Refugee and migrant labor market integration: Europe in need of a new policy agenda. In *The Integration of Migrants and Refugees. An EUI Forum on Migration, Citizenship and Demography*, eds R. Bauböck and M. Tripkovic. Florence: European University Institute, Robert Schuman Centre for Advanced Studies, 88–100.

Zimmermann, K. F. Bonin, H., Fahr, R., and Hinte, H. 2007. *Immigration Policy and the Labor Market. The German Experience and Lessons for Europe*. Berlin: Springer Verlag.

9

The Politicization of Evidence-based Policies

The Case of Swedish Committees

Kristof Tamas

Introduction

Purely scientifically based research funding in liberal democracies tends to limit the utility of research for policy-making. As a result, part of government-funded research is steered towards policy-oriented studies to cater for the government's interest as well as, allegedly, that of the public. Over the past couple of decades there has also been a general growth in the interest in producing more evidence-based policies (Davies et al. 2000: 2). Different models have been developed in this regard in terms of organizational, institutional, and funding structures (cf. Hoppe 2005).

The Swedish experience of government committees offers interesting examples of the diversity of efforts to make research relevant for policy-making. The Swedish case is also an example of how the research–policy dialogue may suffer from the gap between different research and policy 'cultures'. These need to be bridged through dialogue and exchange in order to avoid the demise of relationships between researchers and policy-makers (Davies et al. 2000: 360). The aim of this chapter is to draw on the Swedish example of government committees to critically discuss the potential opportunities, benefits, and pitfalls when attempting to bridge the gap between research and policy-making. The chapter will also cast some new light on the claim that the research–policy nexus in liberal democracies is characterized by 'the simultaneous scientification of politics and the politicisation of science' (Weingart 1999: 151–61).

After a brief conceptual introduction, I will review the Swedish committee system, in general, and the functioning of migration and integration committees working in the 1970s through to the 1990s, in particular. I then discuss a specific case of a committee where this form of research led to a major public controversy. I also discuss the pros and cons of another approach, whereby policy-makers pick and choose from the menu of interpretations offered by think tanks funded by non-governmental sources, or by academia. The chapter concludes by considering alternative forms of policy-driven research in more recent committees.

The Research–Policy Nexus

It is clear that policy-makers often refrain from taking into account available evidence, or even go against sound evidence provided by the academic community, as 'many alternative examples of policy initiatives... seem to either fly in the face of the best available research evidence on effectiveness or, at the very best, are based on flimsy evidence' (Nutley and Webb 2000: 13). While this may have contributed to more widespread post-factual politics (Villumsen Berling and Bueger 2017: 332–41), the public trust in science varies according to political ideology and interest group, and also according to social class, ethnicity, and gender, which may also lead to political divisions influencing policy-making (Gauchat 2012).

Existing research has proposed a range of different conceptualizations and 'models' of the research–policy nexus. Hoppe (2005) makes a broad distinction between 'advocacy models' and 'learning models':

> In advocacy models, science is considered one among multiple political voices that enable political debate, judgment, and decision. In the learning models, all actors are constructed as 'inquirers' engaged in a process of social learning through social debate. (Hoppe 2005: 211)

The advocacy models portray the research–policy nexus as a non-exclusive relationship, where researchers compete with other actors attempting to influence policy-makers (Tellmann 2016: 14). Researchers are thus not entirely neutral and objective as 'each voice in the political arena is considered to be an advocacy plea in favour or against positions defended by other political actors' (Hoppe 2005: 210). In the learning models, research, and policy communities are regarded as equal participants in a forum for debate in the quest to find acceptable solutions to identified problems. Studies of 'enlightenment', 'knowledge creep', 'knowledge shifts', or 'research as ideas', have shown how scientific research historically has had various, sometimes unintended, impacts on policy-making. For some researchers, such impacts could probably be welcome if their findings are used as an aid in defining problems and policy options. They could, however, also be detrimental in cases where research is being over-simplified and reshaped into unscientific arguments, or used selectively merely to legitimize predefined political positions (Hoppe 2005: 203; Daviter 2015; see also Weiss 1977, 1980, 1991: 311).

While researchers often want to avoid secluding themselves in an 'ivory tower' and cannot always control how their output will be used or interpreted, they need to maintain their autonomy in relation to policy-makers (Villumsen Berling and Bueger 2017: 115–19). Moreover, there are also risks with Wildavsky's notion of 'speaking truth to power' (Wildavsky 1979), as an exaggerated emphasis on the production of knowledge for policy-making as steering primarily through knowledge and experts could be to the detriment of open and more inclusive political, democratic deliberations. A further risk would be if the evidence produced for the sake of reinforced policy-making were to end up in the form of empty rituals that policy-makers came to ignore (Ahlbäck Öberg 2011: 764).

Assessments of research–policy dialogues have also pinpointed the different 'cultures' that need to be bridged through open exchange and improved commissioning of research in order to close the existing gaps. Davies et al. (2000) consider that:

> policy makers and practitioners complain that research is, among other things, slow, impenetrable, irrelevant, expensive, and inconvenient or uncomfortable. However, to some extent this reflects failures in the commissioning process and failures to understand the nature of research rather than failures of research.
>
> (Davies et al. 2000: 360)

Finally, research may become politicized, especially in highly contested issue areas such as migration and integration. However, politicization does not necessarily mean reduced utilization of knowledge or evidence in policy-making. It may, nevertheless, shift the position of utilization from instrumental to symbolic. Symbolic utilization either substantiates pre-existing policy positions, or is used to legitimize policy positions (Boswell 2009; Scholten and Verbeek 2015; Chapter 2 in this book).

The Swedish Tradition of Government-funded Committees: Functioning and Critiques

There is a 400-year tradition in Sweden of relying on committees (similar to those in Norway and Denmark) in order to collect information and research, analyse data and prepare proposals as an input to processes of legislative change and broader policy-making. These committees represent different forms of bridging the research–policy gaps.[1] Therefore, they serve as a good case for analysing the extent to which they may be mainly characterized as advocacy models or learning models, and the extent to which they may avoid politicization.

Most of the major legislative and policy reforms in Sweden have been based on the report of a committee of some sort (ESO 1998: 57). Committees of inquiry, commissions, more long-standing delegations or expert groups may be led by professional experts, such as professors or legal experts, or politicians within the theme to be covered.[2] This is a useful aid since Swedish ministries in international comparison have been small in terms of staffing and resources (SOU 2016: 338). This injection of knowledge and evidence could, in an optimistic scenario, bring more well-founded decisions (Zetterberg 1990: 307; Amnå 2010: 556).

The proposals put forward by committees are usually circulated to all concerned stakeholders for input, including government ministries and agencies, labour market bodies (employers' associations and unions), organizations, civil society, and the private sector. Committees, in the sense of Bordieau's concept of social capital and from a broader research perspective on social trust, may be seen as instruments for political deliberations with the aim of bringing opposing views closer together (Trägårdh 2007: 254, see also 261).

In recent decades, there have been important changes in the way that committees have worked and in the way they have influenced policy-making. For example, there has been a relative reduction in the share of parliamentary committees involving both political parties and organized interest groups in relation to inquiries headed by a special investigator (ESO 1998: 57). In addition, Swedish interest groups have noted deterioration in the opportunities to influence government policy-making through the committees (Lundberg 2015a: 44, 56; 2015b). There has also been a relative reduction in the share of committees that take on the major political challenges, while there is an increasing share of committees dealing with somewhat marginal and technical issues (ESO 1998: 57).

An evaluation of the committee system in 1997 by the Parliament's Auditors, found that the quality of the committees' work had deteriorated, partly as a result of reduced time given to the committees in which to prepare their analysis and provide their results. A 2004 follow-up evaluation by the Swedish National Audit Office noted that these deficiencies remain, that the remit with which working committees are tasked does not correspond to the time allowed for delivery, and that several committees have deficiencies in the data they use as background to the analysis and proposals (Riksdagens revisorer 1997/98: 12; Riksrevisionen 2004: 8). The appointed researchers do not manage to contribute with novel research and analysis, and then the committees, become more reliant on expertise from within the ministries (Amnå 2010: 558). Indeed, one study has shown that Swedish governments have exercised increasingly tighter control over the committees (Riksdagens revisorer 1997/98: 70, referring to Johansson 1992).

Similarly, the Administrative Policy Commission (*Förvaltningspolitiska kommissionen*) noted in its report that, since the 1980s, the committees had been increasingly brought closer to the government offices and that they were compiling existing research, rather than collecting their own primary data and analysing it to generate new knowledge. It argued that the government should, instead, make greater use of the committees to undertake *independent* evaluations and take on board the full value of research (SOU 1997: 98–9). The Control Commission (*Styrutredningen*) suggested that the committees should be used more strategically to compile knowledge as counter-narratives whenever a reform of government agencies and their work is to be considered (SOU 2007: 260, 264–5).

It has also been argued that cases of mounted political steering—preordained results and the premature preparation of legislative proposals before committees' final proposals are completed—risk damaging the overall political system (Erlingsson 2016). In contrast, it has been suggested that it is a myth that the government has good control over and the ability to direct Swedish committees. This is illustrated by how directives are often rather vague and ambiguous, and, in addition, are frequently not properly applied by the committees. Nevertheless, the government continues to appoint committees regularly, as there are relatively few alternatives in Sweden compared to other countries as far as think tanks and other independent foundations for research are concerned (ESO 1998: 57).

To conclude this broad review of committees in Swedish policy-making: in its ideal form, the Swedish committee system may function as a depoliticized forum from which the government may harvest science-based analysis and preparatory work for its legislative reforms and policy development. Recent critiques have, however, pointed to considerable challenges with this system. Moreover, what happens when the policy field to be analysed by a committee becomes highly politicized, as in the case of migration and integration?

Government-funded Migration Research in Sweden

The Swedish government, as well as the Swedish media, started to show an interest in migration research in the 1970s. The government wanted close cooperation between government officials and researchers with a view to providing an improved knowledge-base for policy reforms, and to evaluate ongoing policy frameworks. Researchers, in general, still had a limited impact on the policy-making process, however. The Swedish government, nevertheless, took the initiative to commission various sector-based research projects that would otherwise not have been carried out within the regular university system. Such commissioned research encouraged a burgeoning group of scholars to explore the field of migration research. This period was characterized by a realization that immigrants who had arrived as temporarily needed labour were likely to remain for the long term, and that more systematic policy-making and planning was now a necessity. The government asked researchers for empirical analyses of past and contemporary migration patterns, trends, and consequences. The resulting research provided input to the preparations for both integration and migration control policies (Hammar 2003: 10; 2004: 19).

In the period 1975–1983, the government appointed an expert group (Eifo—the Expert Group on Immigration Research) within the government offices to work on immigration and integration issues. It initiated, coordinated, and published policy-relevant studies on the emerging integration issues in Sweden (Hammar 2003: 10; 2004: 19). Several of the researchers employed by Eifo were moved to Stockholm University in 1983, where a new centre (Ceifo—the Centre for Research in International Migration and Ethnic Relations) was established. At the same time, Deifo (the Delegation of Immigration Research) was set up to initiate and share information about research in the area of migration and integration. A government decision in 1990 transformed this body, together with the Delegation for Social Research, into a social sciences research council.[3]

These changes had partly been motivated by the view that research also needed to be established in this field within the more regular university research structures. It was probably also due to the need to make research more independent from the government. For a period, however, much research continued to be initiated by the government. For instance, the first professorship in research into International Migration and Ethnic Relations (IMER) was set up in 1988 on the basis of a political initiative in the Swedish Parliament (*Riksdag*) (Hammar 2004: 30, 33).

In the 1980s and 1990s, migration started to become much more of a politicized issue in Sweden (Byström and Frohnert 2017). An increase in immigration, especially that of refugees and family members, from a much wider range of source countries and regions gave rise to a range of challenges for integration, such as segregation, unemployment among immigrants, and xenophobia. Some parliamentarians and researchers were quite critical of what they saw as an increasingly restrictive migration and integration policy at the end of the 1980s (Spång 2008). This was perhaps one reason why the different governments around that time became more sceptical of approaching academic researchers and asking for advice:

> Maybe policy makers in this new restrictive migration period give less priority to migration research, not because the field has become less important for politicians

and for all of us, but quite the reverse, because it has become a politicized and politically sensitive issue. (Hammar 2003: 11)

Tomas Hammar has noted that, sometimes, politicians appoint a committee and commission research merely as a means of prolonging the decision-making period, or as an excuse for inaction. Nevertheless, commissioned research initiated by politicians, he argued, should be open-ended and not designed in a way that a ready-made answer must be sought by the researchers. He believed that researchers need to be allowed to apply their regular methods of inquiry, seek new knowledge, and interpret it with the same high scientific standards that they would normally apply in a university environment (Hammar 1982: 22).

Overall, the experiences from the period with Eifo, Deifo, and Ceifo in Sweden were—according to Hammar, who was very much involved with all three entities—that research conducted under these premises remained independent and of high quality. The political steering was mainly limited to the themes and topics chosen for the studies, which were often outlined in a very broad, sweeping manner (Hammar 1988: 19). However, the relationship between the political leadership in the ministry and the appointed researchers was also criticized after a while. At the time, there was a lack of immigration research at the universities in Sweden; in addition, there were requests from various stakeholders that the policy-relevant research should be conducted at a university rather than within the structure of a ministry (leading to the setting up of Ceifo) (Wigerfelt and Peterson 2010; see also Hammar 1994: 13–18; 2008: 61).

During this period, relations between researchers and policy-makers were, in general, good, thanks to the engagement of numerous researchers in the work of committees. This enabled many researchers to participate in the ongoing 'problem definition': 'Swedish migration researchers have made critical assessments of migration and integration policies and even highly critical positions seem to have been taken into account' (Jørgensen 2011: 103). In the early part of the period, the nexus was characterized by consensus, whereby researchers informed policy-makers. Subsequently, however, conflicting researcher positions emerged, which also had an impact on the overall research–policy dialogue (Jørgensen 2011: 105).

This observation regarding the conflicting research positions motivates the case study in the following section, which is presented in order to illustrate the more recent characteristics of the research–policy nexus in the field of migration and integration policies in Sweden.

The Committee that Capsized

A low degree of politicization in the migration field seems to have enabled a larger share of learning (a forum for debate) than advocacy (competition), according to the models initially outlined in the research–policy nexus.[4] What happens, however, when migration becomes much more politicized, as has been the case in recent decades? It has been noted that '[i]n politicized settings, research and expertise are much less likely to be used as an authoritative source of policy-making, as this could be interpreted as a threat to political primacy' (Scholten and Verbeek 2015: 2, referring to Hoppe 2005). We shall now take an in-depth look at a case where the research, the committee, and the ensuing debate became highly politicized, and the use of knowledge became more symbolic.

An unusual form of committee in Sweden is one constructed in such a way that it should entirely focus on knowledge-production. The government has, in these cases, chosen to make the committee researcher-driven. Work is often linked to an academic environment, or based on reports being commissioned from external researchers. Some of these committees have not even been called upon to make concrete proposals for changes in policy or legislation, in order to make them even more independent, only being requested to take into account research and knowledge, and not being required to take responsibility for policy-making decisions (Ahlbäck Öberg 2004).

One example is the Integration Policy Power Commission (Ministry of Culture 2000). It was set up in 2000 as an important inquiry into integration policy, including discrimination, in Sweden. The head of the committee was Anders Westholm, a professor in political science and a well-known and highly respected researcher on power and influence. Two of the researchers who were appointed as experts on multiculturalism and discrimination in the committee—Paulina de los Reyes, an economic historian, and Masoud Kamali, professor at the Centre for Multiethnic Research—chose to resign after having expressed concerns regarding the working methods and priorities of the committee.

The critique also centred around the argument from de los Reyes and Kamali that the committee's research had taken a faulty path due to Westholm's alleged lack of expertise in research on discrimination and multiculturalism. According to de los Reyes and Kamali, too few researchers with adequate research expertise and an immigrant background were involved (*SvT Nyheter* 2004). When resigning in April 2003, they published a debate article in the daily newspaper *Dagens Nyheter* (*Daily News*). They claimed that the committee was driven by the norm that 'Swedishness' is self-evident and natural, while immigrants are different and thus subordinated to others in mainstream society. They claimed this to be an example of the very institutional, structural discrimination that should be the real mission of the committee's study. This was also the reason why, they stated, they chose to resign (*Dagens Nyheter* 2003).

These claims were refuted by Anders Westholm. The committee had been tasked with analysing the distribution of power resources and influence among people with a foreign background and the rest of the population, and to develop and test hypotheses around what affects the power and influence of immigrant groups in Swedish society (*Dagens Nyheter* 2003). The minister responsible, Mona Sahlin, a Social Democrat, agreed with de los Reyes and Kamali in much of their critique, including their observation that there is structural discrimination in Swedish society. She argued that she did not take sides in the academic debate but, rather, that she wanted to highlight not only the conflict itself, but also that there is structural discrimination within the academic world (*Dagens Nyheter* 2004a; 2006). Westholm felt compelled to resign (Ahlbäck Öberg 2004) and the government announced the appointment of Kamali to a new committee on Power, Integration and Structural Discrimination (Justitiedepartementet 2004). Moreover, the terms of reference for Kamali's new inquiry stated basically, as self-evident, that there is structural discrimination in Sweden (Justitiedepartementet 2004).

Subsequently, the eight researchers who remained on the Integration Policy Power Commission wrote a debate article in *Dagens Nyheter*. They defended Westholm (*Dagens Nyheter* 2004b), and his interpretation of the terms of reference. They were critical of integration minister Mona Sahlin, arguing that, instead of meeting her responsibility and creating an atmosphere where Westholm could go on working, she had acted in a way that forced Westholm to resign, as he had sensed that she did not trust him to complete his mission. Those researchers in the expert group who had not resigned tried to meet with Sahlin to discuss the matter but they were not presented with any opportunity to do so, according to media sources (*Dagens Nyheter* 2004b).

Finally, according to the eight researchers, the government should instead have given the research councils (*forskningsråden*)—for instance, the research council for working life and social sciences (*forskningsrådet för arbetsliv och socialvetenskap*)—the task of distributing research funding for these kinds of special requests. Researchers could then apply for funding in the usual competitive environment. They stated that the politicization of research by minister Sahlin was very worrying and could harm both the legitimacy of research and the committee system itself (*Dagens Nyheter* 2004b). As a result, there was extensive criticism of the minister, mainly from conservative media and commentators (Söderlund 2005). Around seventy researchers—among them very senior members of high-profile academia such as political science professors Bo Rothstein and Olof Petersson—wrote to minister Sahlin protesting against the politicization of the committee's working methods, a situation which the actions of the minister had allegedly created (*Svenska Dagbladet* 2003; *Dagens Nyheter* 2004b; Rothstein 2010).

One observer—the political scientist Shirin Ahlbäck Öberg—argued boldly that 'with her conduct, Sahlin dictates the scientific formulation of concepts and approaches and points out the "right" research orientation. You get the impression that the government with such a decision marks what kind of response they want on the questions formulated in the terms of reference' to the commission (quoted in Borg 2006: 12).[5] However, at the same time, many of the academics who took part in the debate reflected a scientific, rather than political, gap between a positivist epistemology and ontology (represented by Westholm) and critical, postmodern, and postcolonial approaches (as promoted by Kamali) (see, e.g., *Svenska Dagbladet* 2003). A later study questioned whether there was a 'danger of explaining too much' in the Kamali approach: 'Is it possible to capture the empirical complexity of this field aided by one diagnosis alone?' (Brekke and Borchgrevink 2007: 38).

Kamali's final report to the government was published in 2006 (SOU 2006), but the responsible Social Democratic minister at that time, Jens Orback, received it with great scepticism, arguing that it lacked clear legal proposals and fundamental calculations of costs (*SvT Nyheter* 2006) and that many of its suggestions already formed part of Swedish integration policy (Mavi 2007). Meanwhile, Kamali referred to his results as having shown that structural discrimination is both a cause and a consequence of inequality in Sweden, and that it is created and made permanent through the complex interaction between structural conditions, institutional arrangements, and individual actions. Kamali saw current integration policy as counter-productive and as having the wrong focus, and as having therefore stalled. He argued that radical change, including affirmative action, was necessary (SOU 2006:79).

A few years later, the researcher Stefan Jonsson reasoned that, as soon as the 'immigrants' had gained the right to formulate the problem of integration, 'the political and media elite' in Sweden had chosen to ignore the problem. Jonsson began to argue that discrimination was not a major problem but, rather, only marginal (Jonsson 2008). Despite this, Jonsson argued that Kamali's committee had not worked in vain. Although very little came out of the committee's proposals in terms of politics, the ideational and scientific results were notable in that they moved from a narrow group of researchers into a broader societal context (Jonsson 2008).

A harsh verdict on the whole case was written by the political scientist Ahlbäck Öberg (2004), who sided with Westholm. She argued that, in hindsight, it could be noted that the idea of investigations into power relations in the form of major research programmes had been based on what transpired to be a naive assumption: that, within the framework of the committee, it would be possible to maintain a barrier between policy and research. If the government wishes more research in a particular area, it would be better, she argued, if they allocated funds to the traditional research councils instead.

This case has illustrated how the research–policy nexus became highly politicized and how knowledge utilization became symbolic—politicians using research-as-ammunition (cf. Chapters 2 and 3 in this book; Weiss

1979). Considering this controversy, which I have depicted partly through biased voices, we may draw the conclusion that governments should ensure that the researchers they appoint to their committees are enabled to work independently, so that any doubts about the legitimacy of their work and findings can be eschewed. This would possibly require a broader reform of the committee system to ensure greater transparency in the formulation of impartial terms of reference for committees, as well as in the selection of their members—for example, by consulting parliament and relevant research councils.

Politicized Research Funded by Non-governmental Think Tanks

It has been suggested that the politicization of a policy field reduces the extent of institutionalized research–policy dialogues (e.g. through government-funded committees) to the benefit of ad hoc 'bridges', such as think tanks (Scholten and Verbeek 2015: 2–3). It could thus be argued that, as an alternative to government-funded committees, governments should turn to think tanks or independent academic researchers when seeking scientific evidence for their policy reforms. Government-funded research is, in this regard, subject to competition in the public arena from think tanks funded by other, non-governmental actors.

This section will show, however, that such research is also frequently used for political purposes in order to gain legitimacy for a proposed course of action—the legitimizing function of symbolic knowledge as outlined by Chapter 2 in this book. Moreover, we may also discern the second symbolic use of knowledge as referred to in Chapter 2, the function of substantiation— 'lending credibility to particular preferences or claims'. This case can therefore also be instructive in relation to advocacy models—competition among various research positions—concerning the research–policy nexus and, indirectly, to the role of publicly funded research.

I will highlight these points by discussing the recent debate about low-skilled jobs in Sweden as depicted in two reports. The debate raises questions about the selectivity of research results, rather than the quality of research itself. Political parties and the labour market parties (employers' associations and unions) use specific research to legitimize their arguments. The research results referred to in the debate may be consistent but (depending on the methods used, the discipline of the researchers, and the time-period covered) results may be contradictory. This is quite common in daily political debate but may be problematic from the perspective of public deliberation.

The Swedish think tank, the Centre for Business and Policy Studies (SNS), published their regular Economic Policy Council Report on the theme of inclusive labour market policies in 2017. The report noted that wages in the Swedish labour market are highly compressed and that the labour market is characterized by very low wage dispersion, which has been more or less static since early 2000. This had allegedly made it more difficult for immigrants and newly arrived refugees to establish themselves in the labour market. Moreover, there are very few jobs in Sweden that are suitable for low-skilled employees—in fact, Sweden has the smallest share among all EU member states. The major challenges in the labour market are concentrated on how to enable low-qualified persons with a foreign background to enter the labour market given the relatively high entry-level wages. Therefore, the study suggested policy changes and adjustments in the approach of the labour market parties aimed at lowering the barriers to enable the low-skilled to find jobs, including by abandoning all unnecessary formal qualification requirements. According to the report, 'it is fully possible to differentiate wages more without lowering the wages of experienced or qualified workers within the same agreements' (SNS 2017: 4).

Creating more low-skilled jobs for immigrants in this way was a move that would not be against the so-called 'Swedish model', whereby the labour market parties agree on wage conditions in line with collective agreements. Another report suggesting similar measures was also published in 2017 by the Swedish Labour Policy Council (AER), set up in 2015 as an expert council, funded by the Confederation of Swedish Enterprise but officially working independently from the funder. This report suggested similar ways to target the non-natives with the weakest attachment to the labour market, including the low-skilled. The report included a survey among employers, a significant proportion of whom said that lower costs for salaries would induce them to hire more low-skilled employees with subsidized employment. Consequently, the report argued that the labour market parties should take the initiative to encourage companies to hire newly arrived immigrants for subsidized employment, thus also assuming their social responsibility (AER 2017: 27).

Both proposals became part of the public debate. These are, however, very controversial issues from the perspective of the labour market parties, as well as in the opinion of the traditional left-wing and right-wing blocs in Swedish politics. The issue of low-skilled jobs has been one of the most frequently debated in Sweden in 2016–2018. Previous decades have seen a cemented impasse between the left-wing (leftist, social democratic, and Green) and right-wing (conservative, centre-right, and liberal) political parties in the country. Both sides tend to refer to research that supports their standpoint. Does the lowering of entry level wages risk trapping non-natives in a permanent low-waged position? Would there be a risk of reduced wages across the line, including for more well-established workers? Are more low-skilled jobs the key to reducing unemployment and exclusion among newly arrived non-natives? What are the alternatives? Regarding these kinds of issues, it is likely that evidence-based research becomes politicized, especially if provided by various think tanks, but also if it originates at independent academic institutions. This case is an illustration of an advocacy model, as described initially in this chapter. It is also a case of research-as-ammunition in the symbolic use of knowledge by policy-makers (cf. Chapter 2):

> The struggle between group interests functions as variety generator and selection environment for scientific arguments that underpin political positions and decisions. Every interest involved will look for the type of scientific expertise that harnesses and legitimizes its pre-formed political stance.   (Hoppe 2005: 210)

Government-funded committees may want to join the debate by presenting balanced research, showing the pros and cons of the various policy alternatives, or they may abstain from participating in the debate so as not to be dragged into the process of politicization. The next section will discuss what is already being done in a few policy-oriented committees in order to avoid the politicization of government-funded research outputs.

Committees that Enable Policy-relevant Research without Direct Political Involvement

A more recent form of committee is characterized by broad and open terms of reference, encouraging the committee to assign external, independent researchers to produce reports over a longer period of time. This could be one way to generate guidance for policy development, as well as evaluations of the policy that has been implemented. There are currently three such committees in Sweden: the Migration Studies Delegation (Delmi) under the Ministry of Justice and the Expert Group for Aid Studies (EBA) under the Ministry for Foreign Affairs (both set up in 2013), and the Expert Group on Public Economics (ESO), under the Ministry of Finance,[6] which was up and running in the period 1981–2003, and has again been in place since 2007. The ESO was inspired by the model of the Netherlands Scientific Council for Government Policy (WRR), discussed in Chapter 6 by Monique Kremer.

As I am the current Director of Delmi, these committees will be discussed on a more personal note. All three committees have board members appointed by the government, but their terms of reference are defined in a way that enables the committees to work independently from both the government and the researchers they assign to carry out research. Their tasks include evaluating current policy-making, compiling relevant research in their areas of expertise, and commissioning and producing research reports as an input both to policy-makers and to the broader public debate. In theory, there remain some hazards with this model, although it bears the potential to contribute a sought-after evidence base to permit more balanced policy decisions. Arguably, there is still the danger that these committees may sometimes be too close to the government, presenting a risk that they may abstain from criticism of the policies carried out. At the same time, there may sometimes be the risk that they are too distanced from the government to the extent that their research becomes too theoretical and conceptual, and thus of less value for the daily challenges of a government.

The case of the ESO has been analysed with regard to its position—either too close to or too far removed from the government in its non-traditional task of questioning government policies and programmes, and their implementation (Lemne 2010). Tensions between various categories of actors—politicians, civil servants, and experts who were involved in the committee's work—has been a recurring phenomenon. Its influence on day-to-day government policy-making was somewhat hampered by the fact that it usually worked more slowly with a more in-depth focus than was normally the case among civil servants within the government offices. A somewhat paradoxical outcome of the ESO's role in the public debate was that, although it functioned under the leadership of the government, its critical reports instead often became a tool in the hands of the opposition. That the ESO was a government-funded committee was hence both a strength and a weakness for its policy relevance.

Nevertheless, I argue that these committees are closer to the idea of the learning model, which I regard as a more ideal kind of research–policy nexus than the advocacy model in the highly politicized field of migration. In this regard, I agree with Hoppe that policy-making could be likened to social experimentation:

> the learning model treats the policy process as a sort of research process in two respects: first, a policy or policy program is viewed as a set of hypotheses about the causal links between certain (collective, organizational) acts and a specified (desirable) future state of affairs. Second, policymaking is social experimentation. By close monitoring of the degree of goals achievement and a careful analysis of the causes of deviation, errors can gradually be eliminated. (Hoppe 2005: 211)

The research–policy nexus is thus, as always, filled with potential pitfalls. The policy-making process is characterized by gradual learning and indirect effects from research. When there is more politicization, research and policy dialogues tend to become more fragmented, while the use of knowledge in policy-making tends to become more symbolic (Scholten and Verbeek 2015; Chapter 2 in this book). Therefore, even if researchers take the opportunity to engage in commissioned studies, they need to stay detached in order to maintain their scientific independence and legitimacy in relation to government-funded committees.

Conclusion

The Swedish case includes, at least, three types of research–policy interactions. The first model is the traditional Swedish government-funded committee that can be steered politically in terms of members and research assignment, and where the results are to be reported to the government and dealt with within a formal process. The second model concerns research by think tanks which receive funding from, for example, the private sector or various interest groups, but which may nevertheless be selectively interpreted and politicized by various political interest groups. The third model entails a more independent form of government-funded committee that has no direct political involvement.

In conclusion, it is clear that one lesson learned for today's policy relevant research in the area of migration and integration is that government committees benefit a great deal from being able to work independently, without direct political steering. This is in contrast to research from think tanks, which is often politicized and therefore does not provide a real alternative to publicly funded research. Research at universities tends to be carried out at a distance from the daily policy challenges, with the risk of being driven by intrinsic issues and being inaccessible to policy-makers as well as the general public. The field of migration should strive towards the learning models and try to minimize the risks associated with the advocacy models. I see Delmi as an attempt to establish such a learning model if it succeeds in balancing its output accordingly.

According to the initially discussed advocacy models, the research–policy nexus often shows that researchers merely play a complementary role to the sources of influence or inspiration of policy-makers. Still, the learning models tell us that research may not only bring indirect effects, but also have unintended effects on policy-making and the research–policy nexus—such as committee research results being used by the opposition rather than only by the government, thus becoming part of broader political deliberations. Here, there is much to learn from experiences of how committees have been set up and how they functioned in the past. While many researchers would like to contribute to policy-making, they have good reason to be aware that their research may become over-simplified and be remoulded into unscientific arguments, or used selectively merely to legitimize predetermined political positions. Such risks are heightened when the field of enquiry itself is highly politicized, such as in the fields of migration and integration.

The experience from the Integration Policy Power Commission illustrates the risks of politicians steering research in a political direction. Politics-based evidence may undermine the legitimacy of policy-making. This is why we need more transparency in the committee system when formulating the terms of reference and selecting the researchers tasked with an enquiry. Committees need to remain at a distance from the government. Their reports should be permitted to be either critical or supportive of government policies. As long as such reports are solid, they nevertheless carry the potential to contribute to policy learning, from failures as well as from good (if not best) practices.

Notes

1. Information can be found at www.government.se/how-sweden-is-governed/committees/
2. Ibid.
3. www.ne.se/uppslagsverk/encyklopedi/l%C3%A5ng/delegationen-f%C3%B6r-invandrarforskning
4. The title of this section is taken from a report by the Swedish television station SvT Nyheter (2004).
5. My translation.
6. These three committees work in a similar way to Eifo and Deifo, although more independently from the government.

References

AER. 2017. The Duality of the Swedish Labour Market—Summary of the Swedish Labour Policy Council report *Tudelningarna på arbetsmarknaden*. Swedish Labour Policy Council.

Ahlbäck Öberg, S. 2004. Fri forskning i kollision med regeringens ideologiproduktion. www.temaasyl.se/Documents/Artiklar/Shirin%20Ahlbäck%20Öbergs%20artikel.doc

Ahlbäck Öberg, S. 2011. Kunskap och politik—mellan nonchalans och teknokrati, *Svensk Juristtidning*, 8: 764–771.

Amnå, E. 2010. Speaking truth to power? Statsvetarna och kommittéväsendet. In *Kontraster och nyanser: Svensk statsvetenskap i brytningstid*, eds M. Jerneck and B. Badersten. Lund: Statsvetenskaplig Tidskrift.

Borg, H. 2006. *Som man frågar får man svar: Masoud Kamali, Mona Sahlin och politiseringen av kommittéväsendet*. Stockholm: Timbro.

Boswell, C. 2009. *The Political Uses of Expert Knowledge: Immigration Policy and Social Research*. Cambridge: Cambridge University Press.

Brekke, J. P., and Borchgrevink, T. 2007. *Talking about Integration: Discourses, Alliances and Theories on Labour Market Integration in Sweden*. Institute for Social Research Report 2007:9. Oslo: Institute for Social Research.

Byström, M., and Frohnert, P. 2017. *Invandringens historia: från 'folkhemmet' till dagens Sverige*. Delmi Kunskapsöversikt 2017:5. Stockholm: Delmi.

Dagens Nyheter. 2003. Vi hoppar av Sahlins utredning. *DN Debatt*, 2003-04-06.

Dagens Nyheter. 2004a. Sahlin har ny syn på integrationen, 31/5-2004.

Dagens Nyheter. 2004b. Mona Sahlin politiserar forskningen, *DN Debatt*, 2004-01-20.

Dagens Nyheter. 2006. Nytt val kräver nytt taktikspel, Peter Wolodarski, 1/7-2006.

Davies, H. T. O., Nutley, S. M., and Smith, P. C. 2000. Introducing evidence-based policy and practice in public services. In *What Works? Evidence-based Policy and Practice in Public Services*, eds H. T. O. Davies, S. M. Nutley, and P. C. Smith. Bristol: Policy Press.

Daviter, F. 2015. The political use of knowledge in the policy process. *Policy Sciences* 48(4): 491–505.

Erlingsson, G. Ó. 2016. Utredningsväsendets förfall skadar det politiska systemet, *Dagens Samhälle*, 19 February. Stockholm.

ESO (1998) *Kommitterna och bofinken*, ESO-rapport, Ds 1998:57. Stockholm: ESO.

Gauchat, G. 2012. Politicization of science in the public sphere: A study of public trust in the United States, 1974 to 2010. *American Sociological Review* 77(2): 167–87.

Hammar, T. 1982. Forskningen och politiken. *Invandrare och minoriteter* 4.

Hammar, T. 1988. Kunskapens makt eller vem är det som styr?. *Invandrare och minoriteter* 4–5: 19–23.

Hammar, T. 1994. *Om IMER under 30 år. En översikt av svensk forskning om internationell migration och etniska relationer*, Socialvetenskapliga forskningsrådet.

Hammar, T. 2003. Migration and refugee studies: Reflections about the field's political impact and university status. In *Migration and Immigrants: Between Policy and Reality*, eds J. Doomernik and H. Knippenberg. Amsterdam: Aksant Academic Publishers.

Hammar, T. 2004. Research and politics in Swedish immigration management 1965–1984. In *Towards a Multilateral Migration Regime*, ed. ICMPD. Vienna: International Centre for Migration Policy Development.

Hammar, T. 2008. Diskrimineringsutredningen (DU) och IMER-forskningen. In Anders Gustavsson, Sonja Olin Lauritzen, and Per-Johan Ödman (eds), *Främlingskap och tolkning—en vänbok till Charles Westin*. Stockholm: Stockholm Universitets.

Hoppe, R. 2005. Rethinking the science–policy nexus: From knowledge utilization and science technology studies to types of boundary arrangements. *Poiesis Prax* 3: 199–215.

Johansson, J. 1992. *Det statliga kommittéväsendet—kunskap, kontroll och konsensus*. Stockholm: Akademisk avhandling, Stockholms Universitet.

Jonsson, S. 2008. Blindhet över partigränserna. *Dagens Nyheter* 28 May.

Jørgensen, M. B. 2011. Understanding the research–policy nexus in Denmark and Sweden: The field of migration and integration. *British Journal of Politics & International Relations* 13: 93–109.

Justitiedepartementet. 2004. Kommittédirektiv 2004: 54, *Makt, integration och strukturell diskriminering*. Riksdagen.

Lemne, M. 2010. *För långt från regeringen—och för nära: Expertgruppen ESO: s födelse, levnad och död*. Stockholm: Stockholms Universitet.

Lundberg, E. 2015a. Det postkorporativa deltagandet: Intresseorganisationerna i den nationella politiken, Background study to Swedish Government Offices (2016) *Låt fler forma framtiden!* Demokratiutredningen, SOU: 2016:5, Stockholm: Wolters Kluwers.

Lundberg, E. 2015b. Injured but not yet dead: A bottom-up perspective on the Swedish governmental commissions. *International Journal of Public Administration* 38(5): 346–54.

Mavi, D. 2007. *Integration i återvändsgränd*, Dagens Arena, 2 November.

Ministry of Culture. 2000. *Fördelning av makt och inflytande ur ett integrationspolitiskt perspektiv*, Kommittédirektiv 2000:57. Riksdagen.

Nutley, S., and Webb, J. 2000. Evidence and the policy process. In *What Works? Evidence-based Policy and Practice in Public Services*, eds H. T. O. Davies, S. M. Nutley, and P. C. Smith. Bristol: Policy Press.

Riksdagens revisorer. 1997/98. *Riksdagens revisorers förslag angående kommittéväsendet*, Förslag till riksdagen, 1997/98:RR3.

Riksrevisionen. 2004. *Förändringar inom kommittéväsendet*, Riksdagstryck.

Rothstein, B. 2010. *Bristen på integration vilar tungt på Sahlin*, Göteborgsposten, 5 October.

Scholten, P., and Verbeek, S. 2015. Politicization and expertise: Changing research–policy dialogues on migrant integration in Europe. *Science and Public Policy* 42(2): 188–200.

SNS. 2017. *Economic Policy Council Report 2017, Policies for an Inclusive Swedish Labor Market*, English summary, Stockholm.

Söderlund, T. 2005. Vi har inte råd att misslyckas med rasismen. *Stockholms Fria*, 12 August.

SOU. 1997. *I medborgarnas tjänst: En samlad förvaltningspolitik för staten*, Betänkande av Förvaltningspolitiska kommissionen, 1997:57, Finansdepartementet.

SOU. 2006. *Integrationens svarta bok: Agenda för jämlikhet och social sammanhållning*, SOU 2006:79, Slutbetänkande av utredningen om makt, integration och strukturell diskriminering.

SOU. 2007. *Att styra staten: regeringens styrning av sin förvaltning*, SOU 2007:260. Stockholm: Fritzes.

SOU. 2016. *Låt fler forma framtiden!* Demokratiutredningen, SOU: 2016:5. Stockholm: Wolters Kluwers.

Spång, M. 2008. Swedish Immigration Policy and Democratic Legitimacy, *Current Themes in IMER Research* 8, Malmö University.

Svenska Dagbladet. 2003. Forskare kritiserar Sahlin, based on news from TT, 20 December.

SvT Nyheter. 2006. Orback kritiserar Kamalis förslag, 17 August.

SvT Nyheter. 2004. Utredningen som havererade, by Peter Bagge.

Tellmann, S. M. 2016. *Experts in Public Policymaking: Influential, Yet Constrained*. Nordic Institute for Studies in Innovation, Research and Education.

Trägårdh, L. 2007. Democratic governance and the creation of social capital in Sweden: The discreet charm of governmental commissions. In *State and Civil Society in Northern Europe: The Swedish Model Reconsidered*, ed. L. Trägårdh. New York and Oxford: Berghahn Books.

Villumsen Berling, T., and Bueger, C. 2017. Expertise in the age of post-factual politics: An outline of reflexive strategies. *Geoforum* 84: 332–41.

Weingart, P. 1999. Scientific expertise and political accountability: Paradoxes of science in politics. *Science and Public Policy* 26(3): 151–61.

Weiss, C. H. 1977. Research for policy's sake: The enlightenment function of social research. *Policy Analysis* 3(4), Fall: 531–45.

Weiss, C. H. 1979. The many meanings of research utilization. *Public Administration Review* 39(5): 426–31.

Weiss, C. H. 1980. Knowledge creep and decision accretion. *Science Communication* 1(3): 381–404.

Weiss, C. H. 1991. Policy research: Data, ideas, or arguments? In *Social Sciences and Modern States: National Experiences and Theoretical Crossroads*, eds P. Wagner, C. H. Weiss, B. Wittrock, and H. Wollmann. New York: Cambridge University Press.

Wigerfelt, A., and Peterson, T. 2010. *IMER: möjligheter och gränser festskrift till Björn Fryklund*. Internationell migration och etniska relationer etableras. Malmö: Malmö Institute for Studies of Migration, Diversity and Welfare, Malmö University.

Wildavsky, A. 1979. *Speaking Truth to Power: The Art and Craft of Policy Analysis*. Boston, MA: Little, Brown & Co.

Zetterberg, K. 1990. Det statliga kommittéväsendet. In *Att styra riket. Regeringskansliet 1840–1990*. Stockholm: Departementshistoriekommittén, Allmänna.

10

Migration Research and Policy in the United States

Between Admissionists and Restrictionists

Philip Martin

Introduction

Experience in the United States suggests that bridging the gap between research and policy is far easier on demographics (including the number of legal and unauthorized foreigners, and their age structure, fertility, and internal mobility) than on the socio-economic impacts of migrants. This chapter reviews examples of government-funded efforts to develop consensus among researchers on the number and impacts of foreign-born persons in the United States, including the Bi-National Commission on Mexico–US Migration and National Academy of Sciences studies released in 1997 and 2016.

The US experience demonstrates that, even when researchers achieve consensus on the socio-economic impacts of migrants, the results can be interpreted very differently by *admissionists* (who favour more immigration and the legalization of unauthorized foreigners) and *restrictionists* (who oppose amnesty and want to reduce immigration). For example, the consensus of social scientists in the 1997 National Academy study was that the 15 million foreign-born workers in the US labour force in 1996 depressed average hourly earnings by 3 per cent and led to a net expansion of US gross domestic product (GDP) of $8 billion. Admissionists touted the $8 billion net gain from immigration, while restrictionists emphasized that the then $8 trillion US economy was growing by 3 per cent ($240 billion) per year, making the net gain due to immigration equivalent to 12 days of US economic growth (*Migration News* 1997).

The effect of economic research on policy-making in the United States is muted because migration's major economic effects are (re)distributional, with migrants and owners of capital the major winners. Admissionists stress the gains to individual migrants, the minimal costs to US workers, and other benefits of immigration ranging from preserving industries to repopulating cities and increasing diversity. Restrictionists highlight migration as a key reason, along with technology and trade, for depressing wages and hurting low-skilled Americans, increasing inequality, and reducing social trust.

As immigration numbers and impacts rise, the debate over migration policy is increasingly dominated by the most extreme admissionists and restrictionists. Researchers are also tugged toward these 'no borders' and 'no migrants' extremes by the funders who support and publicize their work. If current trends continue, migration risks joining abortion, guns, and other issues on which Americans are very polarized, and migration research risks joining other issues where links between funders and researchers make research findings suspect, reducing the credibility of experts and research in a wide range of fields.

The chapter begins with discussions of US immigration patterns and research during the periods 1970–2000 and 2000–2016. It then provides a brief reflection on recent developments under the presidency of Donald Trump before concluding with implications for bridging the gaps between research, public debates, and policy-making on immigration.

Immigration Patterns and Research: 1970–2000

The United States is a nation of immigrants whose motto, *E pluribus unum* (from many, one), reflects openness to newcomers.[1] The United States had 42 million foreign-born residents in 2014, almost 20 per cent of the world's international migrants. Over 50 per cent were from Latin America and the Caribbean, including 28 per cent from Mexico.[2] A further 25 per cent were from Asia, the major source countries being China, India, and the Philippines. Almost 50 per cent of all foreign-born residents are naturalized US citizens (Brown and Stepler 2016).

Immigration to the United States occurred in four major waves, beginning with the largely British wave before immigrant admissions began to be recorded in 1820. A second wave was dominated by Irish and German Catholics in the 1840s and 1850s, a third wave included many southern and eastern Europeans between 1880 and 1914, and a fourth wave was set in motion by 1965 laws that switched priority for admission from a migrant's country of origin to US sponsors requesting the admission of relatives or needed workers. Waves suggest peaks and troughs, with troughs in the aftermath of the Civil War in the 1860s and World War I in 1914, followed by legislation in the 1920s that prevented a resumption of large-scale immigration from Europe (Martin and Midgley 2010).

There is no end in sight to the immigration wave launched by the 1965 switch from favouring Europeans to giving priority to foreigners whose US relatives sponsored them for immigrant visas. The change from national origins to family unification was not expected to change immigration patterns, but it did. There was little research to counter the assertion of Senator Edward Kennedy (D-MA) in 1965 that a family unification based selection system would not change 'the ethnic mix of this country' (Congressional Digest 1965; CIS 1995).

Kennedy was wrong. During the 1950s, 56 per cent of the 2.5 million immigrants were from Europe; by the 1970s, fewer than 20 per cent of 4.2 million immigrants were from Europe (DHS, *Yearbook of Immigration Statistics*, table 2).[3] Chain migration—as when immigrants and naturalized US citizens sponsor their relatives for visas—was soon apparent, especially because the United States has one of the world's most expansive definitions of immediate family, including children up to the age of 21 and the parents of US citizens. The United States allows US citizens to sponsor their adult children as well as their adult brothers and sisters for immigrant visas, resulting in sometimes twenty-year waits for visas to become available. The United States offers 50,000 'diversity immigrant visas' awarded by lottery to citizens of countries that sent fewer than 50,000 immigrants to the United States during the previous five years, creating new family networks to sponsor relatives for immigration.

The 10 million foreign-born residents in 1970, the beginning of the fourth and current wave of immigration, were about 5 per cent of US residents at the time. Most immigration research until the 1970s involved historians who explained the integration of third-wave immigrants who arrived before 1914, and debated the effects of very low levels of immigration between the 1920s and 1960s and efforts to 'Americanize' southern and eastern European newcomers, many of whom were making a transition from agriculture abroad to cities in the United States.

Researchers debated the factors most important for immigrant integration, including factories and unions, mobilization for war, public schools, and religious and ethnic organizations (Higham 1984).

Two immigration issues drew the attention of social scientists in the 1970s: farm workers and Asians. Between 1942 and 1964, the US government allowed farmers to employ a total of 4.6 million Mexican guest workers under a series of bilateral Bracero agreements. Most of these guest workers returned year after year, but between 1 million and 2 million Mexicans worked in the United States. Bracero admissions peaked in 1956, when 445,000 Braceros constituted 20 per cent of US hired farm workers. The number of Braceros fell to fewer than 200,000 after 1962 as the US government tightened enforcement of regulations aimed at protecting US and Bracero workers, and increased the cost of Braceros and spurred labour-saving mechanization. The Bracero programme was ended as a form of 'civil rights for Hispanics' in 1964.[4]

A combination of no new Bracero guest workers, few unauthorized workers, and consumer support for farm worker boycotts during the civil rights era brought about a golden age of rising wages for US farm workers. The United Farm Workers won a 40 per cent wage increase in its first table grape contract in 1966, and represented most Californian table grape and lettuce workers by the early 1970s (Martin 2003). Rising labour costs encouraged labour-saving mechanization, and rising demand for fruits and vegetables kept farm worker employment expanding despite higher wages.

Farm employers knew there were experienced workers in rural Mexico, and some encouraged their legal Mexican-born supervisors to recruit friends and relatives in Mexico and encourage them to enter to the United States illegally. There were no penalties on employers who knowingly hired unauthorized workers until 1986, so rural Mexicans who faced a choice between uncertain incomes in Mexico and a guaranteed job in the United States moved north. Illegal immigration from Mexico surged in the 1980s, especially after a short-lived oil-inspired Mexican government spending boom in the late 1970s collapsed with the price of oil. Farm worker unions protested that 'illegal aliens' were undercutting their demands for higher wages and benefits, and demanded that the federal government impose sanctions on employers who hired such workers, but Congress, at the behest of farmers, refused to act.

The research that helped to end the Bracero programme showed that the presence of Braceros depressed the wages of US farm workers, and seemed vindicated by the sharp jump in farm wages in the late 1960s. Clemens et al. (2017) contest this conclusion. They assembled data on farm employment and wages before and after 1964, and concluded that average hourly earnings in states with more Braceros rose at the same pace after 1964 as in states with few or no Braceros, suggesting that removing Braceros did not lead to wage spikes in states that could no longer employ Braceros.

There are several issues with such a before and after comparison as in Clemens et al. (2017), including the fact that the Bracero programme had been shrinking for a decade before it ended, so that state-wide labour markets—in which Braceros constituted less than 5 per cent of farm workers—may be an inappropriate unit with which to measure Bracero effects. Nonetheless, the major response to rising wages demonstrated that flexibility to adjust to fewer workers is mostly a demand side response, not a supply response. Reducing the supply of farm workers does more to accelerate labour-saving substitution or to encourage farmers to switch to less labour-intensive crops than to draw US workers into the farm workforce.

During the 1970s and 1980s, research played little role in the debate over unauthorized migrants in agriculture despite case study analyses of how unauthorized workers replaced US citizens and legal immigrants. Farmers turned to contractors to obtain workers, rather than hiring them directly, spurring indirect competition between employers to obtain jobs for crews of legal versus illegal workers, rather than direct competition between legal and illegal workers to be hired (Mines and Martin 1984). Contractors hiring illegal workers contributed to the rising share of unauthorized California crop workers, which jumped from less than 25 per cent in the mid-1980s to 50 per cent a decade later.

The major intervening variable was the Immigration Reform and Control Act (IRCA) of 1986, a compromise between restrictionists (whose priority was to reduce illegal migration) and admissionists (who wanted to legalize the estimated 3–5 million unauthorized foreigners in the United States). The IRCA imposed federal sanctions on employers who knowingly hired unauthorized workers, and allowed unauthorized foreigners who had lived in the United States for at least five years or who had worked in agriculture for at least 90 days to become legal immigrants.

The IRCA proved to be a victory for admissionists. Some 2.7 million unauthorized foreigners, 85 per cent of whom were Mexicans, were legalized, and the widespread use of false documents to obtain legalization under the farm worker programme, which accounted for 40 per cent of all legalizations, taught low-skilled Mexicans that they could continue to get US jobs by providing false documents to their employers (Martin 1994). Legal and unauthorized Mexicans spread throughout the United States, from agriculture to construction, manufacturing and services.

The IRCA unleashed a wave of research. One strand asked how employers adjusted to employer sanctions, and found that labour costs fell because of the upsurge in illegal migration (Martin 1994). However, the National Academies found that the earnings of newly legalized foreigners increased by 10 per cent to 15 per cent, largely because legal status increased their mobility in the US labour market, allowing them to seek jobs with 'better employers' (Smith and Edmonston 1997). Farm worker unions shrank due to increased illegal migration, with their problems compounded by internal union problems and the rise of labour contractors and other intermediaries (Martin 2003).

The second major area of research involved the economic progress of, especially, Asian immigrants. Newcomers to the United States typically earn less than similar US-born workers, but the earnings gap narrows over time. Chiswick examined various cohorts of immigrants, such as those arriving in the 1960s and 1970s. He concluded that newcomers arriving in the 1960s experienced rapid income gains, catching up to similar US-born workers within thirteen years and then surpassing their US peers, suggesting that average US incomes could be raised via immigration (Chiswick 1978).

Borjas (2016) extended the analysis and concluded that 'immigrant quality' as measured by earnings growth in the United States was falling. Chiswick's data analysis was correct, but reflected a unique and one-time event. Asians found it hard to immigrate until 1965, and those who arrived in the 1960s were especially talented. As immigration from Latin America surged in the 1970s, the initial earnings gap between newcomers and similar US-born workers widened, and immigrant earnings rose much more slowly. Immigrants who arrived in the five years before the 1960 census earned 10 per cent less than US-born workers in 1960, while those who arrived between 1995 and 2000 earned 30 per cent less in 2000 (Borjas 2016).

The legalization of 2.7 million mostly low-skilled Mexicans together with the continued arrival of unauthorized foreigners raised questions about how low-skilled migrants affected similar US workers. Case studies from the 1970s and 1980s suggested that the availability of low-skilled newcomers, legal or illegal, displaced similar US workers and depressed their wages (GAO 1988). However, comparisons of cities with more and fewer immigrants, and studies that compared the wages and unemployment rates of US workers who were assumed to be similar to immigrants in a particular city, could not detect wage depression and displacement, which led to the conclusion that low-skilled migrants do not hurt similar US workers (Smith and Edmonston 1997).

The best-known study of migrant impacts on US workers involved the 'natural experiment' of 125,000 Cuban Marielito migrants who arrived in Miami between April and September 1980, increasing Miami's labour force by 7 per cent. Card (1989) found that the unemployment rate of Blacks in Miami rose more slowly than in several comparison cities that did not receive Cuban migrants, suggesting that the Marielitos benefited, rather than hurt, Blacks in Miami.

Borjas (2016) disagreed with this 'no-harm-and-perhaps-benefit from migrants' conclusion. He noted that, when another wave of Cubans tried to reach Florida in 1994, the US Coast Guard intercepted them and sent them to Guantanamo, a US naval base at the eastern end of Cuba. In 1994, the unemployment rate of equal Blacks in Miami rose, while it fell for Blacks in comparison cities. This prompted scepticism of the validity of natural experiments in 1980 and 1994 that failed to find the impacts predicted by economic theory—first, rising unemployment and, then, falling unemployment when migrants did not arrive. One could conclude that there are many factors in addition to migration that affect the unemployment rate of Blacks and other similar US workers.

The Mariel controversy has become a symbol of the debate over whether the arrival of low-skilled migrants hurts or helps similar US workers. Card's conclusions bolstered so-called immigrant supply siders, who believe that migrants add to economic activity, and benefit themselves and other residents, analogous to supply-side economists who believe that tax cuts encourage additional work, benefiting those whose taxes go down and others via the multiplier effects of increased economic activities. Borjas, by contrast, believes that the demand curve for labour is downward sloping; that is, adding to the supply of labour reduces wages, especially in the short run.

Leubsdorf (2017) reviews the arguments over the Marielitos, emphasizing that the comparison group of US workers selected to check for the impacts of migrants affects the conclusions drawn. Analysts who use more inclusive groups of Americans, such as women and teens still in school, are less likely to find negative effects of the Marielitos than those who focus only on adults who did not finish high school. Borjas (2017) dismissed a suggestion that a change in the number of Blacks in the sample led to his conclusion that the arrival of Marielitos reduced the wages of similar Blacks, emphasizing that the wages of Blacks must be constructed, rather than measured by the survey. By this, he meant that analysts are estimating the effects of Marielitos on a constructed, rather than measured, wage of US Blacks. This debate is still ongoing.

The second major focus of research during the 1990s involved the fiscal impacts of immigrants—the question of whether immigrants pay more in taxes than they receive in tax-supported benefits. California Republican Governor Pete Wilson blamed the need to provide services to unauthorized foreigners for the state's budget deficit in the early 1990s, and won re-election in November 1994 as voters approved Proposition 187 by 59–41 per cent to deny state benefits to unauthorized foreigners, including K-12 education to unauthorized children (*Migration News* 1994).

Most of Proposition 187 was declared unconstitutional, but law suits demanding that the federal government reimburse states for the cost of providing services to unauthorized foreigners prompted studies of the fiscal impacts of immigrants. The Republican-controlled Congress, in response to Proposition 187, enacted several laws in 1996 to make it more difficult for low-income residents to sponsor their relatives for immigrant visas, and denied federal welfare benefits to legal immigrants arriving after 23 August 1996. At a time when 11 per cent of US residents were foreign-born, 45 per cent of the estimated federal savings from the new welfare system were estimated to come from denying benefits to immigrants until they had worked in the United States for at least 10 years or had become naturalized US citizens after five years (*Migration News* 1996).

In response to Proposition 187 and the 1996 immigration laws, the Commission on Immigration Reform sponsored the first National Academies study. It concluded the US economy was $1 billion to $10 billion larger in 1996 than it would have been with no immigrants, with the best estimate that immigrants were responsible for a net $8 billion gain (Smith and Edmonston 1997).

The model for estimating the net economic gain from immigration assumed that adding immigrants to the labour force reduced average wages by 3 per cent, from an assumed $13 an hour to the actual $12.60 in 1996. The lower wages of all workers expanded the economy and increased the returns to owners of capital, making them and the immigrants who moved to the United States for higher wages and more opportunities the major beneficiaries of immigration.

Estimating the public finance effects of immigrants required more assumptions. The study by the National Academies calculated the net present value (NPV) of the average immigrant in 1996 by assuming that the earnings of immigrants will catch up to those of similar US workers, and that the children and grandchildren of immigrants will have the same average profiles with regard to earnings, taxes paid, and benefits received as the children and grandchildren of native-born children (Smith and Edmonston 1997). The study further assumed that immigration did not raise the cost of public goods such as defence, and that persisting federal government budget deficits would force the government to raise taxes and reduce benefits, rather than continue to borrow to provide benefits for ageing residents, meaning that both young immigrants and young US-born workers would pay more in taxes and receive fewer benefits.

These assumptions helped generate two major findings. First, the average immigrant had a positive NPV of $78,000, meaning that a typical immigrant was expected to pay $78,000 more in federal taxes than they would receive in federal benefits in 1996 dollars over their lifetimes and those of their children and grandchildren. The NPV of immigrants with more than a high school education was plus $198,000, while the NPV of immigrants with less than a high school education was minus $13,000; that is, even assuming that the children of low-educated immigrants have the same average earnings, taxes, and benefits as US-born children, low-skilled immigrants and their children impose a net cost on US taxpayers.

The study led to an obvious conclusion: to generate the maximum economic benefits from immigrants for US-born residents, the selection system should favour young and well-educated newcomers who are most likely to earn higher incomes, pay more in taxes, and consume fewer tax-supported benefits. This recommendation was rejected, as those favouring the current system—including advocates for particular migrant groups, churches, and immigration lawyers—argued that levels of immigration should be increased to accommodate more high-skilled foreigners, rather than introduce a points-selection system that would admit more high-skilled and relatively fewer family immigrants. Furthermore, many US employers preferred the current demand-oriented system under which they sponsor foreigners who have temporary work permits for immigrant visas, a system that ties foreigners to a particular employer for years as guest workers. By contrast, a Canadian-style supply-oriented points-selection system would allow newcomers to move from one employer to another.

During the three decades from 1970 to 2000, the share of foreign-born residents in the US population doubled from 5 per cent to 10 per cent. The number of unauthorized foreigners, after dipping briefly with legalization in the late 1980s, more than doubled from 3.5 million in 1990 to 8.6 million in 2000. The effects of legal and unauthorized foreigners were debated. Most economists agreed with Card that, since they could not find the expected negative effects of low-skilled foreigners on similar US workers, there were few or no such effects. There was more consensus among demographers on the number of unauthorized foreigners and more agreement on public finances, since it was easy to visualize how higher levels of education and higher incomes would mean more taxes paid and less reliance on welfare benefits.

Immigration Patterns and Research: 2000–2016

The election of Presidents Vincente Fox in Mexico and George W. Bush in the United States in 2000 was expected to usher in a new era in Mexico–USA migration, marked by cooperation to reduce illegal migration and violence along the Mexico–USA border, legalization of unauthorized foreigners in the United States, and new guest worker programmes. Indeed, just before the terrorist attacks on 11 September 2001, Fox was in Washington, DC, imploring Bush and the US government to enact immigration reforms that would legalize unauthorized foreigners before the end of 2001 (*Migration News* 2001).

Instead, security took centre stage after the attacks on 11 September 2001, and several laws led to increased monitoring of immigrants and visitors. As the US economy recovered from recession and as illegal immigration rose, there were renewed calls for legalization for unauthorized foreigners. However, there was deadlock in Congress between restrictionists, who emphasized the need for enforcement to deter unauthorized foreigners, and admissionists, who wanted to legalize unauthorized foreigners.

Economists were also deadlocked over the impacts of low-skilled foreign workers on similar US workers. Borjas published an influential article that reinforced economic theory. Given the mobility in the US labour market,

Borjas argued that the effects of immigrants on US workers must be studied nationally, rather than in any particular city.

Borjas (2003) divided foreign- and native-born workers into age and education cells, so that workers aged 25–30 years with less than a secondary school education were in one cell, and those aged 30–35 years in another; he found up to 10 per cent lower wages for the US-born workers in the young and less-educated cells due to the presence of immigrants. Foged and Peri (2015) disputed Borjas' conclusion. They suggested that if migrants and natives within each age and education cell were complements, rather than substitutes, playing different labour market roles despite similarities in age and education, and if employers responded to the arrival of migrants by investing more to create jobs for them and US workers, the presence of immigrants raised, rather than lowered, the wages of similar US workers.

The debate over the impacts of low-skilled migrants was mirrored in a similar debate over high-skilled migrants. The United States created the H-1B programme in 1990, at a time when there were believed to be sufficient US workers, as indicated by the unemployment rate of 5.6 per cent, but not enough to fill all of the jobs being created in the rapidly expanding information technology (IT) sector. Some 20,000 temporary foreign workers with college degrees and fashion models were being admitted at the time, and the H-1B programme made it easy for US employers to recruit and employ up to 65,000 per year in the expectation that the number of H-1B visas would begin high and fall over time as US colleges and universities ramped up training and Americans filled more IT jobs.

Instead, the H-1B programme expanded slowly, not reaching the 65,000 cap until 1997 (Martin 2012). At a time of low unemployment and in anticipation of the Y2K problem of computers not adjusting to the year 2000 properly, US employers persuaded Congress to raise the cap, add 20,000 H-1B visas for foreigners who earned Master's degrees from US universities, and exempt non-profit employers such as universities from the visa cap, allowing over 200,000 H-1B workers per year to enter. Since each H-1B worker can stay up to six years, the United States soon had over a million H-1B visa holders.

Researchers studied the impacts of H-1B workers and reached opposing conclusions. Some found that US employers preferred to hire H-1B workers because they were younger and cheaper than similar US workers. In an IT labour market experiencing considerable mobility, H-1B workers were 'loyal' to a particular employer since most wanted to be sponsored for a permanent immigrant visa. Critics called H-1B workers high-tech Braceros, a reference to the by then discredited programme that brought Mexican farm workers to the United States under what are now seen as exploitative circumstances, and found that the presence of H-1B workers reduced wages and the employment of US workers (Bound et al. 2017).

Other researchers stressed the spill-over effects of highly skilled foreigners with H-1B visas (Peri et al. 2015). They found, inter alia, that cities with more H-1B foreigners generated more patents and experienced faster wage and job growth—findings that supported employers who wanted to raise the cap on visas (Nell and Sherk 2008). Some researchers echoed employers in arguing that it made no sense for US universities to educate foreigners in STEM-related fields and deny them an opportunity to stay in the United States and work.

Employers have resisted efforts to link more protection for US workers with an increase in the number of H-1B visas available, arguing that requiring employers initially to try to recruit US workers would slow down their need to hire H-1B workers quickly. Instead, they persuaded the DHS, in 2005, to allow foreign students who graduate from US universities with STEM (science, technology, engineering, and mathematics) degrees to remain in the United States and work in jobs related to their degree for up to 30 months, so-called 'optional practical training' (OPT), giving these foreign graduates time to find a US employer to offer them H-1B visas valid for six years.[5] The Trump administration in 2018 proposed that the period of OPT for all fresh graduates be decreased to twelve months.

By 2005, when Congress began to consider immigration reforms to deal with unauthorized foreigners, most social science researchers agreed that any negative economic effects of low-skilled migrants on similar US workers were small; that high-skilled migrants had positive spill-over economic effects; and that legalization of unauthorized foreigners would increase their mobility and wages, as well as expand the US economy. However, restrictionists in the House of Representatives approved an enforcement-only bill in December 2005 that would have increased enforcement on the Mexico–USA border, required all employers to use the internet-based E-Verify system to check the legal status of new hires, and made illegal presence in the United States a crime, perhaps hindering the ability of unauthorized foreigners to become legal immigrants in the future.

This enforcement-only bill was widely denounced as ignoring the benefits of migration and culminated in a 'day without migrants' on 1 May 2006 that involved many businesses closing for the day to highlight the contributions of migrants. In May 2006, the Senate enacted a three-pronged comprehensive immigration bill favoured by President Bush and many social science researchers; in other words, increase enforcement to deter illegal migration, legalize most unauthorized foreigners and put them on a path to US citizenship, and create new guest worker programmes for low-skilled workers. The House refused to act. A similar comprehensive immigration reform bill failed in the Senate in 2007, but was approved in 2013 with the support of President Obama; the House again refused to act and there was no reform.

During these immigration reform debates, most social scientists supported the legalization of unauthorized workers and more guest workers. There was very little research on how employers, labour markets, and the economy might adjust to fewer foreign-born workers, since immigration reforms were expected to legalize current workers and admit more.

Trump and Migration

In 2015–2016, Donald Trump campaigned on seven major issues, two of which involved migration: have the United States build and Mexico pay for a wall on the 2,000 mile Mexico–USA border and deport the 11 million unauthorized foreigners in the United States. President Trump issued three executive orders during his first week in office, planning a wall on the Mexico–USA border, increasing deportations and dealing with sanctuary cities, and reducing refugee admissions. Trump said: 'Beginning today, the United States of America gets back control of its borders.'

Trump launched his bid for the Republican presidential nomination in June 2015 by accusing unauthorized Mexicans of 'bringing drugs. They are bringing crime. They're rapists...but some, I assume, are good people' (*Rural Migration News* 2015). There was an immediate negative reaction. Most pundits thought that Trump's inflammatory comments would doom his first campaign for elective office, especially since he was competing with well-known senators and the brother of ex-President George W. Bush.

Trump won the most votes in state-by-state primaries and became the Republican candidate for President in July 2016 with a nationalist platform that centred on the slogan, 'Make America Great Again'. After a short visit to Mexico, candidate Trump outlined a 10-point immigration plan on 31 August 2016 that began with a wall on the Mexican border and ended in ambiguity about what would happen to unauthorized foreigners in the United States. He said 'No citizenship. They'll pay back taxes.... There's no amnesty, but we will work with them' (*Rural Migration News* 2016).

The National Academies released its second consensus report on immigration in September 2016 during the presidential election campaign (Blau and Mackie 2016). The report estimated that immigrants generated up to $54 billion in benefits for Americans in 2015, equivalent to 0.3 per cent of US GDP of $17.5 trillion in 2015. This net benefit reflects a loss in wages to US workers of $494 billion and a gain in profits for the United States of $548 billion. The conclusion: 'the immigration surplus stems from the increase in the return to capital that results from the increased supply of labor and the subsequent fall in wages'—meaning that the arrival of immigrants depresses wages, expands the economy, and increases profits.

The report concluded that immigration bolsters 'economic growth, innovation and entrepreneurship', and has 'little to no' negative effect on US wages in the long term, largely because the models used to estimate immigration's impacts on the labour market assume that there will be no long-run impacts on wages.[6] The report highlighted negative impacts of newcomers on previous immigrants and US-born workers with little education, including teenagers.

The report found slowing rates of wage convergence, meaning that newcomers to the United States begin their American journeys with a larger earnings gap than previous arrivals, and are slower to close this gap as they integrate into the United States. One reason for this widening earnings gap is that a higher share of newcomers to the United States has low levels of education, and most are learning English more slowly than earlier arrivals.

The National Academies report concluded that immigrants pay less in taxes than the cost of the public services they receive, and their US-born children do not close this gap because the federal government runs a deficit, meaning that all of the taxes paid by all residents do not cover federal government expenditures. At the state and local levels, where governments generally must have balanced budgets, immigrants pay less in taxes than the cost of their tax-supported services, and this immigrant deficit is covered by taxes paid by natives. If the US-born children of immigrants fare as well as other US-born children, over 75 years this immigrant fiscal deficit disappears at the federal level but persists at the state level.

The National Academies report was used selectively in the political debate (Edsall 2016). Restrictionist oriented think tanks such as the Center for Immigration Studies welcomed the report, summarizing it as follows: 'Immigration is primarily a redistributive policy, transferring income from workers to owners of capital and from taxpayers to low-income immigrant families. The information in the new report will help Americans think about these tradeoffs in a constructive way' (Camarota 2016).

Admissionist oriented groups such as the American Immigration Lawyers Association said that 'the study found that immigrant workers expand the size of the U.S. economy by an estimated 11 per cent each year, translating to $2 trillion in 2016 alone. In fact, the children of immigrants are the largest net fiscal contributors among any group, native or foreign-born, creating significant economic benefits for every American' (American Immigration Lawyers Association 2016). The Migration Policy Institute did not review the report.

Neither candidate Clinton nor candidate Trump responded to the National Academies report when it was released but, in January 2017, President Trump ordered the DHS to plan for construction of a wall on the Mexico–USA border and to beef up interior enforcement by adding 10,000 agents to the current

10,000 to detect and remove unauthorized foreigners convicted of US crimes. Trump said that Mexico would pay for the wall.

Trump also reinstated a programme that allows federal immigration agents to train state and local police officers to detect unauthorized foreigners and to hold them for federal agents, or involves state and local police joining task forces with federal enforcement agents to pursue criminal gangs. Trump's order expanded the definition of criminals who are the highest priorities for deportation to include those charged with, but not necessarily convicted of, US crimes.[7] Trump threatened to withhold federal grants from sanctuary cities that 'willfully refuse' to cooperate with the DHS, prompting Californian legislators to say they would nonetheless defy Trump and prohibit state and local police from cooperating with federal immigration enforcement agents.[8]

Trump sought to suspend the admission of refugees for 120 days, block the entry of Syrian refugees indefinitely, reduce planned refugee resettlements in the United States in financial year 17 from 110,000 to 50,000, and ban entries for ninety days from seven countries: Syria, Iran, Iraq, Somalia, Sudan, Libya, and Yemen.[9] However, this executive order was blocked by the courts, leading to a revised order issued in March 2017 to block only new entries from six countries, with Iraq removed from the list. This revised order was also blocked by the courts, and re-issued in September 2017; the US Supreme Court is expected to confirm Trump's authority to regulate the admission of foreign visitors before 1 July 2018.

Trump's executive orders were widely condemned by most researchers, who emphasize that unauthorized Mexico–USA migration has fallen to historic lows as Mexico completes its fertility transition, and better education and more jobs in Mexico keep most potential migrants at home. Most researchers conclude that migrants are less likely to commit crimes than similar US-born persons, and that efforts to detect and remove unauthorized foreigners would be costly[10] and break up mixed families, those in which some members are unauthorized while others are US-born and thus US citizens. Finally, some researchers decried reducing refugee admissions, arguing that the United States has long been a haven for those seeking refuge, and that most refugees integrate successfully and are not terrorist threats.

The United States does not have a governmental migration commission that studies the socio-economic effects of migration on an ongoing basis. Each House of Congress has an immigration sub-committee that conducts oversight hearings on migration-related issues that range from visa issuance to unauthorized migration to guest workers. Researchers are often invited to testify, although the majority party controls most of the witnesses who are allowed to testify, and most witnesses are either employers of or advocates for migrants. Private foundations and the federal government support a wide range of migration research, most of which concludes that migrants and their children are integrating successfully, with few adverse and many positive effects on the US economy and society.

Conclusions: Bridging the Gap

Most social science research on migration is optimistic, finding that immigrants help themselves by moving to the United States, and enrich the US economy and society. There are several reasons for this optimism, including the fact that migrants expand the labour force and the economy. Economists find that migrants promote growth without hurting US workers significantly; sociologists find that most newcomers integrate successfully; and political scientists are more likely to celebrate the benefits of diversity, rather than emphasize its potential loss of social capital and trust (Blau and Mackie 2016).

There are three major lessons to be learned from the US experience on bridging the gap between migration research and policy. First, the locus of migration research shifted from history to contemporary migration. When immigration was at a low point in 1970, migration research was dominated by historians who examined how immigrants integrated into and changed US society; these were studies of past events. By 1990, a new generation of non-historians focused on the impacts of contemporary migration. Many were immigrants, including George Borjas (from Cuba), David Card (Canada), Alejandro Portes (Cuba), and Giovanni Peri (Italy).

Second, most government- and foundation-supported migration research concluded that immigration was beneficial for the migrants and the US economy and society, supporting those who wanted to expand immigration and legalize unauthorized foreigners. The Mexican Migration Project (MMP), supported by the US government, obtained work and migration histories from thousands of Mexicans in Mexico who had been in the United States. Analyses using MMP data concluded that Mexico–USA migration had mutually beneficial effects as Mexicans circulated between Mexican homes and US jobs until the US government stepped up border enforcement in the 1990s, 'trapping' unauthorized Mexicans in the United States (Massey et al. 2002).

The general theme of social science research today is that immigrants generate more benefits than costs, and that these benefits could be increased if unauthorized foreigners were allowed to legalize their status, which would give them more mobility in the US labour market and provide incentives to learn English. Researchers acknowledge the risk of segmented assimilation, as when frustrated immigrant children or the children of immigrants who identify with US minorities feel unable to get ahead, drop out of school, and, perhaps, join gangs (Blau and Mackie 2016; Meissner et al. 2006).

Third, unauthorized migration, especially, has become an increasingly contentious issue. The research and elite consensus was that three-pronged comprehensive immigration reforms—namely, more enforcement, legalization for unauthorized foreigners, and new guest worker programmes—would be enacted after Hillary Clinton was elected president in 2016. In anticipation of Clinton's election, many of the major foundations supporting migration research shifted funding to implement legalization.[11]

This meant that there was little research on what is happening as a result of increased enforcement under President Trump. Preliminary research suggests that employers are reacting as economic theory would predict. As wages rise, employers are substituting capital for labour in industries from agriculture and care giving to construction and restaurants (Martin 2017).

Bridging the gap between research and policy is often difficult. For two centuries, economists have preached the virtues of freer trade, arguing that comparative advantage ensures that most people in trading countries are better off because winners win more than losers lose, so that winners can compensate losers and leave everyone better off. Free trade became the mantra of opinion leaders in both major political parties and all significant research institutions; most paid only lip service to the need to compensate the losers from freer trade by retraining displaced workers for new jobs. Opposition to freer trade came largely from unions representing manufacturing workers, who found that displaced manufacturing workers who were forced into service jobs generally had lower wages, even after retraining, belying the promise that trade's winners would fully compensate losers.

Bridging the gap is similarly difficult in climate change. Even with research agreement that the climate is warming, there is disagreement over how much of this warming is due to human activities and the appropriate policy response in which to invest now to avoid problems in the future. Most researchers conclude that human activities are a major cause of climate change and urge a significant investment now to minimize future adjustment costs. As with migration, the few researchers who disagree on the need for a carbon tax or other investments now to avoid future problems are considered out of the mainstream; their research is often dismissed because some was funded by energy firms that would be adversely affected by carbon taxes.

It is sometimes said that, in economics, it is easy to become famous without ever being right. Many migration researchers reach the same conclusion in each of their papers and some of those who make false predictions seem to incur no penalties. In most cases, one needs to read only the name of the researcher to know the conclusions, as with economists who consistently find that low-skilled migrants help or hurt similar US workers. Second, there appear to be few penalties for false predictions, as illustrated by the careers of those who confidently predicted in the 1970s, when there were fewer than 2 million

Mexican-born US residents, that Mexicans were sojourners, not settlers, and would not settle in the United States. Forty years later, there were 12 million Mexican-born persons in the United States, plus an additional 18 million children born to them in the United States.

Americans are better educated than ever before, there is more scientific research than ever, and many research-influenced policies are ever more contentious. One reason may be that better educated voters and politicians realize that research generally, and migration research in particular, rarely reaches truly definitive answers. Researchers who oversell their results, and the think tanks, media, and politicians who amplify their message, may wind up reducing the credibility of all research on contentious issues.

Notes

1. The original meaning of *E pluribus unum* was that one nation emerged from the thirteen colonies, but the phrase has evolved to symbolize unity from diversity, or the ability of the United States to integrate newcomers (Martin 2011).
2. There were 11.7 million Mexican-born residents in 2014: 4 million born in the Caribbean, 3.3 million born in Central America, and 2.8 million born in South America. That is, 21.8 million (52 per cent) of all foreign-born residents were from Latin America.
3. Stocks changed slower than flows. In 1960, 85 per cent of the 9.7 million foreign-born residents were from Europe or Canada; by 1980, their share dropped to 43 per cent of 14 million (Brown and Stepler 2016).
4. The average employment of hired workers on US farms in the early 1960s was 2.5 million. http://usda.mannlib.cornell.edu/MannUsda/viewDocumentInfo.do?documentID=1063
5. Employers do not have to try to recruit US workers before hiring OPT graduates, and there are no special wages that must be paid to OPT employees. www.uscis.gov/working-united-states/students-and-exchange-visitors/students-and-employment/stem-opt
6. 'In the case of structural studies, when capital is assumed to be perfectly flexible, [average] wage effects on natives are zero, although this result is built in by theoretical assumptions' (National Academies 2016).
7. Two-thirds of the 2 million foreigners who were put in removal proceedings after being detected by Secure Communities enforcement had committed only misdemeanour crimes. The Priority Enforcement Program unveiled in November 2014 targeted foreigners convicted of felonies (640,000) and those who arrived in the United States after 1 January 2014 (640,000). In July 2015, the Migration Policy Institute noted that the Priority Enforcement Program made one-eighth of the 11 million unauthorized foreigners in the United States priorities for DHS enforcement.
8. Sanctuaries are states, counties, and cities that limit their cooperation with the Immigration and Customs Enforcement (ICE) agency of the DHS. In 2015, there

were four states, 326 counties, and thirty-two cities that had declared themselves to be sanctuaries for unauthorized foreigners (www.americanimmigrationcouncil. org/research/sanctuary-cities-trust-acts-and-community-policing-explained).

9. The United States has admitted 785,000 refugees since 11 September 2001, including twelve who were arrested or removed from the United States due to concerns over terrorism. Some 3.2 million refugees have been admitted since 1975, including 85,000 in financial year 16, of whom 72 per cent were women and children. In financial year 16, 38,900 Muslim and 37,500 Christian refugees were admitted.

10. In 2016, ICE estimated that it costs $12,200 to identify and remove each unauthorized foreigner, a cost that could drop if state and local governments cooperated with ICE. See www.politico.com/story/2016/12/is-donald-trump-deportation-plan-impossible-233041

11. See www.hillaryclinton.com/issues/immigration-reform/.

References

American Immigration Lawyers Association (AILA). 2016. National Academies Report Underscores Immense Economic Importance of Immigrants to America. www.aila.org/advo-media/press-releases/2016/nas-report-econ-importance-immigrants-to-america

Blau, F., and Mackie, C. 2016. *The Economic and Fiscal Consequences of Immigration.* National Academies. www.nap.edu/catalog/23550/the-economic-and-fiscal-consequences-of-immigration

Borjas, G. 2003. The Labor Demand Curve is Downward Sloping: Reexamining the Impact of Immigration on the Labor Market. *Quarterly Journal of Economics* 118(4): 1335–74.

Borjas, G. 2016. *We Wanted Workers. Unraveling the Immigration Narrative.* New York: Norton.

Borjas, G. 2017. *Race and Mariel.* https://gborjas.org/2017/06/12/race-and-mariel/

Bound, J., Khanna, G., and Morales, N. 2017. *Understanding the Economic Impact of the H-1B Program on the U.S.* PSC Research Report No. 16–857. www.psc.isr.umich.edu/pubs/abs/10003

Brown, A., and Stepler, R. 2016. *Statistical Portrait of the Foreign-Born Population in the United States.* www.pewhispanic.org/2016/04/19/statistical-portrait-of-the-foreign-born-population-in-the-united-states-trends/

Camarota, S. 2016. *National Academy of Sciences Study of Immigration: Workers and Taxpayers Lose, Businesses Benefit.* CIS. https://cis.org/National-Academy-Sciences-Study-Immigration-Workers-and-Taxpayers-Lose-Businesses-Benefit

Card, D. 1989. *The Impact of the Mariel Boatlift on the Miami Labor Market.* NBER Working Paper No. 3069. Cambridge, MA: NBER.

Chiswick, B. 1978. The effect of Americanization on the earnings of foreign-born men. *Journal of Political Economy* 86(5): 897–921.

CIS. 1995. *The Legacy of the 1965 Immigration Act,* 1 September. https://cis.org/Legacy-1965-Immigration-Act

Clemens, M. A., Lewis, E. G., and Postel, H. M. 2017. *Immigration Restrictions as Active Labor Market Policy: Evidence from the Mexican Bracero Exclusion*. NBER Paper 23125. Cambridge, MA: NBER.

Congressional Digest, May 1965, 152. https://catalog.hathitrust.org/Record/008315096

DHS. *Yearbook of Immigration Statistics*. www.dhs.gov/immigration-statistics/yearbook (Accessed 15 July 2017).

Edsall, T. 2016. What does immigration actually cost us? *New York Times*. 29 September.

Foged, M., and Peri, G. 2015. Immigrants' effect on native workers: New analysis on longitudinal data. *American Economic Journal: Applied Economics*, 8(2): 1–34. CReAM Discussion Paper Series 1507.

GAO. 1988. *Illegal Aliens: Influence of Illegal Workers on Wages and Working Conditions of Legal Workers*. www.gao.gov/products/PEMD-88-13BR

Higham, J. 1984. *Send These to Me: Immigrants in Urban America*. Baltimore, MD: John Hopkins University Press.

Leubsdorf, B. 2017. The great Mariel boatlift debate: Does immigration lower wages? *Wall Street Journal*, 17 June.

Martin, P. 1994. Good intentions gone awry: IRCA and U.S. agriculture. *The Annals of the Academy of Political and Social Science* 534(1): 44–57.

Martin, P. 2003. *Promise Unfulfilled: Unions, Immigration, and Farm Workers*. Ithaca, NY: Cornell University Press.

Martin, P. 2012. High-skilled migrants: S&E workers in the United States. *American Behavioral Scientist* 56(8): 1058–79.

Martin, P. 2017. *Immigration and Farm Labor. Challenges and Issues*. Giannini Foundation. http://bit.ly/2tvaUSw

Martin, P., and Midgley, E. 2010. *Immigration in America* (June). Washington, DC: Population Reference Bureau.

Martin, S. 2011. *A Nation of Immigrants*. Cambridge: Cambridge University Press.

Massey, D. S., Durand, J., and Malone, N. J. 2002. *Beyond Smoke and Mirrors Mexican Immigration in an Era of Economic Integration*. New York: Russell Sage.

Meissner, D., Meyers, Deborah W., Papademetriou, Demetrios G., and Fix, Michael. 2006. *Immigration and America's Future: A New Chapter*. Washington, DC: Migration Policy Institute.

Migration News. 1994. Prop 187 Approved in California 1(11). https://migration.ucdavis.edu/mn/more.php?id=492 (Accessed 15 July 2017).

Migration News. 1996. Welfare Overhaul and Minimum Wage Changes 3(9). https://migration.ucdavis.edu/mn/more.php?id=1246 (Accessed 15 July 2017).

Migration News. 1997. NRC on Immigration 4(6). https://migration.ucdavis.edu/mn/more.php?id=1246 (Accessed 15 July 2017).

Migration News. 2001. Fox Visits Bush 8(10). https://migration.ucdavis.edu/mn/more.php?id=2463 (Accessed 15 July 2017).

Mines, R., and Martin, P. 1984. Immigrant workers and the California citrus industry. *Industrial Relations* 23(1): 139–49.

National Academies. 2016. *The Economic and Fiscal Consequences of Immigration*. Washington, DC: National Academies Press.

Nell, G., and Sherk, J. 2008. *More H-1B Visas, More American Jobs, A Better Economy.* Washington, DC: Heritage Foundation.

Peri, G., Shih, K., and Sparber, C. 2015. STEM Workers, H-1B Visas, and Productivity in US Cities. *Journal of Labor Economics* 33(S1) (Part 2): S225–S255.

Rural Migration News. 2015.

Rural Migration News. 2016.

Smith, J., and Edmonston, B. (eds). 1997. *The New Americans: Economic, Demographic, and Fiscal Effects of Immigration.* Washington, DC: National Research Council.

Part III
International Experiences

11

Understanding the Role of Evidence in EU Policy Development

A Case Study of the 'Migration Crisis'

Elizabeth Collett

Introduction

One of the most frequently uttered phrases in Brussels in late 2015 was 'Why didn't we see this coming?' While heads of state focused on the dangerous dynamics of maritime migration across the central Mediterranean from Libya, a sharp increase in the number of those boarding boats on the Turkish coast for a short journey to the cluster of Aegean islands nearby took them by surprise. And not only were policy-makers taken by surprise: the Greek government, European Union (EU) agencies, and international non-governmental organizations (NGOs), among others, all found themselves caught inadequately prepared for an emergency response in a remote location with limited resources and significant, immediate needs.

In reality, most of those working in the field of immigration and asylum policy, including senior policy-makers from a range of EU member states, were aware that the combination of continued Syrian conflict, poor conditions in neighbouring countries, and increased smuggling activities in Turkey would likely lead to an increase in arrivals in the short to medium term. They did not base this on specific research but, rather, a combination of experience, instinct, and anecdotal evidence, supplemented by reporting from key international agencies and NGOs. Policy-makers were also aware that existing EU policies, if tested, were likely to crumble in the face of significant pressure (Collett 2015). But despite this foreboding, and despite strong evidence from academic, civil society, and unofficial data sources that a significant shift in arrival flows was likely to occur in 2015, it proved difficult to bring these together to effectively catalyse a timely policy response.

As researchers and policy-makers alike begin to autopsy the crisis, this chapter unpacks the role that evidence and data play in EU policy development, and the ways in which policy-makers are now making use of information, including their ability to make projections regarding future migration flow. This chapter looks at the formal and informal modes of research–policy interaction at EU level that have developed since the late 2000s, and assesses the relative merits of each. Which processes are 'pro-forma' and which genuinely inform policy-makers and influence their approach? How do the various constituencies—EU officials, national civil servants, politicians, academics, and civil society—interact, and through what means is evidence acknowledged and incorporated into decision-making? This chapter looks particularly at the events of the period 2015–2018—with a focus on the 'refugee crisis'—to assess how the utilization of data and research is changing, and what lessons might now be learned for the next generation of European policy-makers, and researchers.

The analysis in this chapter is based on thirteen years of work managing migration programming in several Brussels-based think tanks—including the European Policy Centre (2005–2010) and the Migration Policy Institute Europe (2010–2018)—and interacting with both researchers and policy-makers.

Disconnected Policy-making in Brussels

The interaction between publics, policy, and evidence in the Brussels environment suffers from a number of disconnects peculiar to the European Union project. This is particularly the case regarding migration. Until recently, the EU institutions have remained largely insulated from the impacts of decisions made in the area of Justice and Home Affairs (JHA), at least in terms of public debate and scrutiny. The technical complexity inherent in the development of key instruments—from the Dublin Regulation to Eurodac—means that few media outlets reported on policy developments on migration and asylum prior to 2015. Indeed, Brussels-based journalists have highlighted the difficulties in 'selling' national editors JHA stories with no human content that have been based on dry, technical press releases.[1] This goes some way to explaining why EU migration policy only came to the forefront in the spring of 2015, following a series of harrowing incidents in the Mediterranean. Although the situation in the southern 'front-line' EU member states had been periodically reported in the media since the mid-2000s, it was the news coverage of the large-scale tragedies from 2013 onwards which became the eventual catalyst for political and policy responses.

The complexity of the policy portfolio has also insulated many policy-makers from top-down political scrutiny (in the absence of notable misadventure). Until recently, a relatively small number of EU and national officials, alongside specialized non-governmental actors—including academics, have developed expertise in the substance, mechanics, and process of EU-level policy on migration and asylum. As a result, this group has had relatively disproportionate influence over the direction and development of a large area of policy: many innovations can be traced back to a small group, generating support for a new policy idea within a limited and closed network of experts. For example, a 'like-minded' group of predominantly north-west European governments that meet prior to meetings of the Strategic Committee on Immigration, Frontiers and Asylum (SCIFA) (which are held in the European Council) to discuss common positions and potential new initiatives. Similar dynamics exist within the EU institutions, either within a single Directorate-General (typically, the Directorate-General for Home Affairs HOME), or across EU institutions at the political level. Few outside of government have up-to-date insight regarding those who are making the key-decisions, and at what moment: the circle of influence is thus hard to penetrate.

Since 2015, the number of those involved in migration policy development has increased significantly and the issue is now subject to more intense scrutiny.[2] Yet, this is not necessarily supported by a concomitant broadening of expertise across the EU institutions and its member states, or broadened circles of consultation. Indeed, there is often an inverse correlation between the level and urgency of political decision-making and the breadth of expert consultation undertaken, sometimes out of necessity—and, sometimes, panic.

The inclusion of new actors in immigration policy-making has revealed additional mismatches in expertise. First, the vast majority of those developing (and commenting upon) policy on migration and asylum in Brussels have historically been legal experts, charged with drafting standard-setting legislation on a range of policy areas from border management to the reception of asylum seekers.[3] Today, a broader range of portfolios is integrally involved in migration policy, including the European External Action Service (European Commission 2016a). Yet, as with any institution that is 'learning' about a new issue, the desire to draw linear conclusions and find simple solutions can be tempting (Gentiloni and Avramopoulos 2016). For example, external experts have continually had to highlight that policy-makers cannot simply address the 'root causes' of migration by increasing development investments across the board, and that the drivers of migration from less developed countries may be more complex than mere income inequality (Fratzke and Salant 2018). Meanwhile, on the Interior side, policy-makers have sometimes struggled to adapt to the complexities of foreign policy diplomacy and to incorporate the complex interests of partner countries with starkly different politics, socio-economics, and outlook.

In addition, the Directorate-General HOME itself has had to become operational on the ground in EU member states for the first time, coordinating maritime operations, managing an 'emergency' relocation scheme (Council of the EU 2015a) and developing 'hotspots' in Greece and Italy (Collett and Le Coz 2018). This, again, requires different types of expertise about what will, or will not, be successful, and the learning curve has been steep. Indeed, the European Commission has needed to rely heavily on the front-line knowledge amassed within its own agencies—notably Frontex, Europol, and the European Asylum Support Office (EASO), international and non-governmental organizations—such as the United Nations High Commission for Refugees (UNHCR), International Organization for Migration (IOM), and International Rescue Committee (IRC), and EU Member States offering crisis response expertise.

This shift in substance of EU policy-making during the 'crisis' period has also thrown into relief some of the core goals that had previously evaded strong examination. At national level, the core philosophy of 'good' immigration policy-making is (or should be) the maintenance of a robust system capable of managing the entry and residence of foreign nationals according to defined criteria. At EU level, this goal has often been subsumed within a more philosophical desire to bring the EU member states ever closer together through the development of 'common' policies. Research and evidence (and sometimes even basic common sense) can on occasion be set aside in the pursuit of 'the European project'.

Finally, while the EU is responsible for drafting and promulgating legislation, it is the EU member states that are responsible for translating and implementing those rules into very different national systems. National governments may or may not have the capacity and resources to discharge this responsibility effectively; also, the consequences of an EU-wide policy may have uneven effects, sometimes strongly negative, in particular geographies, sub-national regions, or among particular migrant groups. It has become ever more important for the EU institutions to collect evidence on national implementation and resource allocation (ECRE/UNHCR 2018). The systemic weaknesses within the Greek asylum system demonstrate that peer review of member state practice has proved inadequate; however, there are few independent evaluations with concrete recommendations that can help close the gap (and lag) between policy on paper and policy in practice.

Research and Evidence at EU Level: A Brief Typology

EU-level utilization of research and evidence has been haphazard and uneven, with a strong emphasis on process rather than evidence. This is not to say that there is a paucity of EU-funded research but, rather, that its incorporation within the policy-making process is largely due to factors beyond the tangible relevance that an individual piece of research might have for improving policy. Authorship, purpose, and proximity to policy-makers all play a role in whether it will be 'heard' (cf. the discussion in Chapter 14 in this volume).

There are a number of different categories of research and evidence that policy-makers find valuable. First, there is basic information and data on migration flows, stocks, and the key characteristics of migrant groups; these help policy-makers understand the challenges at hand (such as gaps in employment rates between native and foreign-born groups).[4] Second, there is a vast range of research that investigates the efficacy of particular policy choices, either before or after it has been negotiated. These can take many forms, including impact assessments, evaluations, and reports on implementation. Finally, and more amorphously, there is the broader body of more complex research that investigates the impacts of migration on societies, economies, and individuals themselves. While policy-makers may have a general research agenda and questions they would like answered, it is impossible for them to know what will be most valuable until research has been completed and communicated.

Unlike most résumés of EU research (Singleton 2009; King and Lulle 2016), the following typology does not follow a thematic approach; rather, it looks at where and how research connects with the policy-making environment.

Commissioned and In-house Research

Both the European Commission and European Parliament have significant budgets for commissioning research, whether as part of a formal policy process, such as the pre-proposal impact assessments or evaluations of implemented policy, or more general investigations into issues prioritized within the Commission's annual work programme. Both institutions offer multi-year framework contracts to consortia of research organizations (most commonly led by for-profit consultancy firms), each of whom can then bid for tenders for specific studies. The expertise required for such a potentially broad range of topics is hard to maintain within a single consortium, and lead times are frequently short. Lead partners in Home Affairs framework contracts are often dependent on finding high-quality partners and sub-contracting external experts. The most relevant experts—frequently, former practitioners and academics—can be hard to bring in at short notice. In addition, although framework contracts come with potentially large budgets,[5] the tendering process is competitive (albeit limited) and bids have to ensure cost effectiveness.

Commissioned research of this type can be very influential, particularly if it forms part of the formal policy cycle, or is timed to coincide with relevant internal discussions. Typically, the 'preferred option' outlined in an impact assessment becomes the template upon which legislation is drafted (although impact assessments usually contain multiple options). However, this type of research has its own limitations. Impact assessments rarely, if ever, recommend the status quo (inaction), or suggest that an initiative be discontinued. While a broader academic community may argue that an EU proposal is unwarranted or wrong-headed, EU processes tend to have neither a brake, nor a reverse gear. This pre-determined narrowing of the policy options means that studies tend to begin with a justificatory framing that may exclude particular evidence in order to allow for expected recommendations (see also Chapter 2 in this volume).

Politics can also affect whether evidence translates into policy action. For example, despite an evaluation of the implementation of the Family Reunification Directive in 2013, which highlighted a number of deficiencies in its functioning (European Commission 2008), a recast of the legislation was shelved amid fears that re-opening the legislation would lead to further dilution, rather than a strengthening, of standards. Conversely, some initiatives have continued to be pushed despite deep scepticism about their value. The now adopted proposals for an EU-wide Entry–Exit system endured three separate impact assessments (in 2006, 2013, and 2016), while several European Parliament studies (Jeandesboz et al. 2013) and a European Data Protection Supervisor assessment (European Data Protection Supervisor 2013) highlighted issues of cost, privacy, and proportionality (issues echoed by numerous EU member states). Rather than abandon the endeavour, proposals were re-worked and re-tabled, and were eventually adopted in late 2017, due in part to the weight of these critiques. This demonstrates the value of having commissioned research emanate from multiple institutions. European Parliament studies are often more critical (and more creative) than those produced for the European Commission.

Alongside research associated with policy processes, the European Commission maintains agreements with key international organizations, including the International Organization for Migration (IOM) and the Organisation for Economic Cooperation and Development (OECD), the International Centre for Migration Policy Development (ICMPD), and the International Labour Organization (ILO), which allows them to commission research without a tendering process. These organizations tend to have stronger access to the institutions when offering evidence; also, they have played an increasing role in providing data and analysis in recent years.

EU agencies responsible for migration have developed research, mostly in-house. EASO offers month-to-month data on asylum applications and outcomes, and is developing a repository of country of origin information. EASO has also initiated a bespoke outsourced research programme focused on the drivers of migration, although the budget for this research currently allows for little more than small grants for theoretical review. Frontex invests in a series of risk analyses—for example, the Africa-Frontex Intelligence Community Joint Report (Frontex 2014)—which outlines the trends, nationalities, means, and conditions of those taking the main migratory routes to the European Union, and includes analysis of regional instability and security risks in the Africa-Frontex Intelligence Community (AFIC) region. These risk analyses are primarily concerned with mixed flows to Europe. While they are tuned into changing routes for smuggling and trafficking in a particular region, and ruminate as to the cause, they do not look deeply at the drivers of mass movement emanating from broader socio-economic or political instability. Meanwhile, the Fundamental Rights Agency presents periodic data on the situation for migrants themselves, with a particular focus on those affected by 'large migration movements' (Fundamental Rights Agency 2018).[6] Finally, the European Court of Auditors has undertaken studies on the implementation of hotspots in Greece and Italy, and the efficacy of spending on migration within European Neighbourhood policy (European Court of Auditors 2016, 2017).

Commissioned research is supplemented by the use of expert groups, public consultations, and formal and informal public hearings. Non-governmental actors frequently argue that public consultations perform little more than a legitimizing function in the development of legislation (cf. Chapter 2 in this book). Online consultations rely on the activism of outside organizations in responding to questionnaires and submitting evidence. The European Migration Forum—an annual two-day meeting gathering policy-makers, NGOs, and experts to discuss various elements of policy—is one of a number of physical meetings hosted by the European institutions (European Economic and Social Committee 2018). However, while useful for networking, it is unclear how much influence these discussions have on policy. At the other end of the scale, involvement in thematic expert groups is by invitation only, and restricted to those deemed by the European Commission to be knowledgeable on the topics at hand. For example, the Expert Group on Economic Migration includes experts from the OECD, Migration Policy Institute Europe (MPI Europe), the IOM and leading academic institutions such as Oxford University. Discussions are led by the European Commission, but can influence their thinking very directly (European Commission 2015). As such, they offer exclusive access to a select few, with relatively little investment on either side.

Mechanisms for Knowledge-gathering

Since the turn of the millennium, the European Commission has supported the development of a number of academic research networks and multi-year research projects designed to inform national and European policy-makers. These include open-ended academic networks such as International Migration, Integration and Social Cohesion in Europe (IMISCOE—a pan-European network of migration research centres, launched in 2004) (IMISCOE n.d.) and long-term investments such as CARIM (a consortium of researchers focused on analysing migration trends first to the South, later to the East, launched in 2004) (CARIM-East n.d., see Chapter 12 in this book), as well as multi-year, multi-disciplinary research projects such as MAFE (assessing migration drivers between Africa and Europe) (Institut National d'Études Demographiques 2014) and CLANDESTINO (assessing the size of the undocumented population in Europe) (ELIAMEP n.d.). Beyond this, there are hundreds of smaller research projects covering all aspects of migration and asylum, undertaken by groups of research organizations supported through funding programmes disbursed directly at EU level (King and Lulle 2016).

EU support has been a strong driver in the development of comparative research on trends in migration, asylum, and integration, and on policy impacts, largely through consecutive seven-year research framework programmes (which follow the seven-year EU budget cycle: 2014–2020).[7] They have fostered stronger cross-national and cross-disciplinary research ties between researchers across Europe, as well as with researchers residing in the European neighbourhood. EU support has contributed to a substantial increase in comparative research (albeit with a strong western European focus), subsequently disseminated in national and local policy debates. However, in my view, the resultant canon of research has had an underwhelming impact on policy. There are a number of reasons for this.

Many academics question whether policy impact should be a research priority (even when focused on key public policy questions). Reports are often long and written in technical and/or opaque language, impenetrable for time-limited policy-makers looking for quick illumination of a policy problem, and frequently lack usable policy recommendations. In addition, there is often a gap of up to five years between the initial call for research proposals and the first research outputs from successful proposals. This is too long a cycle for policy-makers confronted with fast-paced change.

But there is also little capacity within the EU institutions themselves to accumulate knowledge over time, or to build on existing work. While most projects funded by the European Union typically involve a dissemination phase, a final report, and conference, these are last-minute affairs and it is often the case that most researchers have already moved on to the next project. Until recently, there was no central repository for EU-funded research on migration,[8] and the internet is littered with lapsed project websites. Few officials are able to draw on research stemming back more than a couple of years.

In an effort to bring more consistent evidence to the policy-making process, the European Commission created the European Migration Network (EMN) in 2008. Coordinated by an external organization,[9] the EMN brings together nationally appointed government (and sub-contracted) researchers to produce information on topics set through an annual work programme, and as needs arise. The EMN produces national and synthesis reports on specific policy areas and publishes annual national reports outlining reforms, and curates answers to ad hoc queries from EU member states as to how other governments address particular policy issues. Over time, the body of work published by the EMN has become more comparative and is valuable in informing other member states about the policies of their peers. However, while the EMN collates information on practice, it does not generally offer policy recommendations, or draw upon empirical analysis to ascertain the effects of particular policy choices.

Communicating Independent Research

While the EU is a driver of research in many countries—and an increasingly critical source of funding—it is by no means the sole catalyst for research relevant to EU policy-making. There is a glut of research, from legal analysis through to fieldwork with migrant groups, that can inform policy-makers' understanding of migration. Given the abundance of research, policy-makers are reliant on trusted interlocutors to filter significant research results and communicate them effectively and in a timely manner. Several Directorates-General in the European Commission have attempted to take on this role and have organized academic conferences on migration; however, these tend to cram together multiple presentations on diverse topics, leaving the few policy-makers in attendance dizzy with a vast array of evidence, which may or may not have relevance to their work. The European Parliament political groupings host frequent hearings to showcase research, but these are often poorly attended.

In this context, think tanks and other policy-focused research institutes have emerged as key interlocutors, particularly those based in Brussels. With a primary focus on policy, and with networks across the broader research community, these organizations can connect relevant, high-quality research to burning policy questions. To be successful, such interlocutors have to be credible, independent, and without a strong political agenda; they must be able to draw on thick networks of policy-makers and other stakeholders from civil society, media, and the private sector; and be capable of extracting policy-relevant conclusions from the evidence presented. This is not a simple task, and requires time and effort to keep abreast of new research and emerging policy issues.

For academics with a strong reputation and an established catalogue of work, there is often no need for an interlocutor. But this can also lead to a bias in the voices that are heard in Brussels: experts with a media presence can find themselves invited to present to policy-makers who have become familiar with their work through the press and, increasingly, social media, Meanwhile, emerging, young, and minority researchers with nascent networks can struggle. This brings home the fact that not only can research, media, and policy influence be mutually reinforcing, but it can also side-line those with less capacity for the active dissemination of their work.[10] Sadly, media and policy influence is not always a strong indicator of quality, knowledge, and expertise; in some cases, it may merely indicate a loud voice.

A Crisis Realization

As the crisis unfolded in 2015, policy-makers quickly realized the inadequacy of the evidence-gathering mechanisms at their disposal. Real-time data from national and international sources were frequently inconsistent, and were not packaged or analysed in a way that could flag key shifts in movement.[11]

Information was not effectively communicated between countries concerning arrivals and onward movement. This is not an insurmountable task, or one which necessarily requires deep investment. For example, the Swedish Migration Agency developed models to predict future flows to the country, incorporating factors—for example, regional instability—to build a series of scenarios that were periodically adjusted to account for new events and changing factors along the migration journey.[12] However, few other countries had similar capacity. At the EU level, not only were there no mechanisms in place to manage a pan-European early warning network, but to put them in place would be to explicitly accept the existence of onward movement within the EU. Countries such as Greece and Italy had no incentive to monitor either arrivals or onward movement. Thus, during the summer of 2015, NGOs and volunteers were often in command of the best information about arrivals on the Greek islands and along the Western Balkan route. Subsequently, UNHCR and others began to collate flow information.[13]

For the EU institutions, the triggering of the Integrated Political Crisis Response (IPCR) system in October 2015 became a critical catalyst for improving information flow between officials, at both national and EU level (Council of the EU 2015b). One of the enduring benefits of the activation of the IPCR has been the development of Integrated Situational Awareness and Analysis

(ISAA) reports, collating data from affected EU member states and providing updates on key changes and responses; this report is distributed weekly to officials. Described by officials as 'the saviour of 2015', the ISAA reports ensured everyone had access to the same data at the same time, and allowed actors to identify key knowledge gaps and to seek further information (Collett and Le Coz 2018). While this seems basic, it did not exist in a usable consolidated format prior to the crisis.

Separately, while proliferating instability within the European neighbourhood has increased the risk of additional mass movements of displaced people, whether primary or secondary movements, interior policy-makers in charge of migration portfolios have few tools to predict—and thus prepare for—the effects of external events on inflow. The earliest warning occurred when people had already reached European borders, when it was too late to put in place appropriate and timely responses. While immigration policy-makers instinctively understood that dynamics were likely to change in 2015, they had little data that would help them predict scale, composition, and route.

Early warning systems exist across the EU institutions. For example, the EU Intelligence Analysis Centre (INTCEN) is designed to provide the European External Action Service (EEAS) and EU member states with early warning analysis and response. Effects on migrants and refugees are included in the analysis, which is mostly limited to the region in question, and dissemination to interior actors is limited. The development of the EU Conflict Early Warning System (EWS) in 2014 was, in part, to redress criticisms that the EU's approach to early warning had been ad hoc and scattered. Within the Directorate-General ECHO, analysts from the Emergency Response Coordination Centre publish a 'daily map' of situations to watch. This can include a damage assessment after a major natural disaster, or forecasts of dangerous weather systems affecting Europe (European Commission Directorate-General for Humanitarian Aid and Civil Protection n.d.).

At agency level, EASO has now been tasked with supporting the development of an early warning, preparedness, and crisis management mechanism.[14] As such, the agency produces regular analyses of trend, push–pull factors, and risk scenarios based on information from EU member states and other agencies, including UNHCR, IOM, and Frontex. In 2016, Europol established the European Migrant Smuggling Centre (EMSC) to help member states target and dismantle the organized crime networks involved in human smuggling and trafficking. The EMSC also produces Migrant Smuggling Monitoring Reports—delivering 174 in its first year of operation (Europol 2017). The existing infrastructure is geared towards sharing information that could indicate the evolution of a migration crisis but it has limited predictive capacity. For example, neither Frontex nor EASO engage in scenario building; where this capacity exists in the EEAS, foresight capacity is narrow due to weak links to broader geopolitical conflict and instability.

Increasing the Use of Research and Evidence Post-crisis: A Mixed Bag

In an effort to address what quickly became a political concern about the availability of evidence on flows, since 2015 the European Union has initiated a number of new mechanisms to gather and improve the use of evidence for policy-making across the European Union.

Between institutions, it is clear that the crisis has created a habit of information exchange on a regular basis, rather than ad hoc. Two weaknesses persist. First, the value of information exchange relies on accurate reporting from EU member states. It became clear in the autumn of 2016 that reported numbers in Greek mainland reception centres were far higher than the numbers witnessed on the ground; concerned by the conditions of continued onward movement through the Western Balkans, it was UNHCR and non-state actors that raised the alarm, rather than the Greek government (UNHCR 2015). Second, issues flagged through the IPCR and other coordinating groups translate into improved policy outcomes. The continued documentation of poor conditions on the Greek islands and along the borders of south-east Europe, for example, reflect a lingering gap between communicating a problem and finding ways to address it effectively when there is political resistance to doing so.

There has also been a concerted effort to gather 'upstream' data on flows. The European Commission has joined various EU member states in funding the IOM's Displacement Tracking Matrix to begin monitoring a number of countries seen to be key origin and transit countries along the central Mediterranean route to the EU.[15] This investment marks a significant upgrade in interest in terms of research: prior to 2016, the major investment from the European Commission had been the development of 'migration profiles' of key sending and transit countries, lengthy reports outlining stocks, flows, and socio-economic data, which tended not to be used by policy-makers (Global Forum on Migration and Development n.d.). However, there have been questions over the quality of some of the data produced and uncertainty over who to believe when data conflict with that produced by national agencies.

Interpretation remains challenging. While there is now perhaps even a surfeit of information available to officials, there is little systematic analysis of that data. It is left to policy-makers to select the data they deem most pertinent and to draw their own policy and operational conclusions, potentially erroneously.[16]

Beyond this, the European Commission has developed a renewed, almost repentant, appreciation of broader migration research and has developed a new range of initiatives (some of which may turn out to be duplicative). This is driven by a desire by numerous Directorates-General within the Commission to ensure their own continued relevance on a topic with high salience as much as it is about improving policy on the basis of evidence. Central among these is the creation in 2016 of a Knowledge Centre of Migration and Demography (KCMD). The Centre is tasked with collating what it perceives to be fragmented knowledge on migration, rather than generating new information, and it has launched a dynamic data hub that presents stock and flow data culled from Eurostat, the OECD, the United Nations Department of Economic and Social Affairs (UNDESA), and others (Knowledge Centre on Migration and Demography n.d.). Based in Italy, it is not yet clear how close its links with policy-makers will be, or whether the primary audience for its data will be in policy or academic circles. Certainly, much of the information published is already circulating in a different form at meetings such as the IPCR, although not sourced via the KCMD.[17] Separately, the Directorate-General Research has created a Migration Research Platform that brings together all the various research projects supported under the preceding research frameworks, as well as the various EU-led sources of information, including (somewhat circularly) the KCMD.

More meaningfully, the amount of funding earmarked for independent migration research under the Horizon 2020 research programme has been increased significantly.[18] This includes the development of an externally managed migration research platform designed to make evidence more comparable across countries (CROSS-MIGRATION) and a 'stakeholders' platform that will bring together researchers, NGOs, and local authorities on social issues related to migration (RESOMA) (European Commission Directorate-General for Research and Innovation 2016). At the same time, under the Emergency Trust Fund for Africa—launched to improve cooperation with sending and transit countries across the continent—a Research and Evidence Facility has been created under the aegis of the School of Oriental and African Studies (SOAS) to look at, inter alia, the drivers of migration (SOAS University of London n.d.).

It is still unclear how these reinvigorated efforts will function alongside the existing mechanisms—from the EMN through to the consultancies tasked with developing impact assessments—and play a concrete role in developing policy, and the EU institutions may be mistaking a flurry of action for progress. These efforts can also be critiqued on the basis of 'too little, too late'; the original Horizon 2020 programme contained little focus on migration, and first results from the new calls for proposals will take several years to emerge. Although the Directorate-General Research has hosted several conferences designed to reflect on the use of evidence in policy-making,[19] there has been little broader reflection within the EU institutions as to how research, once collected, is used to design and reform policy, despite increasing demands from leaders for 'data'.

Conclusion: Challenges to Incorporating Evidence in EU Policy-making Processes

Overall, as one might expect, there is a strong correlation between how far the EU institutions are actively invested in external expertise and how far that expertise can then influence its own policy work. The exception to this is work commissioned by the Directorate-General Research, which is, too often, viewed as sitting outside policy circles. Proximity to policy-makers (how far experts are embedded in a policy-making network at EU or national level), reputation (the canon of expertise that researchers bring to the table) and familiarity (whether the research framing fits within the pre-existing views of policy-makers) are all factors affecting influence. This last criterion is particularly important: there has been a surfeit of critical analysis of EU policy during the crisis period and yet very little of it has affected the overall policy direction;[20] instead, it has often led to a withdrawal of openness on the part of policy-makers to interact.

To be effective, researchers and experts need to provide information that is not readily available to policy-makers. This includes not only primary on-the-ground research, but also ensuring that the voices of those affected by migration (notably, migrants themselves) are heard, as noted by Singleton (2015). Policy-makers are ready to hear from civil society and academic actors who can offer a first-hand account of policy effects, or raise issues that otherwise do not reach Brussels. This creates a paradox: access to EU policy-makers is hugely advanced by regular presence in the policy-making environment—whether Brussels or a national capital—and by the development of networks that are constantly in flux.[21] Thus, researchers who are predominantly undertaking fieldwork tend to have limited access to the policy-making environment. This is an issue replicated in civil society, where local NGOs are reliant on platform NGOs in Brussels effectively translating and communicating their concerns. As the scope of EU interest in migration broadens to non-EU countries and to the implementation of EU policy at local level, the gap between knowledge and access is likely to broaden. This means that the role of effective interlocutors—beyond occasional conferences and presentations—who can distil information and draw relevant policy conclusions has become ever more important.

Reputation and trust are key. Expertise must be seen as independent, or clearly marked otherwise. This has become increasingly problematic in academic circles where researchers' ideologies are frequently set in opposition to those of policy-makers. The use of charged terms such as 'Fortress Europe' and 'externalization agenda' has given policy-makers the impression that research conclusions may not be objective—which, in turn, has affected levels of trust between the policy and academic worlds. There is a need for an open conversation within academia about core goals of research, about the desirability and function of policy influence and, if deemed a valid objective, about the creation of constructive environments to communicate necessary critique to policy-makers. The relationship is under strain, but there is an opportunity to repair it.

When a policy area is politically sensitive and contested, it is not only hard for policy-makers to review and absorb critique, but also to take on board contradictory evidence. This is also related to the level of direct policy responsibility that the EU institutions have over a topic. Since the late 2000s, it has proved far easier for the European Commission to commission and reflect upon public research related to immigrant integration outcomes, as it merely has a loose coordinating role. Conversely, policy-makers are far less likely to commission public research on border management or security issues, preferring to commission private consultancies; for example, McKinsey was commissioned to review asylum procedures in Greece in late 2016, in order to develop means of accelerating the implementation of the EU–Turkey statement. Proximity to decision-making also affects how far research is taken on board: the European Parliament—furthest from the hot-seat—commissions more critical research than the Commission which, in turn, commissions more research than the Council, which relies primarily on information communicated by EU and international agencies through briefings and memos (and, now, ISAA reports). But policy-makers must become more open to new information and be willing to adapt policy based on what it tells them.

The European institutions have clearly identified a need for greater levels of forward-looking evidence on migration, and the willingness to invest in it—specifically, the impact that demographic change, conflict, and instability might have on future flows to Europe, and means through which migrants may use particular regular and irregular pathways. One of the most frequently uttered preoccupations, post-crisis, is the number of migrants who may seek passage to Europe over the next couple of decades.[22] Not only is this an impossible question to answer, given the large number of variables inherent in determining such a figure, but to put forward a static prediction also risks fossilizing a politically sensitive debate around a single piece of data. Thus, researchers and experts will need to find ways to help *shape* the most important future research questions, rather than merely react to those developed in political circles. They will also need to be clear about questions that cannot be effectively answered. This requires not only an understanding of future policy issues, but also a comprehensive overview of the current state of knowledge.

As the migration policy domain is unlikely to reduce in political salience and scrutiny in the near future, experts are in a contradictory position: on the one hand, researchers will find that support for large-scale data and evidence collection is higher than it has ever been at EU level, including financial support; on the other hand, it may be harder than ever to influence a policy-making domain that has become path dependent and constrained by national politics. To affect policy design, research will have to be communicated in a manner that is smartly framed, iterative and capable of acknowledging political realities while not conforming to them. In a context where expertise is increasingly framed as advocacy, providing objective evidence and policy relevant, constructive solutions for policy-makers will be both challenging and essential.

Notes

1. Interviews undertaken in 2008 with Brussels-based journalists, unpublished MPI memo, Transatlantic Council on Migration.
2. The staff of the Directorate-General HOME has grown significantly since 2015; this has involved the establishment of a new unit on migration management support, producing information reports for distribution within the European Commission and elsewhere.
3. While the Global Approach to Migration (and later Mobility)—the EU's effort to develop a foreign policy agenda—has existed since 2005, it was considered a marginal and marginally successful policy with little buy-in from those outside the JHA arena.
4. Eurostat gathers much of this information from EU Member States, including the Labour Force Survey, the European Social Survey and various national population surveys.
5. The European Commission has estimated commissioned work on irregular migration between 2017 and 2021 to be worth up to €6 million, while €3 million have been earmarked for research on legal migration and integration. For original tender specifications, see https://ec.europa.eu/home-affairs/sites/homeaffairs/files/financing/tenders/2017/20170310_tender_specifications_en.pdf (Accessed 7 May 2018).
6. This reporting commenced on a weekly basis in September 2015 and is now presented on a monthly basis.
7. The framework programme in 2018 is Horizon 2020, a fund of nearly €80 billion, managed by the Directorate-General for Research and Innovation.
8. The Knowledge Centre on Migration and Demography is attempting to rectify this.

9. Currently, the EMN is managed by ICF, a for-profit consultancy.
10. This is particularly problematic when academic institutions view policy engagement as an extra-curricular activity.
11. This section draws upon research conducted for Collett and Le Coz (2018).
12. Indeed, the October 2012 prediction for asylum applications in 2013 was accurate to within 259 applications. For more detail on the process, see UNHCR (2013).
13. See, for example, UNHCR's *Daily Estimated Arrivals per Country—Flows through Western Balkans Route*, 24 April 2016.
14. As mandated through Article 33 of the recast Dublin Regulation (European Union 2013).
15. Originally conceived as a tool to help monitor displacement in conflict and disaster regions, Directorate-General ECHO has funded the monitoring of transit flows through Libya (co-funded by the UK government) since January 2016 (IOM 2018a), Niger (co-funded by the German government) since February 2016 (IOM 2018b), and Mali (co-funded by the UK and US governments) since June 2016 (IOM 2018c). The IOM not only monitors inflows and outflows; and demographic data, including nationality, age and purpose of travel; and tracks changes in route; it also produces short, frequent updates of the data.
16. Indeed, the European Commission's Second Report on the Migration Partnership Framework implied that a drop in border crossings in Niger from 70,000 in May 2016 to 1,500 in November of the same year was due to efforts pursued under the proposed migration partnership with the country (launched in June 2016), ignoring other possible factors such as seasonal fluctuation. This data was, in any case, later revised (European Commission 2016b).
17. Interviews with officials in the European Commission conducted during April 2018 suggested that knowledge of the KCMD, and hence the use of its products, was very low.
18. The EU announced in 2017 that they would allocate over €200 million for migration-related research in 2018–2020 (European Commission Directorate-General for Research and Innovation 2017).
19. See, for example, the Directorate-General Research Workshop on Migration Governance: Europe and Africa, hosted in Brussels on 10 July 2017.
20. See, for example, extensive research on NGO search and rescue activities in the Mediterranean. Despite several research projects—such as MEDMIG—disputing the 'pull factor' role played by such activities, Italian and EU policies have continued in the direction of curtailing those activities.
21. This is reflected in literature reviewing the use of evidence (Oliver et al. 2014).
22. A question that the Joint Research Centre has briefly attempted to answer (Joint Research Centre 2018).

References

CARIM-East. n.d. *CARIM East—Consortium for Applied Research on International Migration*. Available at: www.carim-east.eu/(Accessed 7 May 2018).

Collett, E. 2015. *The Asylum Crisis in Europe: Designed Dysfunction*. Brussels: Migration Policy Institute Europe.

Collett, E., and Le Coz, C. 2018. *After the Storm: Learning from the EU Response to the Migration Crisis*. Brussels: Migration Policy Institute Europe.

Council of the EU. 2015a. *Council Decision (EU) 2015/1601 of 22 September 2015 Establishing Provisional Measures in the Area of International Protection for the Benefit of Italy and Greece*. Brussels: Council of the EU.

Council of the EU. 2015b. *Migratory Crisis: EU Council Presidency Steps up Information Sharing between Member States by Activating IPCR*. Brussels: Council of the EU.

ECRE/UNHCR. 2018. *Follow the Money: Assessing the use of AMIF funding at the national level*.

ELIAMEP. n.d. *CLANDESTINO—Undocumented Migration: Counting the Uncountable Data and Trends across Europe*.

European Commission. 2008. *Report from the Commission to the European Parliament and the Council on the Application of Directive 2003/86/EC on the Right to Family Reunification*. Brussels: European Commission.

European Commission. 2015. *Register of Commission Expert Groups and Other Similar Entities: Expert Group Economic Migration*. Brussels: European Commission.

European Commission. 2016a. *Communication from the Commission to the European Parliament, the European Council, the Council and the European Investment Bank on Establishing a New Partnership Framework with Third Countries under the European Agenda on Migration*. Brussels: European Commission.

European Commission. 2016b. *Communication from the Commission to the European Parliament, the European Council and the Council, Second Progress Report: First Deliverables on the Partnership Framework with Third Countries under the European Agenda on Migration*. Brussels: European Commission.

European Commission Directorate-General for Humanitarian Aid and Civil Protection. n.d. *Emergency Response Coordination Centre (ERCC): European Civil Protection and Humanitarian Aid Operations*.

European Commission Directorate-General for Research and Innovation. 2016. *Tackling the Migration Challenge: €11 Million for Five New Research Topics*.

European Commission Directorate-General for Research and Innovation. 2017. *Tackling the Migration Challenges: More Than €200 Million for New Research Topics*.

European Court of Auditors. 2016. *EU External Migration Spending in Southern Mediterranean and Eastern Neighbourhood Countries until 2014*. Luxembourg: European Court of Auditors.

European Court of Auditors. 2017. *EU Response to the Refugee Crisis: The 'Hotspot' Approach*. Luxembourg: European Court of Auditors.

European Data Protection Supervisor. 2013. *Opinion of the European Data Protection Supervisor on the Proposals for a Regulation establishing an Entry/Exit System (EES) and a Regulation establishing a Registered Traveller Programme (RTP)*. Brussels: European Data Protection Supervisor.

European Economic and Social Committee. 2018. *European Migration Forum—4th Meeting*.

European Union. 2013. *Regulation (EU) No 604/2013 of the European Parliament and of the Council of 26 June 2013 Establishing the Criteria and Mechanisms for Determining the*

Member State Responsible for Examining an Application for International Protection Lodged in One of the Member States by a Third-Country National or a Stateless Person: Article 33. Brussels: European Union.

Europol. 2017. *European Migrant Smuggling Centre: Activity Report First Year.* The Hague: Europol.

Fratzke, S., and Salant, B. 2018. *Moving Beyond 'Root Causes': The Complicated Relationship between Development and Migration.* Washington, DC: Migration Policy Institute.

Frontex. 2014. *Africa-Frontex Intelligence Community Joint Report.* Warsaw: Frontex.

Fundamental Rights Agency. 2018. *Periodic data collection on the migration situation in the EU: March Highlights.*

Gentiloni, P., and Avramopoulos, D. 2016. Migrants, Helping Africa to Help Europe. *La Repubblica.* Available at: www.esteri.it/mae/en/sala_stampa/interviste/2016/11/gentiloni-avramopoulos-migranti.html (Accessed 7 May 2018).

Global Forum on Migration and Development. n.d. *Migration Profiles Repository.* Available at: www.gfmd.org/pfp/policy-tools/migration-profiles/repository (Accessed 7 May 2018).

IMISCOE. n.d. *About IMISCOE.* Available at: www.imiscoe.org/about-imiscoe (Accessed 7 May 2018).

Institut National d'Études Demographiques. 2014. *Final Report Summary—MAFE (Migration between Africa and Europe).* Paris: Institut National d'Études Demographiques.

IOM. 2018a. *Displacement Tracking Matrix Libya.* Available at: www.globaldtm.info/Libya/(Accessed 7 May 2018).

IOM. 2018b. *Displacement Tracking Matrix Niger.* Available at: www.globaldtm.info/niger/(Accessed 7 May 2018).

IOM. 2018c. *Displacement Tracking Matrix Mali.* Available at: www.globaldtm.info/Mali/ (Accessed 7 May 2018).

Jeandesboz, J., Bigo, D., Hayes, B., and Simon, S. 2013. *The Commission's Legislative Proposals on Smart Borders: Their Feasibility and Costs, Study for the LIBE Committee.* Brussels: European Parliament Policy Department C: Citizens' Rights and Constitutional Affairs.

Joint Research Centre. 2018. *Many More to Come? Migration from and within Africa.* Luxembourg: Publications Office of the European Union.

King, R., and Lulle, A. 2016. *Research on Migration: Facing Realities and Maximising Opportunities. A Policy Review.* Brussels: European Commission Directorate-General for Research and Innovation.

Knowledge Centre on Migration and Demography. n.d. *Dynamic Data Hub.* Available at: https://bluehub.jrc.ec.europa.eu/migration/app/index.html (Accessed 7 May 2018).

Oliver, K., Innvar, S., Lorenc, T., Woodman, J., and Thomas, J. 2014. A Systematic Review of Barriers to and Facilitators of the Use of Evidence by Policymakers. *BMC Health Services Research*, 14/2: 1–12.

Singleton, A. 2009. *Moving Europe: EU Research on Migration and Policy Needs.* Brussels: European Commission Directorate-General for Research.

Singleton, A. 2015. Speaking Truth to Power? Why Civil Society, Beyond Academia, Remains Marginal in EU Migration Policy. In *Integrating Immigrants in Europe:*

Research-Policy Dialogues, eds Peter Scholten, Han Entzinger, Rinus Penninx, and Stijn Verbeek. Berlin: Springer, 131–40.

SOAS University of London. n.d. *Research and Evidence Facility on Migration in the Horn of Africa*. Available at: www.soas.ac.uk/ref-hornresearch/(Accessed 7 May 2018).

UNHCR. 2013. Chapter 1: Sources, Methods and Data Considerations. *UNHCR Statistical Yearbook 2013*. Geneva: UNHCR, 15–23.

UNHCR. 2015. *UNHCR Warns of Growing Asylum Crisis in Greece and the Western Balkans Amid Arrivals of Refugees from War*. Available at: www.unhcr.org/559fa5da6.html (Accessed 7 May 2018).

12

A Knowledge-base for the EU External Migration Policy

The Case of the CARIM Observatories

Agnieszka Weinar

Introduction

The European Union (EU) has been gradually developing its external migration policy, a process that has involved the use of various sources of knowledge over time. EU funding of research projects and research cooperation on
migration showed a steep increase in the early 2000s, when the Global
Approach to Migration was being crafted (European Commission 2008a;
Weinar 2011). This increase in EU-level policy interest and funding—
undertaken by many actors including academia, civil society, and international organizations—boosted the international efforts of data creation,
translation, and adaptation. The policy-makers who, in 2002, put together
the first Commission communication on cooperation with third countries on
migration, were hard pressed to find a comprehensive analysis of trends in
migration from Africa to Europe.[1] By 2018, that information was much more
easily available from a variety of actors and in a variety of forms. Sources
include migration profiles from the International Organization for Migration
(IOM) and the International Centre for Migration Policy Development
(ICMPD),[2] the Migration Policy Centre's series of migration reports,[3] research
reports on migration coming from dozens of projects funded by the external
cooperation funds of the EU,[4] not to mention the information gathered and
adapted by EU agencies such as Frontex, the European Asylum Support Office
(EASO) or the European Training Foundation (ETF). It seems today that a

myriad of knowledge-brokers stand ready to assist EU policy-makers (Korneev 2018).

This chapter discusses the experiences of one of these knowledge-brokers: the Consortium for Applied Research on International Migration (CARIM) Observatories at the European University Institute (EUI), funded by the European Commission between 2004 and 2013. The Observatories were tasked with building a knowledge base on migration in the Southern and Eastern neighbourhoods of the EU, and also in India. In this chapter, I focus mainly on the case of the CARIM-South and CARIM-East Observatories. My main objective is the critical discussion of the experiences of these two projects, and to identify key insights and lessons for consideration regarding the relationship between research and policy-making. I will discuss the Observatories in the wider context of EU policy developments and then reflect on the processes of building a knowledge base for policy-making in an international context. The chapter reflects on the challenges of collaborative research in a complex international environment. It identifies the risks that can hamper this collaboration, such as the language of knowledge production and the research culture, as well as the ways such risks can be minimized. It also provides insights into challenges with linking and communicating research to policy in the European context.

The Role of Research in the EU Global Approach to Migration and Mobility

The EU has consistently emphasized evidence-based policy-making as an important element of the EU external migration policy, going back to the early 2000s (European Commission 2002, 2006, 2008a). The 'remote control' of the EU borders required building relationships with the neighbouring countries, but also having a clearer view of the migration patterns in the European neighbourhood. This policy—the Global Approach to Migration and Mobility (GAMM)[5]—acknowledged the need to engage in bilateral and multilateral relations with the neighbouring countries based on three principles: partnership, conditionality, and sustainability (Kunz et al. 2011). Hence, the GAMM created the concept of 'partner countries'—countries which should be partnering with the EU on migration policy. This cooperation is intended to cover all the countries of the world which either send migrants to the EU, or are transit countries for such migration. GAMM proposed a holistic approach to migration issues that goes beyond simple cooperation on border management, and can foster democratic and economic development of the countries of origin (Weinar 2011; Reslow and Vink 2015). Since the European Commission has dedicated significant financial means to support this approach, building the knowledge base on migration in the partner countries was seen as crucial for the allocation of funds where they were most needed and for the assurance of policy effectiveness (European Court of Auditors 2016).

Initially, however, the knowledge base on migration—its trends, but also its causes and effects—was either non-existent or inaccessible in many countries. This was partly because not all the partner countries in the neighbourhood saw migration as an issue meriting research funding with other areas, often presenting more pressing needs in the context of scarce resources. Also, the existing research often employed local concepts and practices that were not always easily translatable to the EU-based concepts and practices (e.g. different legal frameworks resulting in different definitions, different methodological approaches). More often than not, such information was unavailable in English or French. Therefore, it was up to the EU to create the information to underpin its new policies. The first knowledge-building tool that the European Commission invented in 2005 was 'Migration Profiles', first proposed as an instrument to collect information on African countries in the Communication on migration and development:

> The Commission also proposes the establishment of a Migration Profile (MP) for each interested developing country. Such a document would bring together all information relevant to the design and management of an effective policy on migration and development. This could help define a policy response which would tailor to the situation and needs of the country or countries concerned the instruments presented in a generic manner in this Communication and its annexes.   (European Commission 2005: 36)

Annex 8 of the Communication further elaborated what type of information would be needed to support the EU (in its role as a donor) in deciding on programming that would further support the migration and development agenda. This information was required to be presented in the form of 'indicators' that can be used to describe not only trends in migration, but also the context in which migration occurs; for example, immigration/emigration flows and stocks, migrants' socio-economic characteristics, and labour market data (European Commission 2005). These indicators were to form migration profiles for each country receiving aid from the EU. Arguably, even the countries in the Organisation for Economic Co-operation and Development (OECD)—countries with a robust and capable administration—could have had problems compiling a list of quality data and information required for such documents. In this instance, the European Commission initially tasked itself with the delivery of migration profiles, relying on the desk officers of its own delegations and, sometimes, the administrations of the partner countries. Both had limited resources and skills to dedicate to this task, and this situation posed a problem in the delivery of high-quality migrant profiles. It was only around 2007, when the EU made funding available to develop migration profiles and when external providers became engaged, that the situation improved.

The funding for the engagement of external actors and for relevant research and data collection projects was mainstreamed in the external cooperation funds of the European Commission; this included the Development Cooperation Instrument (DCI). For example, the Prague Process, funded by the DCI, produced a plethora of migration profiles as one of its deliverables.[6] Interestingly, the more research-oriented bodies of the European Commission (such as DG Research or Eurostat) did not take a lead in the process of designing, funding, and implementing this policy-focused research cooperation. Instead, the building of a new knowledge base has been part of 'development support' within the EU's migration and development agenda (European Court of Auditors 2016). This approach involved several risks: for example, the DCI funding instrument promoted the building of a knowledge base, but was not a research programme, thus it lacked a solid analytical approach and the capacity to evaluate the quality of research proposals submitted to the calls and tenders. Furthermore, it required cooperation with the countries of origin on research while, at the same time, assuming a very EU-centric view of the world and migration research undertaken outside the EU. Finally, the DCI funding instrument assumed that evidence in non-EU countries would be easily accessible and digestible in the EU policy context. These risks had to be mitigated by the actual implementing partners (in our case, the CARIM Observatories). Indeed, it soon became obvious that migration data collection and analysis in the partner countries required not only primary or secondary data collection, but also extensive capacity building measures.

Migration Observatories as a Tool of the Global Approach to Migration (and Mobility)

The first Migration Observatory at the EUI had its roots in the cooperation and partnership agenda between the EU and its Mediterranean neighbours. That cooperation, dating back to the 1980s, only began to include migration in the early 2000s, just after the Seville European Summit. The Euro-Med Migration I was the first project that supported collaborative migration research between all the countries of North Africa and the Middle East, and the EU (European Commission 2008b). The first Consortium for Applied Research in the Mediterranean (the CARIM-South Observatory) was established at the EUI in 2004, as a part of the Euro-Med project. Initially, its role was defined loosely as building a knowledge base on migration that could serve both the EU and the partner countries on the Southern rim of the Mediterranean. After 2005, however, and in light of the increased interest in migration profiles, CARIM took on the creation of migration profiles for each of the countries it covered. In 2011, the CARIM Observatory was expanded to the Eastern neighbourhood (CARIM-East) and, in the same year, it also started data collection on India (CARIM-India).

A key objective of the CARIM Migration Observatories was to establish partnerships and collaboration on migration research with countries neighbouring the EU. The partnership was reflected in the principles of 'accessibility, ownership, and sustainability'. Accessibility meant that the data and research collected by the Observatories should be accessible to policy-makers and the public in both the EU and partner countries—this included linguistic accessibility as well as conceptual accessibility (discussed later in this chapter). Ownership meant that the stakeholders from the countries of origin should recognize the value of the research and data collected by the Observatories, so that the work is not seen as serving only the EU. Finally, the idea of sustainability was that when EU funding ceases, the Observatories should be able to sustain themselves.

To achieve these goals, a key strategy of the Migration Observatories was to develop and engage a network of country experts connected across countries and disciplines, thus allowing comparisons between countries and the multidisciplinary analysis of issues. The researchers from the neighbouring countries were invited to participate in a network of correspondents. They were selected through the existing academic networks of the team of experts based at the EUI and through literature reviews.

The architecture of the Observatories reflected three disciplinary divisions: law, economics/demography, and social/political studies. The logic behind this architecture was simple. First, the CARIM team followed the knowledge management principle: a knowledge base should have a structure that can be easily translated into a functional database. Second, the comparability principle had to be reflected across countries and across disciplines. The three disciplinary fields were covered by three teams comprised of an EUI leader (expert in the discipline) and country experts for each participating country. The teams collected data and performed analysis on a variety of migration topics common to all the countries. Thus, the same research topics were approached by disciplinary experts from the same country. Legal experts collected relevant texts on laws and regulations; the economists/demographers collected relevant statistics; and political scientists/sociologists collected policy papers, qualitative surveys, and reports. Each contribution was registered in CARIM's online database, searchable by topic, country, or discipline. It is crucial to note here that the data included in the database were not a result of primary research; rather, they were a collection of existing information scattered across countries and stakeholders. In addition, each expert would prepare a descriptive paper on the topic, to be published online. The results included in-depth studies that, together, created a multidisciplinary report on an issue, but that could also be compared along disciplinary lines across the different countries. The country experts also contributed with research on issues specific to their country, to fulfil the principle of ownership of knowledge production in the Observatories.

As will be discussed, the Observatories have been places of *translation of existing knowledge* and *assuring accessibility*, but they also have been places of *knowledge production and management, to foster ownership*. Further, they also had a role outside of academia: their activities targeted partner country *political* and *public discourses, to assure sustainability*. This broad approach had immediate benefits, but also carried important risks.

Translation of the Existing Knowledge

The idea behind the Observatories was that there was already a wealth of knowledge produced by the academic institutions in the partner countries. However, this knowledge was not easily accessible to EU policy-makers and scholars for two main reasons: language barriers, and the different cultural and legal contexts in which scholarship was produced and practised. Translation—understood as mainstreaming in English, and clarification of the context of knowledge production—was thus the core task of the project. The same concept was then expanded to the Eastern neighbourhood in CARIM-East.

Language: Language issues are by far the most important elements to consider when talking about accessibility of both primary research and existing studies in countries neighbouring the EU. The CARIM Observatory in the Southern neighbourhood paid attention to the prevalence of French in the academic exchanges across the Mediterranean. However, the dominance of English in the production and consumption of research across Europe had to be considered, together with the fact that research produced in French may not have been accessible either to the wider European public or more internationally. It is also important to note that the prevalence of French language among the younger generations in the Southern neighbourhood has been diminishing as the younger and skilled people recognize the importance of English to accessing the global labour market. This tension between two leading European languages became clear with the development of CARIM-South: each year the number of publications in English increased, achieving a balance with the publications in French around 2011. The migration profiles produced for each of the countries (as well as regional reports) were produced in English to reach the widest audience possible. The CARIM-South database contained administrative data that were presented in French or English, allowing for wider use by the international audience, but the legal database contained documents in Arabic only, neither translated nor described, and so of little use for non-Arabic speakers.

CARIM-South did not produce research papers in Arabic, relying on the French and English language skills of the partner country academic results and policy-making elites. This was possibly a barrier to the dissemination of the results among those sections of the population that do not master these languages.[7]

Over the years, the EU faced growing criticism of its partnership approach in external migration policy-making (Carrera and Hernández i Sagrera 2011; Van Hüllen 2012; Wunderlich 2012). The key criticism concerning knowledge production was that it serves only the objectives and interests of the EU. Thus, a growing emphasis was put on the benefits to the partner countries in the Communication of 2008 (European Commission 2008a). Observatories adjusted to this requirement in their next wave of activities, notably at the inception of CARIM-East in 2011.[8] To benefit both the EU and the partner countries alike, the working languages needed to be adjusted. Indeed, Russian—not English—is the lingua franca east of the EU border and thus the database inputs and multidisciplinary research were produced consistently in English and Russian. The work was done by the bilingual research team and supported by translators and proofreaders in both languages. This required the use of additional resources.

The adoption of Russian as the official project language also had another advantage. When looking for scholars able to participate in a multinational research network, the language criterion is usually a limiting factor. A research coordinator can typically only use the pool of scholars who can write in good English, which considerably limits the choices possible. English-speaking researchers and consultants usually earn their credentials working for international organizations and producing informative reports, but not all can produce analytical contributions. Very often, English-speaking researchers unknowingly create research monopolies. This is a major unintended consequence of international research networks, which only open up to people with good English skills and previous experience working for international organizations. Often, it is two or three individuals in a country who are used in cross-country research projects, while arguably the possible pool of suitable candidates could be much wider if knowledge of English were not a precondition. So, the risk perpetuated by the international research networks is that competency in English, rather than exceptional skill or unique knowledge, gives a country expert their dominant position. Adopting Russian allowed us to reach scholars and practitioners who did not work in English but who had a required set of skills to contribute to the research. Most of them were invited to participate after a literature review of the Russian-language sources, performed by the CARIM-East team in the first month of the project.

Cross-country comparisons: When establishing a network of collaborators, an important translating function of the Observatories emerged. Even if the working language were the same and understood by all the scholars involved, the different traditions of scholarship made a truly comparative approach difficult. The differences concerned both actual concepts used in data collection and analysis, and the standards of academic research and analysis. In my experience, when EU decision-makers look for comparative studies in migration, they often aim to achieve the standards of OECD work on migration, which effectively translates national differences in data collection into a coherent annual International Migration Outlook report.[9] The OECD first reports pre-date EU-level efforts to harmonize migration statistics, and they are comprehensive, including information on policy changes and social issues. I believe that, for the time being, this standard is impossible to achieve across various non-OECD countries, mainly due to the differences in data collection methodologies (the definitions and modes of collection). Even in continental Europe, these traditions differ (see Di Bartolomeo 2019).

Within the CARIM, we attempted to address this difficulty in two ways. The first solution, adopted in the CARIM-South Observatory, saw the comparative research delivered at the stage of Migration Profiles. The CARIM-South statistical database contained table statistics from administrative sources and qualitative surveys for each country, but only the qualified team members were able to provide a comparative analysis of the content (which they did in the Migration Profiles). A lay person using the table 'as is' ran the risk of comparing apples and oranges. The second solution was adopted in CARIM-East: each data item included in the database was accompanied by adding explanatory notes for each of the tables, which explained the content of the table and thus aided its comparability across the countries.

It must be added here that the Observatories never aimed at offering a comparative dataset with the statistics processed to achieve comparability (as it is the case in the OECD reports or Eurostat reports). It has always been understood that the national data reflect local specificity that is lost when we try to use global, overarching definitions and concepts. A similar learning process took place in the case of legal and socio-political components of the database. In CARIM-East, the laws and policy documents written in local languages were annotated in English (and in Russian, when needed) to explain their content and importance. Also, newspaper articles in local languages were given a short explanation in English and Russian.

Knowledge Production and Management

To build the knowledge base of migration issues in the neighbourhood of the EU, the EU institutions have been seeking information on very specific topics all linked to the main themes of the Global Approach to Migration, such as irregular migration, remittances, circular migration, and so on. Consequently, the CARIM Observatories focused on these topics in such a way as to make it clear that the primary beneficiary of the research was the EU. Yet, these topics were not always relevant for a given country: for example, the issue of asylum seekers was not relevant for Georgia (with a handful of cases each year), while the issue of Internally Displaced Persons (IDPs) was a real topic of concern. In order to produce analytical reports and data on asylum seekers in Georgia, primary research had to be conducted. This was a clear challenge for two reasons: financial constraints regarding the primary research, and lack of motivation to conduct such research due to its thematic irrelevance. It is important to note, however, that only relatively few topics were considered largely irrelevant for the partner countries. CARIM teams have tried to adjust the thematic range and be open to other topics that are more important to the partner countries (hence, for example, the research on IDPs conducted by CARIM-East).

The financial instruments dedicated to migration policy at the EU level are insufficient to support quality, large-scale primary data collection and analysis.[10] This is understandable, since primary research has not been an objective in these instruments. Consequently, the Observatories were unable to develop a fully fledged primary research programme. There have been isolated cases of small-scale surveys undertaken in the framework of CARIM-South involving selected countries, but usually primary research was funded by other international donors (e.g. the IOM funding a survey of asylum seekers in Italy). Indeed, more primary research could have been done in the framework of Horizon 2020 but that programme has rarely followed the Global Approach interests.[11] Therefore, the Observatories could only engage in limited original qualitative studies on an ad hoc basis.

The pooling of resources and optimizing the existing knowledge were thus a key strategy. The belief underlying the functioning of the Observatories since their conception was along the lines of the beliefs expressed in the Global Approach policy documents: that the relevant research exists but is not easily accessible. It transpired that this was, indeed, true—to a considerable extent. Migration studies is a functioning field of research all over the world, albeit that scholars can have different perspectives and be interested in different facets of the phenomenon. A clear example of such differences is burgeoning literature on immigration control in the countries of the Global North, while the scholars in the Global South work more on the effects of emigration. These differences lead to inevitable gaps in the existing data and knowledge. The main task of the Observatories was to identify and transmit research relevant from the point of view of the EU and the partner country development agenda. The problem was that the EU-centred view on what constitutes an important research question on migration would not always be met with understanding, or be relevant to the reality of a partner country.

It is natural for researchers from the countries of origin, with a predominance of migration outflows, to be interested in emigration and its effects. Thus, the knowledge base often exists, ready to be interpreted and shared internationally. However, in many cases the outflows are towards other regions than the EU, as was the case in Armenia or Palestine. Thanks to their role as a bridge between the EU and the partner countries, the Observatories were able to generate a holistic image of migration in the wider EU neighbourhood, and study flows towards other destinations (such as Russia or Turkey). In addition, between 2004 and 2010, a significant evolution of the EU's thinking about the nature and extent of evidence that was needed for policy formulation occurred. EU policy-makers became more interested in migration phenomena in general, to contextualize the EU's position. The work of the Observatories was needed to provide that contextual information, which was a wider topic than just studies of migration flows into the EU.

Yet, controversies arose in cases where a partner country had different priorities and the available research did not fit the core topics of the research agenda dictated by the EU. That was the situation with Libya and Russia— both huge markets for immigration—where most scholars no longer undertook research on either emigration or emigration to the EU. Arguably, the primary research in Libya was very scarce on any topic related to migration. Contrary to that, the research on immigration to Russia developed exponentially in the early 2000s and thus there was a wealth of excellent primary sources to tap into. But this required flexibility on the part of both the Observatories and the EU policy-makers, and agreement that the Russian team should take a different perspective—that of a host country. This helped the CARIM-East team to open a new research field: the comparative analysis of migration from Eastern partnership countries to the EU and the Russian Federation. This became a win–win situation: it engaged Russian scholars who perceived the comparative perspective as very useful for their own work; it made the research produced by the migrant-sending countries more relevant for them because it allowed a holistic view of migration in these countries; and it helped to change the tone of the EU debate on migrations from the Eastern partnership countries to the EU by recognizing the central role of Russia.

Even so, among the partner country teams that were studying emigration, the challenges prioritized by the EU were not the same as the perceived challenges their countries faced. Irregular migration to the EU was probably not an important research theme for Lebanese or Armenian scholars, neither was irregular immigration to their countries. If the research was to benefit them, the differences had to be recognized by the EU team coordinating the

Observatories. In many instances, other issues related to migration were considered more important. Among them were the IDPs, depopulation, and the social impacts of emigration. Over the years, the Observatories adjusted their methodologies to include the themes that were more relevant for the partner countries than for the EU, thus fulfilling the promise of research partnerships. In CARIM-East, the research themes were actually agreed by the national teams themselves. They took the decision based on their knowledge of the existing research and its usefulness for comparative multidisciplinary work, thus taking full ownership of their work.

Apart from the thematic issues and data discrepancies, an important consideration had to be taken into account when coordinating large international networks: the different research cultures. The existing knowledge had to be collected by the experts according to the common guidelines and then adapted to the needs of the European policy-makers according to Western European standards. Culturally responsive communication was thus the top skill required from all the EUI team members. Indeed, a crucial element of the success of the Observatories was the fact that they specialized in the regions under study, had had experience of living in the countries participating in the Observatories and, at the same time, had the Western European approach to the research process and to academic publications. The translation of one academic culture into another was far more important than simple language translation. All differences had to be carefully managed and negotiated, especially when there was a different understanding of research standards, publication standards, and analysis. An important and delicate issue was the variation in norms of academic freedom across countries. In a few extreme cases, the political pressure on academics made meaningful cooperation impossible—either because they felt obliged to insert political language (e.g. praising a country leader) into academic papers, or because they did show academic free thinking and risked political consequences.[12]

One of the goals of the Observatories was to build the capacities of the researchers from the partner countries to enable them to function in the Western European academic culture. Hence, the EUI teams engaged in ad hoc training (e.g. on policy–research communication), as well as offering support for publications in the English-language academic journals. That part of the work was especially rewarding and had a visible impact on the younger generation of scholars over the years.

Shaping the Political and Public Discourses

The knowledge base produced by the Observatories was primarily to serve the European policy-makers but, in the spirit of the EU partnership, they were also intended to benefit the partner countries. As already alluded to earlier, this part of the Observatories' mission has been the most difficult to achieve.

The EU-level policy-makers were the most receptive targets for research–policy communication. This came as no surprise, as they all read English and French; in addition, immigration has been highly relevant for the EU institutions. The Observatories thus served as a knowledge hub for migration-related data and information for many European institutions, and the dialogue has been ongoing. CARIM teams regularly prepared briefings and information notes for the Commission officials, highlighting evidence on migration in the neighbourhood. This work was often done through very informal channels of communication. The team members regularly participated in research–policy dialogues, contributing to the Commission working groups and Council working group meetings. For example, the CARIM-East team was one of the key stakeholders in the consultations on Schengen visa liberalization with Ukraine and Moldova, supporting the Commission when it was designing its Action Plans on Visa Liberalisation. Its members also participated in the Eastern neighbourhood partnership meetings and Prague Process meetings, as well as during European Parliament hearings.

Yet, for a variety of reasons, getting the national government officials to engage actively in the debates resulting from the research was more challenging. First, the European dimension of the research was not seen as necessarily relevant at the national level in all instances. Second, not all the countries in the EU are equally interested in migration from North Africa or Eastern Europe. Italian policy-makers have been quite involved in the activities of CARIM-South, while CARIM-East enjoyed high levels of support from the Polish Ministry of Foreign Affairs. In addition, as already explained, the language barrier was decisive in limiting the possible impact of the results beyond those able to speak English or French. However, the Observatories tried to build bridges: it is important to note that CARIM-South supported the upcoming Polish presidency when it was preparing its plan of action on the Mediterranean by contributing a policy paper (2011). The Observatories were also a scientific partner of the POLITICALLY.EU Italian national debate on 'Europe and Migration Policies' (2014).

Engaging with policy-makers in the partner countries was the main challenge faced by the Observatories. A tradition of an intensive research–policy communication is not universally shared by all the countries of the world. Indeed, more often than not scholars do not have access to policy-makers. If anything, the fact that the Observatories were seen as an EU project opened some doors for the dissemination activities. Nevertheless, the lack of deep interest in migration matters was a major obstacle to fruitful research–policy debate on migration issues. Morocco and Moldova have been the most interested in systematic and collaborative research on migration of their own citizens, while in other countries such interest was short-lived (e.g. in Ukraine). Migration was not a top-priority and was seen as predominantly an EU concern, to which the countries felt obliged to respond within clear political limits—that is, participating in EU initiatives but not necessarily engaging in the production of an EU-sponsored knowledge base. The knowledge base used by these governments was usually produced by United Nations organizations or the IOM on an ad hoc basis, and that was clearly perceived as sufficient.

The view that migration is mostly 'the EU's problem' caused challenges for the sustainability of the Observatories. At that time, the CARIM partner countries did not invest in comprehensive migration research and the EU funding could not replace sustained national support.

Conclusion

The work of the CARIM Observatories can shed light on the challenges faced by EU policy-makers when trying to establish migration policy partnerships with third countries. The key issue, in my view, is the true partnership in collaborative research and research–policy communication. Such a partnership relies on the acknowledgement of diversity, understood as linguistic, cultural, and institutional diversity that impacts on research goals; its execution and the policy–research dialogue. This diversity needs to be negotiated to satisfy all the partners. Such partnerships are complex: they involve academics from different academic cultures, policy-makers from different institutional settings and actors from other sectors that bring their own perspectives.

Collaborative research in such a context requires a team of knowledge translators (or brokers). Their role is based on trust: the trust of the donor as regards their academic credentials and capabilities to meet the expected standards and goals; and the trust of experts from the partner countries who recognize the academic authority of the team members to the extent that they accept the necessary adjustments and improvements of the produced research. This was the case of the peer review process across languages and cultures performed by the Observatories. The EUI-based teams elaborated a model of cooperation that allowed the achievement of research excellence in a complex environment.

Research–policy communication can be even more challenging. If the partner countries do not have a tradition of research–policy communication, a one-off external initiative will not change the status quo. The political support of the donor can help foster the dialogue, but it may not be entirely successful because of its perceived imposed character. In the case of the CARIM Observatories, the main beneficiaries of the knowledge base were the EU institutions, network members from the EU and the partner countries, and numerous academics and students from all over the world (as documented by the database statistics). The policy impact of the Observatories on the partner countries' policies has never been measured in a systematic way.

Notes

1. In fact, the authors relied heavily on a report by the Centre for Development Research in Copenhagen, which is the only research source quoted in the Communication COM(2005) 390 Final (European Commission 2005).
2. See the migration profiles repository at: https://gfmd.org/pfp/policy-tools/migration-profiles/repository (last accessed 3 June 2018).
3. The repository of the reports can be consulted at: www.migrationpolicycentre.eu/publications/migration-report/ (last accessed 3 June 2018).
4. For example, the reports produced by the CARIM Observatories, to be consulted at: www.migrationpolicycentre.eu/publications/
5. The original name figuring in EU documents since 2005 was the Global Approach to Migration, but it was modified in 2011. However, it refers to the same policy framework.
6. See, for example, https://www.pragueprocess.eu/en/migration-observatory/migration-profile-light
7. However, there has been no evaluation study to provide an accurate assess ment of the CARIM reception among the wider population in the countries of origin.
8. Language has never been an issue in CARIM-India because English is an official language in India.
9. See, for example, www.oecd.org/migration/international-migration-outlook-1999124x.htm
10. Unlike research funding available under purely research instruments; for example, Horizon 2020.
11. A handful of large-scale projects were funded under the 7th Framework Programme, specifically, Migration between Africa and Europe (MAFE) and Temper projects.
12. For example, as is the well-known case of Arif Yunusov from Azerbaijan, a country expert from CARIM-East who became a prisoner of conscience due to his critical stance towards the country's leadership.

References

Carrera, S., and Hernández i Sagrera, R. 2011. Mobility Partnerships. In *Multilayered Migration Governance: The Promise of Partnership*, eds R. Kunz, S. Lavenex, and M. Panizzon. Abingdon: Taylor & Francis.

Di Bartolomeo, A. 2019. (forthcoming). Apples and Oranges? Data Sources on Migration in Europe. In *Routledge Handbook on the Politics of Migration in Europe*, eds A. Weinar, S. Bonjour, and L. Zhyznomirska. Abingdon: Routledge.

European Commission. 2002. Communication from the Commission to the European Parliament: Integrating Migration Issues in the European Union's Relations with Third Countries. COM(2002) 703 Final.

European Commission. 2005. Communication from the Commission to the European Parliament, the Council, the European Economic and Social Committee and the Committee of the Regions: Migration and Development: Some Concrete Orientations. COM(2005) 390 Final.

European Commission. 2006. Communication from the Commission to the European Parliament: The Global Approach to Migration One Year On: Towards a Comprehensive European Migration Policy. COM(2006) 735 Final.

European Commission. 2008a. Communication from the Commission to the European Parliament, the Council, the European Economic and Social Committee and the Committee of the Regions: Strengthening the Global Approach to Migration: Increasing Coordination, Coherence and Synergies. COM(2008) 611 Final.

European Commission. 2008b. Euro-Mediterranean Partnership. Regional Co-Operation: An Overview of Programmes and Projects. https://ec.europa.eu/europeaid/sites/devco/files/publication-regional-cooperation-mediterranean-partnership-projects-2010_en.pdf

European Court of Auditors. 2016. EU External Migration Spending in Southern Mediterranean and Eastern Neighbourhood Countries until 2014. ECA 09/2016.

Korneev, O. 2018. Self-legitimation through knowledge production partnerships: International Organization for Migration in Central Asia. *Journal of Ethnic and Migration Studies* 44(10): 1673–90.

Kunz, R., Lavenex, S., and Panizzon, M. 2011. *Multilayered Migration Governance: The Promise of Partnership*. Abingdon: Taylor & Francis.

Reslow, N., and Vink, M. 2015. Three-level games in EU external migration policy: Negotiating mobility partnerships in West Africa. *Journal of Common Market Studies* 53(4): 857–74.

Van Hüllen, V. 2012. Europeanisation through cooperation? EU democracy promotion in Morocco and Tunisia. *West European Politics* 35(1): 117–34.

Weinar, A. 2011. EU cooperation challenges in external migration policy. EUI Research Papers.

Wunderlich, D. 2012. Europeanization through the grapevine: Communication gaps and the role of international organizations in implementation networks of EU external migration policy. *Journal of European Integration* 34(5): 485–503.

13

Metropolis and Post-truth Politics

'Enhancing Policy through Research'

Howard Duncan

Introduction

In 1995, the government of Canada, concerned to shore up its stock of evidence upon which to build immigration and integration policy, turned to the academic community. Its approach was to offer incentives to social scientists to turn their attention to immigration phenomena, an area that was little studied at the time in Canada. Thus was created the Metropolis Project in Canada, with its university-based Centres of Excellence and a broad partnership of agencies of government at all levels and civil society organizations across the country. Funding was provided to support research in areas of direct relevance to policy development; also, the immigration ministry, Citizenship and Immigration Canada, provided a Secretariat whose principal role was to build bridges across which members of the three sectors (the academy, government, and civil society) would travel to engage one another actively, all with the ambition to improve the outcomes of immigration for both the immigrants and the Canadian public.

At the same time, the government of Canada, in concert with the Carnegie Endowment for International Peace, led the creation of an unfunded correlate—the International Metropolis Project—to motivate international comparative research and policy–research exchanges among an initial group of organizations within countries belonging to the Organisation for Economic Co-operation and Development (OECD). The Metropolis Secretariat at Citizenship and Immigration Canada (now Immigration, Refugees, and Citizenship Canada) was responsible for managing operations, expanding membership of the network and supporting the Metropolis International Steering Committee (ISC)—the Project's governing body. Although the international project was and remains unfunded, it has been able to rely upon the members of its Steering Committee to host and fund its activities— principally, its annual conferences. The Canadian arm of Metropolis ceased research operations in 2012 with the closing of the Centres of Excellence, but the annual Canadian conference continues. The closing of the Canadian arm had no effect upon the operations of the International Metropolis Project, as it has always operated without core funding. The Metropolis model is that of a special project that created a network, but not a formal organization with independent legal status. The Project had dedicated research funding for the Centres of Excellence, and they operated only in Canada. Both the Canadian and the International Metropolis Projects had governance infrastructure, but in neither case were they envisaged as formal organizations.

Metropolis adopted the motto, 'Enhancing policy through research', and adopted a bridge motif for its logo. Of course, the bridge signifies the connections that Metropolis has always tried to build across not only the three sectors of its participants, but also within each of the sectors: across academic disciplines, across government ministries, and across civil society organizations, all of which activity is on an international basis.

This chapter will emphasize the relations between the academy and governments without going into detail about the substantial role of civil society. It will begin by covering the workings of the Metropolis Project in Canada, followed by an account of how it has worked—and continues to work— internationally. Working internationally always brings special challenges, some of which are highlighted. The chapter closes with a look at the recent rise of populism, the implications for academics and academic research, and whether the Metropolis model offers ways to diminish the impact of populism on government and public discourse. It should be made plain that the author is writing from a background of over twenty years with the Secretariat of the Metropolis Project, both the Canadian and the international projects which he continues to lead. For the first sixteen years, this direct involvement was with the Metropolis Secretariat, which was part of the Department of Citizenship and Immigration in Canada; since 2012, the Metropolis Secretariat has been at Carleton University in Ottawa. Much of what follows is based upon personal experiences and reflections of this time. Although a certain amount of subjectivity is inevitable, the author has tried to retain a healthy modesty in these remarks. The term 'Metropolis' is frequently used throughout this chapter; when it is invoked in the context of positions or decisions taken by Metropolis, the reference is to decisions made by the Metropolis ISC or the Metropolis Secretariat acting on behalf of the ISC.

Some Metropolis Basics

As befits an ambition of intellectual bridge-building and to emphasize a point made earlier, Metropolis was conceived as a network, not as an organization. Developing productive working relations among such an array of organizations was thought best done with the flexibility and informality of a network rather than through the more formal structures of an organization, particularly an organization that receives core funding from its member organizations. In particular, Metropolis has eschewed adopting specific positions on migration and integration policy, choosing instead to remain non-partisan and apolitical apart from one core foundation. That core foundation is the belief that it is unhelpful for societies to attempt a full prevention of migration into their territories and that, instead, so far as possible, migration ought to be managed in the best interests of the receiving society and the migrants, and that this management be carried out through policy grounded in empirical research.

Metropolis has always recognized that how a society manages migration is to be tailored to its particular social, political, economic, and demographic situation and history. As a result, Metropolis has encouraged discussions that compare and contrast national and local situations, seeking data, evidence, and analyses that will help inform each other's considerations and policy development.[1] Metropolis has avoided prescribing universal solutions or even best practices, offering instead a fully neutral discussion forum. The neutrality of Metropolis discussions has been one of the attractions, particularly for governments who have long viewed academic research and civil society as often being hostile to their actions and decisions. Metropolis neutrality offers them the confidence to participate both in the discussions and as members of the Steering Committee.

That this project carries the name 'Metropolis' stems from the recognition that most migration, whether international or internal, is now destined to the cities of the world.[2] The original intention was that Metropolis would encourage and support policy research on how migration affects cities, and how cities can best respond through the various mechanisms of integration available to them and in partnership with higher levels of government. Over the years, Metropolis' reach grew beyond the interests of cities to embrace the interests of national governments and the international community, and its subject matter interests expanded well beyond integration to include the phenomenon of migration itself. Despite this expansion in the scope of Metropolis, its name remains pertinent, as cities remain the principal destination of the vast majority of the world's migrants. Indeed, the international community is looking ever more carefully at cities not only as destinations, but also as active players in the management of migration.[3]

Bridging the gap between research and policy has, then, been a principal concern for Metropolis, which has always recognized that this matter of policy relevance has what one may call epistemological aspects and also inter-personal, psychological, and sociological aspects. In other words, to some extent, this issue is one of relations between ideas—ideas from both research and policy; but it is also, and significantly, a matter of relations between persons, those who carry out research and those who develop policy.

Metropolis maintains that policy relevance is 'in the eye of the beholder' and not something simply delivered on a plate by a researcher to a policy analyst or decision-maker. Because research does not alone determine policy, empirical research findings are neutral with regard to policy, and their rele-vance is a characteristic imposed either by the researcher who discerns a link to a policy issue, or by a policy-maker who draws such a link.[4] Metropolis has purposely ignored the quest for a logic of policy-making and sees policy development more from a psychological than an epistemological perspective. There are numerous models of the policy–research relationship, referring to such things as the policy cycle. These rational re-constructions are of little interest to Metropolis because real-world policy-making is inherently messy and iterative, not a clean matter of deductive, or even inductive, relations between evidence and policy conclusion. There are many reasons for this, among them that the determinants of policy go far beyond empirical evi-dence, and those who influence policy go far beyond those who produce empirical evidence. That the Metropolis Secretariat was located within the Canadian immigration department for sixteen years has given us insights into the actual workings of policy development. It has long been recognized that traditional means of disseminating research articles and books is no guarantee of influence or value-added. The busy schedules of most policy officials leave them little, if any, time to read lengthy and complex material; often, the language of the researcher is impenetrable to the official and, often, the researcher is ill-equipped to explain the relevance to policy of their work. Metropolis has found it more effective to bring the researchers and policy officials into the same room for mutual engagement.

This requires no small amount of confidence-building and, one could say, professional culture shift. The gap between research and policy is often, at heart, a gap in trust. Government officials often view academic researchers as, at best, uninterested in policy or, at worst, as hostile to it. Academic researchers can view governments as targets and can feel that working with them risks their academic integrity. Further, university reward systems do not normally value work on the grounds that it has influenced policy, let alone work directly with governments; reward systems continue to recognize pri-marily peer-reviewed academic publications and not contributions to govern-ment policy or publications in the grey literature. To some extent, this mutual suspicion is rooted in a lack of awareness of what each sector does. The Metropolis approach to dealing with these inherent suspicions relied heavily on in-person contact. But, in the case of the Canadian Metropolis Project and its funded research programme, it took a specific administrative measure to get the Project off the ground.

The Canadian Metropolis Project

Canada has a long experience with immigration—one that the national government has taken very seriously, as is evident in the investments that it has made in creating a large supportive bureaucracy with offices not only in Canada, but throughout the world. Canada's immigration programme, which is administered now by the federal government's Department of Immigration, Refugees, and Citizenship, has always had as its principal objective to enhance the Canadian economy and to raise the standards of living for its citizens. In other words, the programme has been run primarily for economic rather than humanitarian purposes, although Canada has also long been one of the world's most open countries to re-settled refugees and asylum seekers. In managing such a large-scale economic programme, the government needed an increasingly strong evidence base for setting and adjusting policy on the numbers of immigrants to bring into Canada, for considering their human capital characteristics and for enhancing their integration outcomes. The Metropolis Project was intended to help the government deepen this evidence base.

Like most OECD countries, Canada has a national social science research funding agency, the Social Sciences and Humanities Research Council (SSHRC). This agency, although government funded and managed, had earned the trust of Canadian researchers, most importantly with regard to the protection of academic freedom and the integrity of the process for selecting projects for funding. When Canada's immigration ministry, Citizenship and Immigration Canada, began exploring the idea of establishing academic Centres of Excellence to stimulate migration research in the country, the flat response from Canadian universities was that they would only participate if the funds flowed through the SSHRC. Otherwise, they feared that the funds would be used to influence the directions and conclusions of the research. As a result, Metropolis funds, which eventually came from fourteen government agencies, were pooled at the SSHRC and distributed by the Council using peer review adjudication of individual research proposals.[5] This measure satisfied the academic sector's demand that academic freedom be fully respected.

How, though, was the government's demand that the research be policy relevant satisfied? After all, the only reason for establishing the Metropolis research centres was to increase the amount of research done on immigration and integration in Canada and, ultimately, to provide a stronger evidence base for government policy. The government's demand was met, first, in specifying in the initial call for proposals to establish for the centres a set of broad research areas within which the centres' research activities were to take place. Second, to reflect the dynamics of immigration and integration, the research centres were to respond to an annual call for research projects in which the themes of the year's research were specified as a result of discussions among the government and academic partners. The use of the SSHRC as an intermediary of the funding was the foundation upon which the rest of the edifice in Canada was built, and it was upon this foundation that the discussions leading to the choice of annual research themes took place. Although the university-based Centres of Excellence had academic freedom, they were expected to work in partnership not only with the Metropolis Secretariat, which was an arm of the government, but also with all of the federal government funding partners. This was to ensure, so far as possible, that the research was in areas that would best inform government policy, as well as providing an effective means for communicating the results of the research and to build trust among the players. Active committees were formed to make this possible, some chaired by the government with others chaired by the five research centres.

Over the first three years of the Project, the levels of trust, which were low at the outset, began to build as a direct result of the in-person discussions, which also came to include discussions of research results and how policy should respond. On a broader scale, in my experience and assessment, it was the annual conferences that made the greatest contribution to establishing trust among the sectors. These events were organized as joint policy–research events that also brought civil society organizations into the mix of voices. Both the plenary sessions and the workshop (breakout) sessions required exchanges among people from government and the academy, and it was through these, especially the more intimate workshops, that trust was built and significant working relationships established. The conferences functioned as neutral discussion fora where all present were there to contribute to a shared objective of improving the lives of immigrants in Canada, and to enhancing their contributions to the Canadian society and its economy. The culture of the conferences was one of cooperation and it was extremely rare that exchanges became confrontational. This overt culture of cooperation allowed the government officials to continue attending these events, about which they were very sceptical early on.

Did the model work in Canada? The goal of increasing the amount of research devoted to immigration and integration was certainly realized, with hundreds of peer-reviewed publications as well as hundreds of working papers published. The number of researchers in the area grew substantially as a result of the funding directed to these themes, as did the number of migration programmes in Canadian universities. That the government indicated that it was interested in this field of study was, in itself, a motivation for some researchers. It is noteworthy that, since funding for the Metropolis Centres ended in 2012, all but one of the research centres has closed and academic interest in the subject is beginning to shift to other areas, especially those with dedicated funding. Evaluations of the Metropolis Centres of Excellence programme indicated that the government's policy ambitions were largely satisfied. Officials' understanding of immigration and integration phenomena was thought to have been enhanced, and there were various specific policy influences that Metropolis research was credited for—among them with regard to the importance of language abilities for integration, especially in the labour market, the role of foreign credentials in labour market integration, and the growth of ethnic enclaves in Canadian cities.[6] Canada changed its selection criteria for skilled workers as a result of this research and introduced significant measures to manage the fact of foreign credentials and their degree of fit with Canadian employer standards. We know that the research directly affected policy development in these cases from the Metropolis Secretariat having worked directly with government policy officials within the Department of Citizenship and Immigration and from the evaluations that were conducted.

The Canadian project was shut down after seventeen years of funding from the government. It was always conceived as a limited term experimental project; although it had initially been intended to last five years, it was renewed twice. After the seventeen years of public funding, the government decided to turn to other areas of policy, also in the hope that Metropolis could continue some of its operations independently. Although this could be seen as a sign of failure, the fact that the Project was only intended to be a five-year experiment suggests that it did better than was anticipated. Furthermore, although the research funds have disappeared, along with four of the five research centres (one in Toronto continues to function to a lesser degree), the annual conference continues with strong participation from all three sectors and a central emphasis on the various aspects of settlement and integration. Such has been the impact of the personal and professional connections that were established previously that the conference in 2017 attracted over 800 participants, the same level as during the years of full funding.

Institutions that support research tend not to support special projects for long durations. Social science research institutions are no different. They may have a long-standing open call for proposals that may endure for decades, but a special project in a single area will only rarely continue for long. Research institutions will be pressed by many other interests to invest special project funds in other areas, especially when the competition for funds is high.

The lesson for academics who rely upon funding from government research granting institutions is not to expect indeterminate funding for special projects. Such special funding is best regarded as seed funding, and research centres in receipt of these funds would do well to invest in their own institutional capacities such that, when the dedicated funds come to an end, as they almost certainly will, they are ready to secure financial support in other ways, success here being grounded in the capacities developed over the period when the institution received special funds.

The International Metropolis Project

The fundamental goals of the International Metropolis Project are the same as those of its Canadian counterpart, but the mechanisms for achieving them have been different because of the lack of core funding. Internationally, Metropolis relies upon there being sufficient goodwill among the members of the network to keep its operations going. Interest in migration has grown dramatically across the globe since the late 1990s—not only among governments, but also among academic researchers, think tanks, and civil society organizations. The rise of migration on the agenda of the international community has been remarkable, with now twenty-two members as compared with only ten members in the original Geneva Migration Group.[7] High-level meetings of the international community have attracted not only a growing number of government representatives, but also members of civil society and the academy as well, such has been the appetite to participate in meetings of the United Nations General Assembly, the Global Forum on Migration and Development, the Mayoral Forum on Migration and Development, and a host of conferences and seminars offered by the members of the Global Migration Group (GMG) and many other organizations worldwide. In 1996, when Metropolis launched its first international conference, there were very few organizations organizing regular conferences in the migration field. Metropolis had little competition then but, today, faces a very different situation.

Given the lack of a formal organizational structure, notably the lack of a budget for operations or research, Metropolis has had to be flexible and responsive to the changing migration environment to remain competitive. Members of the ISC contribute time and, when serving as hosts of a conference, seminar, or ISC meeting, the finances required by the event. The ISC membership, together with the Secretariat offices in Ottawa, Amsterdam, Manila, Seoul, Beijing, and New Delhi, form the core of the network. The ISC membership includes organizations from each of the three sectors and decides cooperatively on such matters as the conference host, themes and speakers, and the strategic directions of the network—directions that will allow Metropolis to maintain its perceived value to the international

211

community, which increasingly has many options from which to choose to whom to give their attention. The choice of conference themes is intended to reflect not only Metropolis' views on which are the issues of current importance, but also what Metropolis sees as emerging issues to which government policy-makers and researchers will need to pay attention. The choice of themes not only provides a framework for selecting speakers, but also provides a framework for the programme of workshops and serves as a signal to the research community of what Metropolis regards as subjects most worthy of empirical research.

The organization of conference workshops has been a significant instrument for bridging the policy–research gap. Rather than the workshops being put together by the central conference organizers, it is the Metropolis constituency who does so, through a 'Call for Workshop Proposals' for each conference. This means that there is a high degree of ownership of the workshops by those who organize and participate in them. A central requirement of the application process is a demonstration that the discussion will include a mix of academic, governmental, and civil society participants and is conducted on an international basis. Those who wish to create a workshop but who find this requirement difficult to meet can rely upon the conference organizers and Secretariats for help. The result of the decentralization of the workshop programme was a steep increase in the number of conference registrants, the repetition of workshops year after year for groups that were established and that created their own policy–research plans, and a progressive growth in the utility of these events as meeting grounds for researchers and government officials. The strong connections between research and policy that the conferences provide remain the hallmark of Metropolis.

One of the ambitions of the International Metropolis Project has been to increase the overall level of understanding of the phenomena associated with international migration, be they, for example, with regard to the flows of people; their settlement and integration; their impacts on economies and societies, especially those of cities; or the various forms that migration takes. The assumption is that the more comprehensive the understanding of migration and its effects, the more effective will be policy based upon this understanding.

The issues that Metropolis established for itself at its first conference held in Milan in 1996 were, like those in the Canadian context, concerned with integration in its essential guises of immigrants into OECD countries (labour market, housing, and neighbourhoods, discrimination, education, access to social services, and so on). But, in subsequent years, Metropolis gradually enlarged the scope of its interests to include migration flows themselves, including not only South–North flows, but also flows South–South, North–North, and North–South; the special circumstances of refugees; transnational communities; multiple migration patterns; smuggling and trafficking; the global competition for talent; the relation between war and migration; and many more.

Metropolis and the Global South

The point is that, to attain a degree of comprehensiveness of understanding of migration, Metropolis shifted from a network primarily interested in integration to one that sought to bring virtually all aspects of migration to bear on its discussions. Furthermore, it began to enlarge its geographical scope beyond the small number of national partners that it began with in 1996 to the same end. Metropolis now has a more extensive presence in Europe, Latin America, and especially Asia, having launched a special project, Metropolis Asia, with Secretariat offices to sustain a programme of policy–research activity. The partnership in Asia was also Metropolis' first sustained foray into the Global South, an ambition long-stalled for lack of funding to support the participation of organizations in those countries.

The introduction of members of the Metropolis ISC from Asia and the Global South has strengthened the perspective that the South brings to the table, a perspective that notably includes the relationship between migration and development—at this time, a major focus of the international community.[8] Also, Metropolis has been able to increase the discussions from the point of view of what some still think of as the sending countries, although the distinction between sending and receiving countries is now so blurred as to be almost without value.[9] Regardless, understanding better how countries of the Global South or traditional sending countries think about and develop policy to manage out-migration is useful for those in the receiving countries. For example, coming to realize that migration is increasingly multiple in its direction, rather than a mostly one-way permanent change of home, is essential for receiving countries, especially those in the OECD whose migration policies have long been premised on the permanency of migration. It has been said that there is nothing more permanent than a temporary migrant, but one could now say, without irony, that there is nothing more temporary than permanent migration. The hope expressed in enlarging the discussion table through a greater diversity of membership as well as subject matter is to increase the sophistication of policy throughout the world through an enlargement of the perspectives of the discussions.

Remaining Challenges

Metropolis has achieved much of what it set out to do twenty years ago and has expanded its scope in ways that it did not foresee when it began. Although its model of bridging the policy–research gap through the engagement activities of the network, rather than through supply-driven dissemination, has met with some degree of success, the challenge posed by historical mutual suspicions continues as new members join. The task of trust-building is a continuing one, and it is unlikely it will ever be fully resolved given the normal changes in personnel, especially in the policy arena. The strategy of sustained conversations in neutral settings among the three sectors, conversations that would build trust and show the mutual value of collaboration, requires constant attention and modernizing, if only to meet the dramatic increase in competition for these sorts of discussion. And although many academics chose to work in these discussion settings, intending to support rational policy-making, others have deferred. The academic reward structure that favours publication in academic journals and rarely recognizes work in support of policy is a significant barrier, especially for early-career researchers. Academics working from a critical theory perspective remain largely ignored by the policy world, but those engaged in empirical and statistical studies often find a receptive policy audience. Nevertheless, existing reward structures remain a disincentive for many, especially younger, scholars.

One way that Metropolis assesses success is the extent to which participants from the three main sectors establish enduring working relations through which policy is enhanced by research. In general, Metropolis has seen more success in the traditional migration regions of North America, Europe, Australia, and New Zealand, but has had less success in Asia, Africa, and Latin America. It has met with significant success in building policy–research partnerships on issues of migration flows, but integration has been the strongest suit, with a considerable degree of cooperation on labour market integration, the role of language in integration, foreign credentials and experience, media, and discrimination. Metropolis has done less well on emerging integration issues; for example, the societal effects of transnationalism and multiple migration patterns. Governments tend to be conservative in their range of interests and can be slow to embrace new fields developed by the research community. Similarly, Metropolis has had less success on recent developments in trafficking and smuggling, international relations, demographic trajectories, and the emerging global competition for talent.

Metropolis' ambitions to reach countries in the Global South have met with only limited success to date. To some extent, this is a result of the limited funds that are available in those countries and the fact that Metropolis, being but a network, has been unable to offer financial support to people and organizations from those parts of the world. Even in Asia, where Metropolis has enjoyed more success than in Africa, most participation has been from the wealthier countries such as Japan, China, South Korea, and the Philippines. Countries such as Bangladesh, Pakistan, Cambodia, Thailand, and Myanmar have been unable to participate to date.

But finances are only part of the explanation, one could argue. The agenda of most Metropolis discussions reflects the interests of primarily the OECD countries, and those are the interests of destination societies: integration and social cohesion, economic effects, demographic trends, smuggling and trafficking, and managing undocumented migration. While there are analogues to these issues from the point of view of countries in the South, their issues have more to do with the protection of their émigrés; the right to work in countries of destination, be they in the North or the South (South–South migration is now at roughly the same magnitude as South–North migration);[10] the rights of migrant workers and their families (as presented in the UN Convention in this area which has not yet been signed by any OECD country, save Mexico which is also a major source country of migrants to the United States);[11] the size and speed of urbanization—that is, internal migration; and the capacity of their cities to manage rapid population growth and so on.

The relation between migration and cities is quite different in the North than it is in the South.[12] Cities in the North are more concerned with matters of social integration, inclusion, and the protection of rights, or, alternatively, with the perceived risks and costs of migrants in their cities. For many cities in the Global South, the issues are more immediate; for example, the provision of housing, drinking water, sanitation, transportation, electricity, and other basic services. For many megacities and peri-urban settlements in the South, concerns of inclusion are but a luxury. The point is that the themes of Metropolis gatherings tend to be those of the Global North and that this may stand as another reason for the relatively low participation of academics and government officials from the South.

This is another form of the policy–research gap—the gap between the issues of the North and those of the South. This gap in interests and priorities is also evident in the global migration discussion that has been taking place since the early 2000s. Many countries of the Global North were reluctant participants in such exercises as the Global Commission on International Migration—fearing that the emphasis would be on access to OECD economies for migrant workers from the South (a hesitation that continues, although has somewhat abated, through to today)—and the Global Forum on Migration and Development, which has emphasized the rights of migrants, including even the right to migrate—an issue only for the traditional countries of origin. Metropolis will need to find more common ground between North and South if it is to bridge this geographical gap and increase participation from non-OECD countries.

Many in the migration field wish to bring the business community to the discussion table, seeing business employers as a significant influence on migration flows, as implicated in the observance of migrants' rights, and as having tacit responsibilities for immigrant integration. Some would suggest that businesses have obligations to employ immigrants and refugees.[13] Metropolis has had little success in attracting the private sector for the simple reason that there is little clear advantage to their participation. As was the case with relations between the academic and the policy sectors, trust may be a barrier here. Many in the business community see the academic sector, especially the social sciences, as highly critical of business. Where businesses have interests in immigration, they normally lie in government relations rather than with the academic community, and the business sector already has a significant lobby with governments. In other words, there is little in it for business to join an exercise in policy–research relations as they are now conceived. The private sector is, however, deeply engaged in research to support its planning and operations; the challenge for Metropolis and others in the migration field is to develop capacities that would appeal to the business community.[14] One such area could be the intensifying global competition for talent, a competition that appears to be affecting migration flows, for example, through incentives to return migration by such rapidly developing countries of origin as China, India, and Mexico.

The Rise of Populism

In 2016–2017, many felt the effects of a slowly but inexorably rising populist politics throughout much of the world, a form of politics that has been deeply suspicious of experts who many populists see not as neutral arbiters of scientific veracity but, rather, as the voices of an elite with a vested interest in the outcomes of their research. What is sometimes referred to as 'post-truth politics' is an evolution of a long-held suspicion that academic research is biased either politically or ideologically, or towards the interests of its funders, especially when those funders are corporate. The global interest in migration has reached a level perhaps never before experienced, partly because of governments' growing interest, levels of migration much higher than even during the post-World War I era, but also partly as a result of populist politicians and lobbies having raised levels of fear regarding immigration among increasingly sceptical publics.

Mainstream media have become quite politically polarized in some countries, with some strongly favouring populist political parties in their reporting as well as in their opinion pieces. More recently, as has been well-noted, social media have begun to play an ever-stronger role in the formation—and, perhaps, the hardening—of public attitudes. Many of these politically extreme mainstream and social media promulgate what could be termed 'alternate accounts' of the workings of a society—spreading conspiracy theories; speculations about the true intentions of governments and other members of the 'elite', including academic researchers; and spurious pseudo-science on just about anything that one may imagine. Many share a view that academic research is biased towards protecting the positions of the elite in a society. There are but a very few governments that, in 2018, openly embrace immigration and welcome refugees despite the messages of the benefits of migration from the International Organization for Migration (IOM), the United Nations, and other members of the international community.

Metropolis has been only minimally affected by this rise of populism and nationalism, including among its member countries. The reason is that, despite a sizeable number of populist politicians and their supporters in the public realm, few governments are anti-immigrant populist in their actual policies. Most of those who participate in Metropolis activities support well-managed migration and integration. The hosts of Metropolis conferences have supported these events because they value the neutral exchanges among academics, policy officials, and civil society. A small number of anti-immigration demonstrations have occurred at Metropolis events, but little else to cause the Project to steer a new course.

How does post-truth politics affect the relations between policy and research? One way to look at this is from the point of view of the marketplace of ideas, which has become increasingly competitive over time, especially with the rise of information and communication technologies (ICT) and the overall effectiveness of communications, including in politics. The sophistication with which messages can now be delivered and the extraordinary speed with which ideas can be spread through ICT puts research back on its heels. The academic community now faces competition to a degree that it has not experienced since the beginnings of The Enlightenment. Scientific research gains its credibility from the care with which it is pursued, as well as the rigorous peer-review processes that must be gone through before results are released to the public. The culture of the best science—social or physical—is inherently conservative, which can mean that scientists are more reluctant than political pundits, or even journalists, to offer public analyses of situations and trends. Fear-laden accounts of migrants committing crimes, taking jobs, eroding national identities, and so on are easy to make, but a responsible rebuttal requires appeal to hard data and analysis, something that takes time and is often more difficult for politicians and their publics to understand. The 'sound bite' style of much modern journalism favours the less-considered opinion over the complex analyses of social scientists. The challenge is for the academic research community to become more competitive in the marketplace of ideas, if it is to be a force against populism and post-truth politics.

This is not an easy matter. Most social scientists, whether in the field of migration or otherwise, are not trained in communications—possibly even for the classroom, let alone for the news media or policy officials. But more universities are seeing communications with the public as of value to them; they are offering media training to their faculty and encouraging the media to call upon them for expert commentary. For public audiences as well as for government officials, communicating through the media may be more effective than more academic forms of communication; for example, through scholarly publications. Some scholars have taken to blogging their messages, something that has a greater potential reach than academic journals. But the competition in the blogosphere is similarly intense, with reasoned evidence-based blogs having to vie for attention against all others, however rooted in evidence they may or may not be.

Conclusion

There remains value in the Metropolis approach of direct engagement of researchers with policy officials, especially when it endures over time. Although politicians may react quickly to the dynamics of their societies, the development of policy—and, especially, legislation—takes time, and it is this time that offers opportunities for research to influence policy. Further, the Metropolis approach is to enhance the overall level of understanding of migration and integration among policy-makers—again, an exercise that takes place over time, not in the heat of the moment, and that is best accomplished through conversation. Metropolis activities are designed to facilitate these sorts of conversations by building a network characterized by mutual trust among its members. By this means, we hope to provide some degree of competition to the forces of populism and post-truth politics.

To some extent, this will depend upon national and institutional cultures regarding the relationship between research and policy. Some countries have a more easy relationship between the research and policy sectors, and a longer history of collaboration and mutual respect. For others, there is considerable discomfort and mistrust. Metropolis conferences and other activities have been helpful in building bridges here because of the inherent interactions between research and policy that these activities entail. By working together on a problem of common interest, trust can be built and suspicions dispelled and, along with this, an appetite for collaboration can emerge.

Ultimately, what is needed is for governments to accept that there is value for policy-making in solid academic research and to support the research community in ways that respect academic integrity while motivating policy relevant academic work. To do this well, government policy units need to protect the time of some of their staff to allow them to read scientific research and, perhaps even more effective, to have conversations with researchers about their work and what it may imply for policy. Policy-makers normally have little time to learn about contemporary research, let alone to think about what it means for either long-term strategic policy or the short-term work that usually dominates their day-to-day lives. Perhaps the contemporary backdrop of post-truth politics will provide governments with a new motivation to engage the research sector. There may be some comfort for governments to be found in the neutrality and integrity that continues to characterize much, although not necessarily all, academic research. Cultivating researchers whose work is characterized by academic integrity will be in the long-term interests of governments and those whose lives they so greatly affect.

Notes

1. Within Canada, for example, a great deal of comparative research was done on the effects of official language competence on employment rates and income levels. Geographers studied the residential settlement patterns of newcomers to the country, noting where enclave formation was taking place and where greater dispersion was evident. Internationally, Metropolis members have focused much of their attention on such matters as immigrant integration, the effects of naturalization policy and public attitudes towards immigration. The principle vehicle for conveying Metropolis' policy–research interests internationally is the annual conference, which selects its plenary session themes partly to stimulate the interests of researchers in these themes.
2. See, for example, www.weforum.org/agenda/2017/10/how-migration-is-changing-world-cities-charts/
3. Consider, for example, that the IOM convened a conference, Migrants and Cities, in Geneva in 2015 at which they launched their 2015 World Migration Report (www.iom.int/world-migration-report-2015), which was devoted to the same topic. The UN Habitat 3 report included many references to cities, as did the Sutherland Report (www.un.org/en/development/desa/population/migration/events/coordination/15/documents/Report%20of%20SRSG%20on%20Migration%20-%20A.71.728_ADVANCE.pdf) prepared on the ending of Sir Peter Sutherland's tenure as the Special Representative of the Secretary General on migration.
4. As philosophers of ethics—following David Hume—have said, one cannot derive an 'ought' from an 'is'. Research tells us the nature of the case; policy decisions are about what a government believes ought to be the case.
5. The federal government partners in Metropolis in its final stages were Citizenship and Immigration Canada, the Social Sciences and Humanities Research Council, Canada Mortgage and Housing Corporation, Human Resources and Skills Development Canada, Justice Canada, Heritage Canada, Public Safety Canada, the Canada Border Services Agency, the Royal Canadian Mounted Police, Atlantic Canada Opportunities Agency, FedNor, Western Economic Diversification, Status of Women Canada, and the Public Health Agency of Canada.

6. See, for example, this 2015 report of Professor Daniel Hiebert of the University of British Columbia: http://irpp.org/research-studies/study-no52/
7. See, for example, www2.ohchr.org/english/bodies/cmw/GMG.htm, for more information on the original Geneva Migration Group. For information on the Global Migration Group of today, see www.globalmigrationgroup.org/
8. Consider only the United Nations High Level Dialogue on Migration and Development (2006 and 2013) (www.un.org/en/ga/68/meetings/migration/), the Global Forum on Migration and Development (https://gfmd.org/), the Joint Migration and Development Initiative of the UNDP, and the IOM (www.migration4development.org/en/content/about-jmdi).
9. Consider that North–North migration constitutes roughly one quarter of the world's total migration flows. See www.un.org/en/ga/68/meetings/migration/pdf/International%20Migration%202013_Migrants%20by%20origin%20and%20destination.pdf
10. www.un.org/en/ga/68/meetings/migration/pdf/International%20Migration%202013_Migrants%20by%20origin%20and%20destination.pdf
11. This Convention has only 39 signatories to date, none from developed countries. See https://treaties.un.org/Pages/ViewDetails.aspx?src=IND&mtdsg_no=IV-13&chapter=4&clang=_en
12. The final report of the IOM conference, Migrants and Cities, held in Geneva in 2015, included in its conclusions that if there are to be further such conferences, they should 'recognize the different situations faced by lower and higher-income cities' (see p. 98. in www.iom.int/sites/default/files/our_work/ICP/IDM/RB-25-CMC-Report_web-final.pdf)
13. For example, the Toronto Region Immigrant Employment Council (TRIEC) has as its mandate to encourage businesses to hire immigrants. See http://triec.ca/
14. The Century Initiative in Canada, which supports significant population growth through immigration, is led by the business sector in that country (www.centuryinitiative.ca/). Some private sector think tanks, such as the Conference Board and McKinsey & Company, are heavily involved in migration research and policy advice.

References

Canada Century Initiative www.centuryinitiative.ca/

General Assembly of the United Nations. 2006. High-level Dialogue on International Migration and Development: 14–15 September 2006. http://www.un.org/esa/population/migration/hld/

General Assembly of the United Nations. 2013. High-level Dialogue on International Migration and Development: 'Making Migration Work', 3–4 October 2013. http://www.un.org/en/ga/68/meetings/migration/about.shtml

Global Forum on Migration and Development https://gfmd.org/

Global Migration Group www.globalmigrationgroup.org

Hiebert, D. 2015. Ethnocultural Minority Enclaves in Montreal, Toronto and Vancouver. Institute for Research on Public Policy http://irpp.org/research-studies/ethnocultural-minority-enclaves-in-montreal-toronto-and-vancouver

IOM, 2016. Conference on Migrants and Cities. International Dialogue on Migration. http://www.iom.int/sites/default/files/our_work/ICP/IDM/RB-25-CMC-Report_web-final.pdf

Joint Migration and Development Initiative www.migration4development.org/en/content/about-jmdi

Martin, P., and Teitelbaum, M. 2001. The mirage of Mexican guest workers. *Foreign Affairs* November/December. www.foreignaffairs.com/articles/mexico/2001-11-01/mirage-mexican-guest-workers

Office of the United Nations High Commissioner for Human Rights. Global Migration Group http://www2.ohchr.org/english/bodies/cmw/GMG.htm

Toronto Region Immigrant Employment Council (TRIEC) www.triec.ca

United Nations General Assembly. 2017. Seventy-first session 13 and 117 of the provisional agenda Globalization and interdependence. http://www.un.org/en/development/desa/population/migration/events/coordination/15/documents/Report%20of%20SRSG%20on%20Migration%20-%20A.71.728_ADVANCE.pdf

United Nations International Convention on the Protection of the Rights of All Migrant Workers and Members of their Families, New York, 18 December 1990. UN Treaty Collection https://treaties.un.org/Pages/ViewDetails.aspx?src=IND&mtdsg_no=IV-13&chapter=4&clang=_en

14

More Research and Fewer Experts

Global Governance and International Migration

Katy Long

Introduction

This chapter discusses the role that both research and researchers have played in (re)forming the global governance of international migration, with a special focus on refugees.[1] The chapter draws on my experiences while working as an adviser to Peter Sutherland, the former United Nations Special Representative for International Migration, as well as a decade working on both sides of the policy–research gap, as an academic at Oxford, the London School of Economics (LSE), and Edinburgh, and as consultant to the United Nations High Commission for Refugees (UNHCR); the UK Department of International Development (DFID); and the World Bank.

I argue that, while research has played a vital role in identifying and systematizing the weaknesses within migration's global governance systems, research has an extremely limited ability to shape or effect reform directly, except where it fits with pre-determined political agendas. Researchers can certainly play a key role in conferring legitimacy on processes of migration reform, as global governance 'experts'. But it is questionable whether this type of engagement has much impact in shaping global agendas, rather than simply legitimizing existing political platforms (see also Chapter 2 in this book).

The rest of this chapter is divided into three parts. In the first section, I consider the motivations for researchers engaging in global governance reform. In the second part, I survey the historical role of research in defining policy. In the third section, I consider some of the problems faced by researchers working in this area today.

Motivation

On 20 September 2016, I found myself standing in the lobby of a grand New York hotel. The previous day had seen the United Nations General Assembly (UNGA) issue the New York Declaration for Refugees and Migrants, ostensibly the culmination of international efforts since 2015 to address a whole set of crises—dead bodies in the Mediterranean, neo-Nazis in Europe, and refugees trapped in poverty in Jordan and Lebanon (UNGA 2016). Ultimately, the Declaration amounted to little more than a scrap of paper, accompanied by an agreement to return in two years' time for further attempts at forging a grand bargain (see, e.g., Borger and Kingsley 2016; Frelick 2016).

I was in New York working as an advisor to Sir Peter Sutherland, the then United Nations Secretary General's Special Representative for International Migration, readying myself that day to attend the day-long Concordia Summit's event on how the private sector could help to address these refugee and migrant crises. I knew what was expected of me. The format—roundtables, workshops, coffee breaks for networking—was familiar. The faces—mostly white faces—were familiar, too. And that was the problem: I'd been here before. I counted up airfares and hotel bills: I wondered by what metrics you judge success. I wondered, not for the first time, where the refugees are in all this. I wondered why I was here.

The question of why we do research is a complex one: there is no uniform answer, just as there is no single homogenous 'researcher'.[2] Researchers also make very different decisions about the relationship of their work with policy (for further discussion of these issues, see Bakewell 2008; Van Hear 2011). For some, research is an intellectual pursuit, with researchers driven by the conviction that pure scholarship will bring its own rewards in the fullness of time. For some of these individuals, policy-makers are not so much to be courted as to be avoided. At the other end of the spectrum are researchers whose careers are entirely focused on having immediate impact—making a difference *now*. These researchers may find employment directly with policy-making institutions. However, researchers can also have an uneasy relationship with institutional stakeholders: some researchers are drawn to forced migration research so as to 'give voice to the voiceless', seeing themselves as refugees' advocates working to holding powerful institutional stakeholders to account (see, e.g., Turton 1996; Fiddian-Qasmiyeh et al. 2014).

These categories are not always clear-cut. Many research careers fall somewhere between these two extremes, and can shift over time: few researchers would insist that their chosen balance between policy and research is the only correct approach. Many researchers with university careers will, at some point, play a role in advising policy-makers, attracted by the idea of 'making a difference', the offer of a seat at the table, and the promise of a pay cheque.

Political views, the realities of think-tank finance, the structure of academic careers and personal ambition may all play a role in shaping the choices researchers make: what to research, where to publish, who to talk to. Similarly, a host of factors—including but not limited to gender, ethnicity, institutional reputation, and geography—play a role in determining who will listen. The power of policy-makers to shape academic decision-making is multifaceted. Policy-makers may simultaneously be the funders, the subject *and* the audience for research. These tensions and rivalries raise important questions about how researchers choose (or are chosen) to wield influence, and whether research has any significant impact in framing or shaping the global governance of migration.

Evidence-based Policy

Most obviously, research can provide important empirical foundations for evidence-based policy. In a field such as migration and refugee protection, where policy is subject to heavy political filters, particularly at national and global levels, the normative contributions of philosophers and ethicists are also important in helping to shape what these 'commonly accepted goals' should look like (e.g. Gibney 2004). The question of who is a 'migrant' and who is a 'refugee', for instance, is not only fundamental to the architecture of global governance in both areas, but also a question central to refugee research (see, e.g., Zetter 2007; Long 2013).

Yet, the global governance of migration is often bureaucratic. Institutions such as UNHCR or the International Organization for Migration (IOM) are rarely the locus of political decision-making power, especially when—as now—migration and refugee crises are heavily politicized. So, for researchers interested in improving refugee protection or influencing global migration regimes, the potential to effect change—particularly at a global level—seems to rest far more in local action or national debates than in the global processes that have, in 2017–2018, often seemed marginal in both political and humanitarian terms.

Added to this is the difficulty of detecting and measuring something as slippery and intangible as 'influence' or 'impact'. A policy analyst may read a paper or see a presentation; a conversation may be sparked over lunch; a recommendation may appear years later. The positive connection between migration and development, for instance—now mainstream in development circles and made explicit in the 2030 Sustainable Development Goals (UNGA 2015)—was seeded by research carried out many years before this widespread acceptance (Piper 2017). Another example of how research may eventually influence policy can be seen in the long gestation period between the study of diaspora, and its emergence in the 2000s as a 'hot' development topic (Van Hear 2014).

Nevertheless, the value placed on knowledge and expertise by those shaping the structures that govern global migration and refugee policies means that research is certainly understood to matter. The next section of this chapter tries to understand how and why, by tracing a brief history of moments when research has directly intersected with policy-making on refugee and displacement issues.

Influence: Historical Case Studies

Since the 1930s, research has been variously used as a substitute for action, a legitimizing force, and—very occasionally—the foundation for meaningful reform of global migration and refugee governance structures.

1930s: Research as a Substitute for Action

By the 1930s, the global governance structures that had been established to try and deal with those uprooted by the Russian revolution and the violent demise of the Ottoman Empire in the 1920s were clearly no longer fit for purpose, even as a new European refugee crisis loomed (Skran 1995). Yet, in the absence of politically feasible solutions, researchers were called on to study the problem as policy-makers wrung their hands.

In 1938, Sir John Hope Simpson, a British-Canadian politician and statesman, was charged with compiling a report—first, for the Evian Conference held in July 1938 and, then, for the September meeting of the League of Nations. The result was a comprehensive survey that blamed immigration controls and nationalism for Europe's new refugee problem: 'before the war refugee problems were avoided because frontiers were open. There was none of the political, economic, and racial nationalism we have.' Simpson's interests were not purely analytical: the aim was to influence discussions by demonstrating that any repatriation of Europe's Jews to Germany belonged to 'the realm of political prophecy and aspiration...a programme of action cannot be based on uncontrollable speculation' (Simpson 1939a, 1939b: 2, 174). Instead, Simpson argued for vastly expanded emigration, including to Palestine.[3]

Much as academics in search of policy 'impact' today, Simpson toured the lecture circuit, talking at venues such as Chatham House. His surveys were published by the Institute of International Affairs and, later, by Oxford University Press. But his writings had little, if any, effect on refugee policy. The Evian Conference failed to secure any serious commitments from states: hope for a solution to the flow of refugees from Germany dissolved. One year later, Europe was at war. As a precedent for the influence of research upon the global governance of migration, Simpson's experience was not a hopeful one.

1950s–1970s: Research as Documentation and Legitimation

If, in the 1930s, research was used as a substitute for action, the career of Louise Holborn sheds further light on the role that 'inside' academics can play in legitimizing policy-makers and their institutions. Holborn—a tenured professor at the Connecticut College for Women from 1947 until her retirement in 1972— spent her career working with a number of refugee organizations, including the United Nations High Commissioner for Refugees. In two 'voluminous studies' of UNHCR's first decades (Elie 2014: 24), she documented their responding to refugee crises and the expansion of the international refugee regime (Holborn et al. 1975). Reading Holborn's work today, what is striking is both the level of access granted to Holborn by UNHCR and the lack of serious critical analysis. Holborn's work never seriously questions the policy-makers' own legal-institutional and Western European-centric framing of 'refugee crises'.

These two observations are not unconnected. Holborn's research work conferred legitimacy and authority on the actions of refugee organizations: it aimed to preserve institutional memory, rather than to challenge institutions' actions. In effect, Holborn's access was quid pro quo for writing to explain, rather than to challenge, the existing institutional arrangements. So, while Holborn's more descriptive writings reflect, in part, the time at which she was writing (the post-War consensus era), they also speak to what remains a salient question. Can researchers maintain critical independence while working closely with institutional gatekeepers? And should the aim of research be to record and analyse policy, or actively to lobby for change?

1990s: Research and Policy Reform—Cometh the Hour, Cometh the Expert?

A third model—arguably the most positive in terms of research shaping policy—is the commissioning of research that then guides the development of new policies in politically open space. Perhaps the most obvious case—in terms of refugee protection—is the emergence of 'Internal Displacement' as a specific policy category in the 1990s, and the subsequent construction of international architecture to respond to the needs of displaced persons. Such architecture includes a United Nations Special Rapporteur on Internal Displacement, the Guiding Principles on Internal Displacement and the 2009 Kampala Convention on Internally Displaced People (IDPs). In this case, there is little doubt that the work of Roberta Cohen and Francis Deng at the

Brookings Institute played a significant role in helping to place internal displacement so firmly on international agendas in the 1990s.

While internal displacement—the forced movement of people within a state's borders—is no new phenomenon, it was only with the end of the Cold War and the emergence of more interventionist norms centred on human rights doctrines that internal displacement came to be seen as a salient problem. In 1994, Deng—a South Sudanese politician, diplomat, and scholar—was appointed to the newly-created post of Special Rapporteur. He faced a significant challenge. How should his office promote the framing of 'Internal Displacement' as a specific problem, one that required coordinated international action, to a global community tired of refugee crises?

The answer lay in a decade-long partnership with Cohen. In 1996, Deng and Cohen co-founded the Brookings Project on Internal Displacement and, in 1998, co-authored the first major study of internal displacement, *Masses in Flight: The Global Crisis of Internal Displacement*, as well as co-editing a second volume of case studies (Cohen and Deng 1998a, 1998b). The book combined detailed research mapping of the phenomenon of internal displacement alongside the development of concrete policy recommendations, including the *Guiding Principles on Internal Displacement* that Deng submitted to the Human Rights Commission in 1998, and which formed the basis for the Kampala Convention, which was adopted on 22 October 2009.

Scholarship has thus played an important role in shaping international responses to internal displacement, first, by defining and framing the problem of IDPs and, then, by conferring authority and a platform for human rights advocacy. But what factors created the space for such influence? First, while Deng and Cohen produced high-quality research into internal displacement, they were not career researchers but, rather, a diplomat and a policy-maker and political advisor. This meant that the two understood the complex negotiations required to effect policy change and were well-placed to use their research as a tool for advocacy. Second, the fact that the Brookings Institute is a think tank, and not a university, reinforced this emphasis on producing 'policy relevant research'. Deng and Cohen's mission was explicitly to help create a new global governance framework to address internal displacement.

Third, the particular contours of legal scholarship also helped to cement this relationship between IDP advocacy and academia, especially during the tenure of Deng's successor Walter Kalin (2004–2010). Law is understood to be less a theoretical study than a profession and, as a result, noted refugee and human rights lawyers regularly cross between academia and practice, helping to foster communication between 'researchers' and 'policy-makers'. Alice Edwards, Jean-Francois Durieux, and Volker Turk, for example, are among those who have both published widely in an academic context, taught at respected universities, *and* held senior positions at UNHCR.[4]

Perhaps most important, however, was the political context within which Deng and Cohen's research-based advocacy occurred. The end of the Cold War offered new opportunities to rethink displacement alongside the development of new doctrines of humanitarian intervention and 'the responsibility to protect'. NGOs and international agencies—also recognizing that the profound political shift around displacement was likely to influence their own work—were also open to developing new labels and framing, helping to facilitate a humanitarian 'pivot'. Research processes certainly shaped the IDP dialogue and directly influenced the resulting global governance framework. But research did not initiate the conversation.

Research as Advocacy: Demanding Change from Outside

This very brief historical survey shows clearly that there is a risk research commissioned or co-opted in the policy spaces opened by states and international organizations may lack independence. As Fiddian-Qasmiyeh et al. (2014: 16)remind us, 'the right conclusions are often those the powerful least want to hear'. Many researchers in this field are drawn into their work by a desire to represent marginalized migrants and refugees, and to challenge the status quo, which they see as excessively deferential to state interests. So, can research also be harnessed for more radical ends, to change the refugee protection system from the outside?

There is a rich tradition of the academic advocate as righteous outsider. The figure of Barbara Harrell-Bond looms large over any history of refugee studies, not least because of her work in establishing the Refugee Studies Centre in Oxford. However, she is also noted—particularly in policy circles—for her virulent critiques of UNHCR and the international community's institutional failure to protect refugees adequately.

In 1986, Harrell-Bond's seminal study *Imposing Aid*, a critique of humanitarian failings in refugee camps, established the foundations for a wider body of research in this area and inspired a whole generation of researchers (Harrell-Bond 1986). Over thirty years, this work has cumulatively contributed to shifting international institutional perspectives on the use of refugee camps, as evidenced in the publication of UNHCR's 2014 paper *UNHCR Policy on Alternatives to Camps* (UNHCR 2014). More broadly, Harrell-Bond's work belongs to a canon of refugee and migration research that has sought to give refugees and other migrants a voice—often in opposition to the interests controlling the process of global governance reform: Western states and global capital. Today, it is rare for conferences or workshops not to include, at some point, mention of the importance of inclusion of refugees and migrants in framing their own lives. This critique has certainly permeated the consciousness of those at the conference table. Care should be taken not to stretch this point too far: research has not so much changed *who* is sitting at the conference table, as altered the discourse around who *should* be at the table. Nevertheless, Harrell-Bond's work is an important reminder that influencing policy-makers to change direction usually involves debate and opposition, rather than an easy welcome.

It is also important to consider how academic research and intervention can also cause things *not* to happen. Researchers as advocate-critics have often spoken out against proposed policy initiatives or perceived trends—for instance, shifts in the language around 'voluntary repatriation' in the mid-1990s that attempted to legitimize practices that amounted to *refoulement* (the forcible return of refugees or asylum seekers to a country where they are liable to be subjected to persecution) (Long 2013). In cases such as this, evidence-based advocacy can act either as a check against the erosion of protection or as controversial reform. The work of organizations such as Human Rights Watch (exemplified for many years by noted migrant advocate and scholar Bill Frelick), has played an important role in recording the consequences of the failure of global governance structures—from the rights of labour migrants in the Gulf to refugees crossing the Mediterranean—and in shaping responses to such abuse. While the influence of such critics is often intangible, their role in calling out government intransigence—Amnesty International called the 2016 New York summit an 'abject failure'—is important, and their authority to do so rests in large part on fieldwork and research (Amnesty International 2016).

Research and Policy Today: No Solution in Sight?

Research has been extraordinarily successful in documenting the institutional failures of global migration policy. Today, in 2018, it is acknowledged by virtually all researchers (and nearly all policy-makers) that today's global refugee and migrant protection system is dysfunctional. There are too many refugees living for too long in overcrowded camps or stuck in overwhelmed asylum systems, with no solution to their exile in sight, as too many countries seek to evade admitting or caring for refugees. It is equally evident that too many poor migrants are not refugees, that too many poor migrants have no legal means to move in search of work and that too many poor migrants—whether they fit the definition of refugee or not—die.

Yet, research has been less successful when it comes to developing workable solutions to such failure. Why? Some researchers view this as a step beyond their remit, offering analysis that is intended to explain and not to solve. Others point to larger structural causes of refugee and migrant flows. Many researchers working on refugee and migration issues see 'the refugee problem' as inevitable in a world of nation-states (see, e.g., Haddad 2008), and policy-makers as essentially compromised, with neither the power nor the will to do more than make incremental and marginal progress.

The result is that the politics of national interest have driven most recent discussions on global governance reform, often underpinned by the assumption—not shared by all researchers—that migration can be stopped. The use of what Alexander Betts identified as 'linkages' between North–South interests has produced a number of agreements focused on the control and containment of migration (see Betts 2008). The EU's offshore processing and detention facilities in West Africa, for example, have fundamentally shifted the notions of asylum and return, central to refugee and forced migrant protection. Inter-European cooperation through the expansion of FRONTEX provides another example of how the supra-national *management* of migration is being reformed and securitized. The Australia–Malaysia deal and the EU–Turkey deal are examples of bilateral agreements that have significant global implications for how asylum is understood and practised.

These reforms have found little support among the broad refugee and migration research community, who have, instead, focused on critiquing both the moral and operational failings of such policies. This is partly political: researchers in this field, especially at the global level, are overwhelmingly concerned by the humanitarian consequences of such decisions. But it is also because such policy changes have been driven less by evidence-based research than by political calculation. For researchers seeking to influence policy outcomes, since the mid-2000s, the locus of migration power has continually shifted further away from international agencies towards national governments playing to domestic audiences. The rise of nationalist politics across the West means that states' interests are collectively aligned—at least temporarily—in ensuring that changes to global migration governance mechanisms remain limited.

Technical Reform

Without the political will to effect more broad-based change, global governance reform has become increasingly technical and bureaucratic in nature. One example of such reform is the admission of the IOM to the United Nations (UN) as a 'related agency' in September 2016 (IOM 2016).

Prior to 2016, the IOM was already a 'permanent observer' at the UN General Assembly, and IOM staff were already working alongside UN staff in many humanitarian crises. Yet, there was strong interest in promoting the IOM's admission to the UN from key political players and an equally strong investment of political and reputational capital from those—such as IOM Director General Bill Swing—who made the decision to support the IOM's admission. Bringing the IOM into the UN was viewed as a means of achieving visible 'action' in the face of a migration crisis with which the UN had evidently struggled.

Researchers have often been among the IOM's most virulent critics—citing its lack of a norm-based mandate, its chequerboard portfolio of projects and its willingness to bend flexibly to meet states' 'migration management' needs. But research was largely irrelevant in discussions leading up to the IOM's September 2016 admission. At several workshops during 2015 and 2106, in both New York and London, key proponents of the IOM joining the UN struggled to articulate a clear sense of why such a change mattered, beyond largely bureaucratic and technical questions of coordination, capacity, and support. Hours were spent discussing the difference between a 'specialized' and a 'related' UN Agency, with few clear articulations of either the difference between these two terms, or why it mattered. As one senior advisor remarked in frustration in the summer of 2016, 'OK, so IOM is joining the UN. Why should anyone care? Why do I care?' To date, large parts of both the activist and academic communities seem to have largely greeted the IOM's new UN status with a collective shrug of their shoulders.

Sitting at the Table: Research as Echo

Nevertheless, despite deep flaws in the existing global governance system, and considerable obstacles standing in the way of substantive reform, researchers are still viewed as integral to the process of reforming migration and refugee protection. The Sutherland Report, for instance—published by the UN at the end of Sutherland's decade-long contribution as the Secretary-General's Special Representative for International Migration—lists at least two dozen academic experts who were consulted during a two-year drafting process (UNGA 2017). The New York Declaration explicitly recognizes 'academic institutions' as 'relevant stakeholders' in the inter-governmental conference (UNGA 2016). So, even if political decisions drive states' migration policies and, consequently, international frameworks for responding to crises, scientific knowledge is still recognized to be the more desirable basis for action—a marker of reputation and authenticity.

This is important: as previously noted, influence is often intangible and diffuse. Yet, there is also a clear risk that those invited to the table are those whose conclusions echo what key stakeholders *want* to hear: the 'experts' who are most adept at adapting their work for the audiences' sensibilities, rather than those best placed to offer academic critique.

The recent foray of Sir Paul Collier into migration policy provides one example of this. An Oxford development economist with a considerable public profile, Collier's first book on migration, *Exodus*, attracted enormous attention in the UK, but was criticized by many migration experts for its questionable theoretical assumptions (Collier 2013; Clemens and Sandfur 2014). In March 2017, Collier's second work on migration, co-authored by fellow Oxford Professor Alexander Betts, presented an excoriating critique of UNHCR. Instead, it offered an alternative, work-centred model for protection, focused on the promotion of special economic zones as a solution for Syrian refugees in Jordan (Betts and Collier 2017).

Betts and Collier are high-profile academics: the Amazon page for *Refuge: Transforming a Broken Refugee System* notes endorsements by International Rescue Committee President David Miliband and former UK Prime Minister David Cameron. The book received largely positive reviews from a number of commentators and journalists (see, e.g., Crabtree 2017; Van Tulleken 2017). Yet, these reviews in many ways illustrate the gap between the world of policy and the world of research, with refugee and migration scholars far more negative in their verdicts, labelling the book a poorly researched apologia for containment policies, and heavily criticizing its thin fieldwork, research gaps, and empirical errors (see Crawley 2017; Munro 2017; Yaghmaian 2017).

In a sense, this debate epitomizes the problematic relationship between academic research and policy. In *Refuge*, Betts and Collier seek to present themselves as challenging the comfortable orthodoxies of refugee protection that no longer work. Theirs, they argue, is the role that scholarship should play in shaping policy: testing inconvenient truths, presenting new ideas, even if these do not fit well with the existing humanitarian consensus.

Certainly, Betts' and Collier's work achieves this, and should not be criticized by academics just because it rejects some of the political orthodoxies around which migration scholars have coalesced. Yet, the real problem with *Refuge*—as identified by its critics—is not the nature of its conclusions but, rather, the quality of its research, particularly given the limited impact of special economic zones on the ground in Jordan (an area of which neither of the authors have regional expertise but whose refugee crisis forms the lynchpin of *Refuge*'s arguments).

Refuge is therefore a good lesson in how, when well-connected researchers become the advocates for policy (particularly when that policy is conveniently close to the interests of governments), the substance of scholarly work may be less important than the authors' ability to promote it. The capacity of Betts and Collier—both white, male, Oxbridge professors, and British citizens—to be physically present at conferences and to build the social networks that facilitate access is considerably greater than those who have to grapple personally with visa regimes, limited university funding, or difficult geography.

This underlines another problem. The success of *Refuge* reflects the fact that researchers who find a seat at the global table are disproportionately likely to be those whose views echo and reinforce the preformed views of policy-makers—in part, because they are drawn from a similar cultural elite. This preferential access to power and influence is not simply a matter of explicit political affiliation. Instead, it reflects much wider filtering and selection processes that act to limit the expression of dissent within fixed political parameters, in line with the 'propaganda model' developed by Herman and Chomsky (1988).

The lack of diversity among policy-makers, or the researchers they listen to, is hardly an issue restricted to the world of refugees and migration. However, it does have particular resonance given the acute inequalities of power that often characterize refugee crises. If refugees' voices are only heard when they are filtered not just through researchers' words, but through the words of privileged researchers selected by policy gatekeepers in the first place, then it can be of little surprise that the reforms proposed in these settings often, even when framed as 'radical', would, in fact, largely maintain intact existing structures of global power.[5]

Inaction, Influence, Integrity

How, then, should researchers seek to influence much-needed reform of global migration governance? Should they simply retreat to the libraries in the face of political manoeuvring and a 24-hour news cycle? The charge of inaction is one that all researchers working on refugee crises have grappled with. Are theoretical papers a sufficient response to urgent human misery? Contributing to policy debates can help to provide a sense of relevance: over years, they may even help change the debate.

But policy work can feed not only relevance, but also self-importance. Conference panels and workshops provide the necessary smoke and mirrors to appear as if you are in 'the room where it happens'. The trappings of self-importance are seductive; they also genuinely matter for ambitious academics, whose careers are increasingly framed by grant applications and promotion committees who count such things as markers of impact. All this ultimately turns on a fundamental question. What does influence mean? Is influence a seat at the table, playing by rules pre-determined by powerful stakeholders? Is it an op-ed in *The New York Times*? A spot as a talking head on CNN?

In a world in which states' migration policies are shaped by populist political culture, a world whose constituents 'have had enough of experts', immediate influence may well depend upon a newspaper column or interview, rather than in-depth, high-quality, ethically-sensitive research. This is at best a loss and at worst dangerous, both for the integrity of academic research and the likely success of any reform of global governance machinery. Deng and Cohen's *Masses in Flight* was a two-volume 2,000-page study. In contrast, Betts and Collier's *Refuge*—a work specifically aimed at promoting a particular policy prescription—is a slim volume of 160 pages.

The 'dual imperative' that drives refugee research—the need to contribute to ameliorating human misery, as well as scholarship—has long been the subject of interrogation, with Jacobsen and Landau (2003) among those who have warned against sacrificing methodology in the pursuit of conviction. I am accustomed to telling my students each year that passion is not enough; that the best advocates for refugees are those whose research stands up to scrutiny by opponents. We too rarely acknowledge that much of the research held up by policy-makers is often equally flimsy, even if it is more palatable to existing power brokers.

Conclusion: More Research, Fewer Experts

In 2018, the question of how 'expertise' permeates policy and politics has become ever more urgent. Yet, it seems clear to me that research matters more than ever, precisely because it offers no quick fixes.

On that September morning in 2016, I did not doubt the value of research to refugee or migrant protection. I can think of dozens of studies—from ethnographic accounts of life in Somali refugee camps to quantitative analysis of the impact of migration on wages in destination countries—that make fundamental contributions to our understanding of the way migration shapes our world and how we respond to it. We need to understand more about the economics of migration, the power structures that shape it, the causes and consequences of the policies—political and humanitarian—that have been adopted to try and contain, constrain, and cope with the movement of people, especially the poor and the persecuted.

Research can be policy-relevant without being policy-driven: independence is a virtue that does not necessarily consign scholarship to obscurity. But too much good academic research is buried underneath dense postmodern phrasing, disseminated in terms that make no sense beyond the seminar room. This is not to say that research must be distilled into bullet points in order to be relevant but, rather, it *is* to acknowledge that there is too often a communication gap that allows policy-makers to set the narrative around what counts as 'important' research.

There is also a tendency among academics to make good critics but poor innovators—in part, because it is always easier to comment on others' failures than risk your own. The work by Betts and Colliers—however flawed— does underline the potential for more innovative collaborations between researchers and policy-makers; collaborations in which researchers help design and build projects, a sort of 'Silicon Valley' model in which research is not the precursor but the parallel to action. It should be remembered, however, that 80 per cent of technology start-ups fail. For researchers to become innovators, a major cultural shift will be required—among researchers, policy-makers, and the systems that review them—to allow room for failure.

I left New York in 2016 certain of very little, but certain that the improvement of the lives of millions of migrants and billions of citizens will not be achieved with polite round-tables and incremental pen-pushing. Researchers undoubtedly have a critical role to play in global governance reform, by analysing and proposing radical change. But, if the world's migrants and refugees need more researchers, they also need fewer 'experts'. I am currently trying to bend my own career to fit this observation: it remains a work in progress.

Notes

1. While the examples discussed in this chapter primarily relate to the governance of refugee and forced migration flows, the issues discussed are also relevant to other forms of migration, including labour migration.
2. For the purposes of this chapter, research is defined as a process of systematic inquiry resulting in the creation of new knowledge and/or the use of existing knowledge in a new and creative way. Researchers—those who carry out such inquiry—can work in purely academic university settings, but may also carry out their work in more policy oriented think tanks and institutional settings, or as independent consultants.
3. This was notable because, in 1930, Simpson had previously headed up a British enquiry into immigration, land settlement, and development in Palestine, and had recommended that limits be placed upon Jewish immigration.
4. For many years, Jeff Crisp similarly linked the non-legal academic and policy worlds as Head of Evaluation and Policy at UNHCR.
5. It should be emphasized that privilege is, of course, structural. However, this means that those of us who wish to pursue a social justice agenda, but who benefit personally from the existence of such structures (and, as a wealthy, white, Western citizen, I certainly include myself in this group) have a responsibility to acknowledge explicitly the ways in which we are privileged and, therefore, more easily able to enter other privileged spaces.

References

Amnesty International. 2016. World leaders have 'shirked, not shared' responsibility on refugee crisis, 13 September. www.refworld.org/docid/57d901df4.html (Accessed 26 July 2017).

Bakewell, O. 2008. Research beyond the categories: The importance of policy irrelevant research into forced migration. *Journal of Refugee Studies* 21(4): 432–53.

Betts, A. 2008. North–South cooperation in the refugee regime: The role of linkages. *Global Governance: A Review of Multilateralism and International Organizations* 14(2): 157–78.

Betts, A., and Collier, P. 2017. *Refuge: Transforming a Broken Refugee System*. London: Penguin.

Borger, J., and Kingsley, P. 2016. Swift response to refugee crisis rests on Obama summit after UN talks fail, *The Guardian*, 18 September. www.theguardian.com/world/2016/sep/18/refugee-crisis-rests-on-obama-summit-un-talks-fail (Accessed 26 July 2017).

Clemens, M., and Sandefur, J. 2014. Let the people go: The problem with strict migration limits. *Foreign Affairs* 93: 152–9.

Cohen, R., and Deng, F. 1998a. *Masses in flight: The Global Crisis of Internal Displacement*. Washington, DC: Brookings Institution Press.

Cohen, R., and Deng, F. 1998b. *The Forsaken People*. Washington, DC: Brookings Institution Press.

Collier, P. 2013. *Exodus: How Migration is Changing our World*. New York: Oxford University Press.

Crabtree, J. 2017. A new deal for refugees, *Financial Times*, 26 April. www.ft.com/content/684fa8e6-29e7-11e7-bc4b-5528796fe35c?mhq5j=e5 (Accessed 14 October 2017).

Crawley, H. 2017. Migration: Refugee economics. *Nature* 544(7648): 26–7.

Elie, J. 2014. *Histories of Refugee and Forced Migration Studies*. Oxford: Oxford University Press, 22–35.

Fiddian-Qasmiyeh, E., Loescher, G., Long, K., and Sigona, N. 2014. Introduction: Refugee and Forced Migration Studies in Transition. In *The Oxford Handbook of Refugee and Forced Migration Studies*. Oxford: Oxford University Press.

Frelick, B. 2016. The refugee summit: A failure of vision, *Newsweek*, 20 September. www.hrw.org/news/2016/09/20/refugee-summit-failure-vision (Accessed 26 July 2017).

Gibney, M. J. 2004. *The Ethics and Politics of Asylum: Liberal Democracy and the Response to Refugees*. Cambridge: Cambridge University Press.

Haddad, E. 2008. *The Refugee in International Society: Between Sovereigns*, Volume 106. Cambridge: Cambridge University Press.

Harrell-Bond, B. E. 1986. *Imposing Aid: Emergency Assistance to Refugees*. Oxford: Oxford University Press, 15.

Herman, E. S., and Chomsky, N. 1988. *Manufacturing Consent: The Political Economy of the Mass Media*. Pantheon Books (rev. edn, 2010. London: Random House).

Holborn, L. W., Chartrand, P., and Chartrand, R. 1975. *Refugees, A Problem of our Time: The Work of the United Nations High Commissioner for Refugees, 1951–1972*, Volume 2. Metuchen, NJ: Scarecrow Press.

IOM. 2016. IOM Becomes a Related Organization to the UN, 25 July. www.iom.int/news/iom-becomes-related-organization-un (Accessed 26 July 2017).

Jacobsen, K., and Landau, L. B. 2003. The dual imperative in refugee research: Some methodological and ethical considerations in social science research on forced migration. *Disasters* 27(3): 185–206.

Long, K. 2013. When refugees stopped being migrants: Movement, labour and humanitarian protection. *Migration Studies* 1(1): 4–26.

Munro, G. 2017. Book review: *Refuge: Transforming a Broken Refugee System* by Alexander Betts and Paul Collier. *LSE Review of Books*.

Piper, N. 2017. Migration and the SDGs. *Global Social Policy* 17(2): https://doi.org.1177/1468018117703443.

Simpson, J. H. 1939a. *The Refugee Problem: Report of a Survey*. London and New York: Oxford University Press.

Simpson, J. H. 1939b. *Refugees: A Review of the Situation since September 1938*, Volume 1. London: Oxford University Press, for the Royal Institute of International Affairs, November/December. This article was originally published in *International Affairs* 18(6), 1 November 1939: 820–821. https://doi.org/10.2307/3019538

Skran, C. M. 1995. *Refugees in Inter-war Europe: The Emergence of a Regime*. New York: Oxford University Press.

Turton, D. 1996. Migrants and Refugees. in *In Search of Cool Ground: War, Flight, and Homecoming in Northeast Africa*, ed. Tim Allen. Trenton: Africa World Press, 96–110.

UNGA. 2015. *Transforming our World: The 2030 Agenda for Sustainable Development*, 21 October, A/RES/70/1. www.refworld.org/docid/57b6e3e44.html (Accessed 1 June 2018).

UNGA. 2016. *New York Declaration for Refugees and Migrants: Resolution/adopted by the General Assembly*, 3 October, A/RES/71/1. www.refworld.org/docid/57ceb74a4.html (Accessed 26 July 2017).

UNGA. 2017. *Report of the Special Representative of the Secretary General on Migration*, 3 February, A/71/7238. www.un.org/en/development/desa/population/migration/events/coordination/15/documents/Report%20of%20SRSG%20on%20Migration%20-%20A.71.728_ADVANCE.pdf (Accessed 26 July 2017).

UNHCR (UN High Commissioner for Refugees). 2014. *UNHCR Policy on Alternatives to Camps*, 22 July, UNHCR/HCP/2014/9. www.refworld.org/docid/5423ded84.html (Accessed 26 July 2017).

Van Hear, N. 2011. Forcing the issue: Migration crises and the uneasy dialogue between refugee research and policy. *Journal of Refugee Studies* 25(1): 2–24.

Van Hear, N. 2014. Refugees, Diasporas and Transnationalism. in *The Oxford Handbook of Refugee and Forced Migration Studies*, eds Elena Fiddian-Qasmiyeh, Gil Loescher, Katy Long, and Nando Sigona. Oxford: Oxford University Press, 176–87.

Van Tulleken, A. 2017. Lives on Hold, *The Times Literary Supplement*, 26 April. www.the-tls.co.uk/articles/public/migration-lives-on-hold/ (Accessed 14 October 2017).

Yaghmaian, B. 2017. 'How Not to Fix the Refugee Crisis—A Response to 'Refuge', *Refugees Deeply*. www.newsdeeply.com/refugees/community/2017/04/20/how-not-to-fix-the-refugee-crisis-a-response-to-refuge (Accessed 26 July 2017).

Zetter, R. 2007. More labels, fewer refugees: Remaking the refugee label in an era of globalization. *Journal of Refugee Studies* 20(2): 172–92.

Part IV
Conclusions, Lessons Learnt, and the Way Forward

15

Bridging Research, Public Debates, and Policies on Migration and Integration

Lessons Learnt and Ways Forward

Joakim Palme, Martin Ruhs, and Kristof Tamas

This book has provided a unique set of testimonies from researchers and experts who have been deeply involved in attempts to bridge the gaps between research and policy-making in the field of migration and integration. In the introductory Chapter 1, we suggested a three-way conceptual framework for the analyses of the various national and international level experiences including research, public debate/media, and policy-making. This conceptualization builds on the work of three thought-provoking contributions to this book: Chapter 2, by Christina Boswell on research, experts, and the politics of migration; Chapter 3, by Han Entzinger and Peter Scholten, on research–policy dialogues on integration; and Chapter 4, by William Allen, Scott Blinder, and Robert McNeil, on the relationship between research, public opinion, and the media. Our ambition has hence been to generate new insights about not only the direct relationship between research and policy-making, but also the critical and potentially mediating role of the media, as well as other features of the public debate.

In a variety of ways, this book has explored the interplay between the production, dissemination, and uses of knowledge in the area of international migration and integration. The chapters were written with three aims in mind. The first intention was to contribute to the theorization and understanding of the role of research in public debate and policy-making on migration and integration. As previously noted, its main contribution is therefore to frame research, public debate, and policy-making as a set of three-way relationships. The second aim was the critical discussion and identification of the reasons for the successes or failures of a range of national and international initiatives to bridge the gaps between research, public debates, and policy-making; we will return to some reflections about this issue later in the Conclusion. The third intention was to identify effective strategies for linking research to public debates and policy-making on migration and integration in different national and institutional contexts. We have been particularly interested in exploring how to manage and strengthen these links in different contexts, and to ask how transferable particular approaches are across borders and institutional settings.

The role and uses of research in policy debates about migration and integration cannot be understood without considering the broader politics of these issues. Migration and integration are phenomena that are at the top of many national and international policy agendas and discussions. In addition to their political importance and salience, public debates and attitudes to migrants are often based, at least in part, on strong value-related emotions that involve both hopes and fears. Processes of migration and integration have consequences for the welfare and security of a number of different actors, ranging from migrants themselves to members of communities in both host countries and countries of origin. These processes also tend to raise classical political economy issues, generating costs and benefits for different groups, and involving potentially conflicting interests—for example, those of domestic workers, employers, and migrants. The role of research and knowledge thus comes into play in a political (mine)field that is full of different and frequently diverging, or even conflicting, values and interests. As a consequence, the research itself might become politicized.

Whether and how research is used in public debates and policy-making is also influenced by the specific institutional context. Migration and integration do not happen in a vacuum. They are embedded in broader institutional and structural contexts, such as national institutions for regulating labour markets and social security, that can and typically do differ across countries and change over time. This means that debates about migration are never *just* about migration but also about many other related public policy issues. How national, regional, and international institutions and policies are designed are political issues at heart; however, specific institutional designs can also have important implications for the characteristics and effects of migration and integration processes, as well as for the production and uses of knowledge in public policy debates about these issues. For example, the nature and characteristics of the political system, political decision-making processes, and the national 'media culture' affect whether and how research findings and ideas are used in public debates. A problematic media culture, where media is exploiting the fears among the public for commercial purposes and politicians do the same for political/electoral purposes, is of course a fertile soil for the abuse of research (cf. Chapter 4). If media are dominated by negative sentiments towards researchers and experts, this is likely to magnify the problems.

Research can play an important role in promoting 'virtuous' polices that consciously manage and minimize trade-offs and promote positive-sum solutions for the concerned stakeholders. But, just to be clear, we do not expect that research and knowledge will resolve all tensions between different interests and values in policy-making on migration and integration. While it may be possible to reduce some trade-offs, an important contribution of research is the identification of the real conflicts, thus paving the way for an enlightened discussion about how to balance different goals and interests.

Given these political and institutional contexts, what can the analyses and case studies in this book tell us about the characteristics of, and strategies for strengthening the links between research, public debates, and policy-making on migration and integration?

Before identifying some of the key insights and lessons, it is important to reiterate what we stated in the introductory Chapter 1, namely, that we have not embarked on a systematic impact assessment exercise. The pragmatic reason for this approach is that it is difficult to isolate the effects of research on migration and integration policies in practice, as evidenced by the growing research literature on the societal impact of social science research (cf. Bastow et al. 2014). When examining the findings of the various chapters in this volume, we should also keep in mind that most of the contributors to this book are actors who, in different ways, belong to the research community, rather than policy-making or media circles. Furthermore, the contributors themselves have often been involved in some of the initiatives analysed in this book. Their research experience and personal involvement in some of the case studies may be a source of bias in their reflections and assessments of past experiences. Yet, this bias could potentially push the results in different directions when it comes to assessing the relationship between research and policy. For example, some researchers' critical views may be based on unrealistic expectations about what could be achieved; *if only the policy-makers listened more to researchers everything would be so much better*! Other researchers may be biased in the opposite direction, in the sense that there could be a tendency to exaggerate their own importance. If our aim had been to undertake systematic impact evaluations, these risks and potential biases could have created a significant difficulty and methodological problem. However, since our aim has been different and more explorative, the scholars' and experts' personal involvement in some of the experiences they describe does not necessarily weaken the analysis. In any case, it is clear from their discussions in this book that the chapter authors are all acutely aware of these challenges.

Lessons Learnt

On a conceptual level, the case studies have not only illustrated that research, public debates, and policies can all influence each other, but also that there can be two-way causalities between each of these three components. For example, the focus of research questions and the types of data collected can be affected by politics, as well as by public debates in media and elsewhere (e.g. Chapter 7 on Norway and Chapter 9 on Sweden). The book also includes examples of researchers influencing public debates and policies by providing new research, expert commentary, and expert advice to policy-making processes (e.g. Chapter 5 on the UK, Chapter 7 on Norway, and Chapter 8 on Germany). It is important to recognize that expert commentary and advice do not necessarily require the production of new research. Given the very short time lines that tend to dominate in policy-making, it is often impossible to find the time to carry out new in-depth studies. Typically, policy advice has to build on the existing body of research; this can be problematic to the extent that the available research may have been produced in response to questions other than the specific policy issue under consideration.

The chapters in this book have further demonstrated that research can have an influence on policy-making both directly but also indirectly, through public debate, via media as well as civil society organizations (e.g. Chapter 13 on Canada and Chapter 10 on the United States). Public opinion may be an important and integrated factor in the development of new migration and integration policies. Depending on the institutional context, some policy-makers may find themselves constrained in their policy choices by public opinion. Where the political salience and politicization of migration and integration are high, politicians who seek election or re-election typically cannot ignore these issues. Here, 'evidence' can be used for 'legitimizing' (cf. Chapter 2) policy choices that have become polarizing and emotionally loaded but can also be used for changing the mind-sets in the opposite direction and making discussions more fact-based and less polarized. How the interaction between our three types of actors work appears to be of critical importance for how this plays out.

The case studies in Chapters 7, 8, and 10 have also shown that whether and how research affects policy-making and public debate, will always be influenced by institutions, interests, and the broader politics of immigration and integration, as well as related policy areas such as education, labour markets, welfare states, and so on. There can be important interactions between research and other policy determinants, such as the economic interests of employers and the political orientation of the government in power. In addition to playing an instrumental role in policy-making, research can have important political functions which are often more symbolic than instrumental. Chapter 2 distinguished two such symbolic functions of research: a 'legitimizing function' where stakeholders use research to enhance their legitimacy, and a substantiating function where expert knowledge and research are used to give authority to particular policy positions. In addition, Chapter 3 shows that the research–policy gap could widen due to the increasing politicization of the policy issue.

We argue that it is crucial to think seriously about how research can play an effective role beyond its substantiating and legitimizing functions. Although there is much scepticism about its potential, we believe that research can be of important instrumental or problem-solving value (cf. Chapter 2) as a tool for improving the processes and outcomes of migration, and human development more broadly. However, this is likely to require new research that can respond to the challenges that policy-makers are facing today—and tomorrow—in a more transformative way. We cannot limit the efforts of 'bridge-building' to communicating the existing body of research to policy-makers. An important part of the problem is that we need more and new knowledge about a large number of policy issues. If evidence is produced just for the sake of reinforced policy-making, the research–policy interaction would end up as an empty ritual and become ignored by policy-makers (Ahlbäck Öberg 2011). The challenge is to provide the institutional context that allows research to play a positive instrumental role in policy-making.

The book's case studies of particular country experiences have clearly highlighted the importance of paying attention to cross-country differences in the politics and institutions that mediate the interrelationships between research, public debate, and policy-making on migration and integration. For example, Chapter 9, on the Swedish experience, points to the different traditions of organizing policy-related research in general, not merely when it comes to migration. There are also major differences between countries when it comes to the role of think tanks, which has had implications for how policy relevant research and expertise is, and could be, organized (which the Swedish case also serves to illustrate in Chapter 9). Recognizing these specific institutional contexts is a precondition for organizing and funding policy-relevant research in a way that makes it credible and helpful for public debate and policy-making processes. For instance, strengthening the links between research, public debates, and policy-making in the United States would need to take account of the particular role of think tanks. Philip Martin's account of the US case in Chapter 10 shows that, rather than resulting in a pluralism of perspectives, the large number of politicized think tanks in the United States has contributed to entrenched views and disagreements between the two camps of what Philip Martin calls *admissionists* and *restrictionists*.

The importance of considering research as part of a three-way relationship with public debates and policy-making is very clear in the description in Chapter 6 of the reception of the Máxima report from the independent government advisory body, the Netherlands Scientific Council for Government Policy (WRR). The chapter demonstrates that it is not possible to understand the conflicts about this particular report without the role of the media. There are interesting similarities and differences between Chapter 6's discussion of a publication of the WRR in the Netherlands and Chapter 7's analysis of the experiences with two Norwegian commissions on immigration and the welfare state. The credibility of the institutions in the two countries was, at the outset, quite similar. Both the Dutch WRR and Norwegian NOU system generally enjoyed strong support and were seen as credible by more or less all sides of the debate. Yet, the Máxima report stirred up considerable emotion, while the Norwegian reports seem to have had the opposite effect and reduced the emotional loading of the issues. The public responses and media coverage of these reports in the two countries appear to have been dependent on the specific foci of the studies carried out. The kinds of identity issue raised in the Dutch report appear to be more sensitive than the cost–benefit analyses and welfare state issues that had been put at the forefront in the two Norwegian reports. That cultural issues around migration are more conflictual than economic matters, is in line with the findings of Lucassen and Lubbers (2012), as well as with a broader review of the field undertaken by Hainmuller and Hopkins (2014), and this could be one explanation for the Dutch controversy. Another explanatory factor for the different experiences in the two countries could have been that, while there had been high awareness, before publication, of the potentially strong conflicts around the report in Norway, the potential for controversy had not been anticipated, at least not to the same degree, in the Netherlands.

Chapter 9 on the Swedish committees shows that, even though they are meant to work independently from the government, their work can become politicized. The media plays an important role in this process of politicization, and it can be used by a range of different actors. The Swedish example illustrates how researchers can use media to argue for their own positions and conclusions, run their internal academic debates, and to criticize governments. It also shows how opposition parties may use the output of government-funded committees to criticize the work of governments. At the same time, the discussion of the German case in Chapter 8 suggests that the media can be highly effective in serving as a bridge between researchers and policy-makers. In line with the chapters on Norway, Sweden, and the Netherlands, the analysis of the German experience suggests that it can be helpful for media to be associated with potential stakeholders from the outset of the research process.

It is important to find ways of avoiding or minimizing the politicization of research. It is clear from the various analyses in this book that media have an important role to play in any efforts to reduce the degree of politicization of research on migration and integration. It is important to add that the aim of reducing politicization does not imply that we should seek to take politics out of migration and integration policy (cf. Chapter 5) but, rather, that politics and policy preferences should not be confused with, or obstruct, the important task of research to describe and analyse 'the state of the world'.

This book has given ample room for the analysis of national experiences. As nation-states subscribe to various global or regional regimes for handling international migration—such as those based on the 1951 Refugee Convention or the 'free movement' of workers in the European Union (EU)—they need to be engaged in decision-making processes on these international levels. This makes bridge-building between research and policy-making important also in these international contexts. The balancing act of handling the three-way relationship between research, public debate, and policy-making becomes even more difficult when international debates and policy processes are added to national ones. In Chapter 11, on the use of research and experts in EU policy-making on migration, Elizabeth Collet is clear about her view: there has to be exchange and proximity between the worlds of politics and research, otherwise the research will often be (or at least be perceived as) policy irrelevant. There is also a risk that, without sufficient contact between the two spheres, communication from the research side will be overloaded with high ambitions to 'speaking truth to power'.

Chapter 12 illustrates the complexities when involving research generated outside European borders. The experience from the CARIM projects give guidance for how barriers can be overcome—not only where language is concerned, but also with regard to working with different research cultures. The case study in Chapter 12 also illustrates the risks of making research overly instrumental in attempts to export European norms and policy ideas to 'partner countries'. Fostering modes of cooperation should essentially be about supporting virtuous circles in the three-way relationships between research, public debates, and policy-making. This is also of key importance at the global level. Chapter 14, on the role of researchers and experts in debates about the global governance of migration, highlights the significance of who is sitting at the table, for the content and legitimacy of migration research and policies. An important insight from Long's historical inquiry is that research can matter a great deal by narrating the state of affairs, thereby contributing to setting the political agenda on the global level. It is, however, easy to share Long's frustration about the difficulties for research in impacting on current policy-designs and recent global policy debates, where the role of research has been tightly constrained by agendas set by other actors. Chapter 13 reminds us of the fact that global is also local. The strong presence of cities in the International Metropolis project discussed in Chapter 13 reflects a situation where cities are increasingly becoming policy-makers, not least in the integration arena. This is recognized in EU-funded research and policy-making, too, illustrating the dynamics of multi-level governance and how the local level can help innovate migration and integration policies.

Ways Forward

A number of lessons can be learnt from the experiences reported in this book. We argue that these lessons can give guidance for 'ways forward' in efforts to make migration policy and public debates more informed by research. What can we do better? The simple truth may be that all actors involved have to try harder in order for policy-makers to gain the knowledge resources necessary to act more wisely. A fruitful strategy will most likely have to be built on the combination of a strong normative agenda, which specifies good codes of conduct in organizing the three-way relationships, with an improved and sound incentive structure for all of the pertinent stakeholders. At this stage, we can only hint at where to find the building blocks for both the norms and the incentives that can bring about the necessary changes.

Even if many individual researchers are highly effective in their public and policy engagement, it is clear that the research community as a whole can improve considerably in terms of its outreach beyond academia, which is paramount to any strategy that intends to build stronger bridges between research, public debates, and policy-making. Research can be more useful for policy-making by getting involved in different kinds of policy studies. Policy relevance can, however, be achieved in many different ways and does not necessarily involve the direct study of policies. It can be enough to highlight conditions that deserve to be addressed by policies. It is nevertheless true that, the closer research analyses come to actual policy instruments, the closer research gets to guiding policy-makers in the reform processes required to improve existing institutions and conditions. To achieve this may require greater involvement of different kinds of 'brokers' in the process, such as policy institutes, commissions, committees, and/or think tanks.

To be instrumental, in the sense of the concept as offered in Chapter 2, the independence of research needs to be safe-guarded. This suggests that public funding and its conditions are critical. In Chapter 10, Phil Martin's frustration with the predictability of researchers should be taken seriously, and this issue is certainly not only about think tanks. It is clearly difficult to make an instrumental contribution if the results are completely predictable. Beyond that, policy-makers and researchers, as well as media, need to be constantly engaged in a serious discussion concerning the way in which questions are asked to research, the analytical frames imposed, and the way in which data and results are interpreted. This must involve critical awareness of fundamental methodological issues, especially about the consequences of choosing one analytical frame for the analysis in favour of another. Some contradictory research results are simply the outcome of choosing a particular model, and the appropriate choice of analytical framework is at least partly dependent on what questions we ask. Certainly, the kinds of questions we ask often follow from our values and politics. We cannot, and should not, take the politics out of migration policy, but we should be very transparent about the political nature of the questions we pose and how we evaluate the results.

Researchers can always improve in terms of making their work and results more accessible. This is, however, easier said than done. Howard Duncan (Chapter 13) is not alone in observing the poor incentive structure in academia in this regard, and in noting that this is particularly true and problematic for younger scholars. While funding and the way that career-paths are designed in the academic world should be improved in a way that rewards policy-relevant research, this is unlikely to be sufficient. There are issues around communication that require the kind of specialization that journalism represents. We need many more 'knowledge brokers' embedded in the university/research system and policy-oriented research institutes to be able to build solid bridges to media, as well as other bridges to policy-making communities, also, where appropriate, involving civil society and the private sector. Being more inclusive and transparent in the research process (e.g. in the problem definition phase) is another important way forward to fostering more cooperation within the research community, but also with media and policy actors. As pointed out in Chapter 14, part of being more inclusive is also about language: researchers that aim to generate policy-relevant research have to be able to use concepts and descriptions that translate easily to public debates and realities.

A number of contributors to this book argue that there is no better instrument for bridging the gap between research and policy-making than the media. Chapter 6 discusses how policy-oriented research (institutes) can play the role of an 'honest broker' between (university-based) research and public policy debates, but it also points to the necessity of getting media and other critical voices on board to facilitate this brokerage. Clearly, engaging the media to achieve policy impact carries many risks as well as opportunities, and using media alone cannot be expected to deliver policy impact in the intended way. We need to build a chain of 'honest brokers' from university-based research all the way to the policy-making circles by means of applied research institutes, commissions and the media. We also argue that the linking of the various actors should be done in ways that do not compromise the role of the media to keep a critical eye on both researchers and policy-makers. Moreover, it is of decisive importance for members of media to scrutinize what other media actors are doing, as well.

To strengthen the links between researchers, public policy-makers, the media and other contributors to public debates, it is critically important that the different actors understand and appreciate each other's primary aims and constraints. This implies that much more needs to be done to foster such a common understanding, which appears to be a vital condition for the promotion of genuine cooperation between the key actors and a stepping stone for the evolution of a good climate for research-based policy reforms.

Ultimately, whatever researchers and media do to improve, there will be no change if politicians do not listen and reflect on what is being brought to the table. The conceptual framework in Chapter 2 is a useful starting point for such reflections. There will always be circumstances when research is used to only legitimize or substantiate policy changes but the more politicians are able to use research for instrumental reasons, letting policy reforms be directly guided by research, the better. We know from Chapter 14 that, historically, some transformative changes have been aided by ground-breaking research efforts. We should ask ourselves if and how it is possible to repeat such positive experiences.

In politics and policy-making, going with the flow and maintaining the status quo is perhaps the least demanding political strategy. This also applies to the policy field of migration and integration. However, such an approach would lead to missed opportunities to make a difference as public policy reforms carry the potential to greatly improve human conditions. The more instrumental (or even transformative) the policy changes, the greater the courage demanded on the part of political leadership. Another vision for the role of research in policy-making that has guided this book is that we constantly need to evaluate and re-evaluate our understanding of how the policy world works. We argue that there is an important potential for improvement of the performance of migration and integration policies if existing institutions and policies are subject to recurrent evaluations. This is about promoting a process that Hoppe (2005) has labelled 'the learning model' of research—policy interactions, where policy-making becomes part of social experimentation (see Chapter 9). However, such a process would require that policy reforms and evaluations be guided by an underlying normative agenda concerning the ultimate goals of policies (which is something different from the normative aspects of regulating the three-way research/public debate/policy relationship). Migration is mentioned in several of the seventeen Sustainable Development Goals but is not a *Leitmotif* in any of them. While it is clear that, together, migration and integration have a very important role to play in promoting human development in very broad terms, a more elaborate and explicit normative agenda for migration policy is needed and this certainly applies to policies at the national level to.

In this context, it is also important to ask if and how research in the migration and integration field can be harmful. We know that the results of research, including those of high quality research, can sometimes be used for a range of different ends, some of which might generate negative consequences for at least some groups. The risk of research creating harm is increased, however, if it is not conducted properly (from a scientific perspective) and/or if it is misinterpreted. If research is not carried out properly, this is a problem for the research community to resolve—a serious one, too. There is also an important responsibility resting with the researchers to be clear in explaining the research results and their implications. The misinterpretation of research results in public debates or during policy-making processes may or may not be intentional. If they are unintended, stronger bridges between research, public debates and policy-making may reduce the problem. We argue that when policy-makers or contributors to public debates deliberately misinterpret the results of research studies, there should be strong demands on both media and researchers to scrutinize the political and other relevant actors, including their interests and values. Pluralism and political independence in the media landscape may help prevent deliberate and gross misinterpretation and misuse of research results in media coverage.

To conclude, we believe that well-designed policies on migration and integration carry the potential to make significant contributions to the reduction of human insecurities and the promotion of human development. We also argue that public policy designs will improve if they are founded on a research-based understanding of how the world works. At the same time, failed policies can generate great risks for human security and development. This is why we want to increase the supply of policy-relevant research and why we are concerned about the common failures to consider and feed relevant research into public debates and policy-making processes. However, we strongly believe that matters can improve and we hope that this book can help identify potential ways forward.

Any significant positive and sustainable effort to 'bridge the gaps' requires changes by all actors involved in the three-way relationships between research, public debates, and policy-making. All actors have the potential to influence each other because of the two-way causalities between each of these three elements. This suggests that any intervention or change can trigger both 'vicious' and 'virtuous' circles that either weaken or strengthen the links between research, public debates and policy.

Our concluding suggestions for building more and stronger bridges between research, public debates and policy-making are as follows:

- All actors should recognize that migration and integration are complex processes that require careful and multi-faceted policy interventions. This sounds like a very basic argument, but it is one that appears to be increasingly rejected in public policy debates that are often focused on 'quick

251

fixes' and immediate policy 'solutions' to what are often complex policy dilemmas. Researchers are often criticized for highlighting complexities without offering clear policy answers. This critique is sometimes fair but, in the case of the migration and integration issues analysed in this book, ignoring issue complexities and inter-dependencies can become an important reason for public misunderstandings and policy failures.

- To strengthen the links between researchers, public policy-makers, the media, and other contributors to public debates, it is of critical import-ance that the different actors understand and appreciate each other's primary aims and constraints. This implies that much more needs to be done to foster such common understandings and this requires a constant dialogue between the key actors.

- The political and socio-economic institutional context can shape the effectiveness of specific interventions aimed at bridging the gaps in important ways, thus limiting the transferability of particular experiences and lessons across countries and over time. This does not mean that there can be no learning across countries but that each intervention needs to be tailored to the specific institutional environment (e.g. to the specific political system and media culture).

- Migration is not beneficial for everything and everyone at all times. The politics of immigration and integration are often dominated by distribu-tional (rather than economic efficiency) issues as well as the perceived impacts on culture, identity, and security. To be effective and credible in what are often highly politicized and polarized debates, research that aims to influence public policy debates must be—and must be seen to be— independent of the politics of migration, at least at arm's length from power. At the same time, research that claims to be impartial and evidence-based has a responsibility, and we would argue obligation, to identify the benefits and costs of any specific policy intervention, or entire policy regime, for all key stakeholders involved and affected. This is of particular importance in a policy field that is plagued by simplifica-tion and one-sidedness.

- Researchers who aim to engage with public policy issues need to interact more closely with policy-makers, journalists, and actors from civil society in order to become relevant, which has to do with both the way research questions are asked by the researchers themselves and the way policy-makers are helped to understand how the results from research may be translated into the world of policy-making.

- Media organizations can play an important role in bridging the gaps between research, policy and the public but, if they do not work with other 'honest brokers', the risk is that the media erodes the entire 'bridge construction'. We recommend including specialized journalists in both research processes and the dissemination of research results.

- Our suggestion for politicians is that they should ask precise questions to the research community, including questions regarding the effects and trade-offs of specific policy interventions under consideration, but make sure that their questions could actually be answered by more research. In addition to turning to the research community to help address specific policy questions, politicians can—and we argue should—also use research and researchers to engage in bigger picture reflections on, for example, the many interdependencies between migration and other issue areas, and the longer-term consequences of migration and integration processes and policies.

We hope that this book has shown that bridging the gaps between research, public debates, and policy-making requires actions by a range of different stakeholders, not just by researchers and policy-makers. It requires a collective recognition of the importance of the issue, and a collaborative approach that can promote the evolution of more effective institutions with the adequate norms and incentives for all the relevant stakeholders to engage. We hope this book can help promote debates that can generate more ideas about how this can be done in practice.

References

Ahlbäck Öberg, S. 2011. Kunskap och politik—mellan nonchalans och teknokrati [Knowledge and politics—between nonchalance and technocracy], in *Svensk Jurist-tidning* 8: 764–71.

Hainmuller, J., and Hopkins, D. J. 2014. Public attitudes toward immigration, *Annual Review of Political Science* 17: 225–49.

Hoppe, R. 2005. Rethinking the science–policy nexus: from knowledge utilization and science technology studies to types of boundary arrangements, Poiesis Praxis 3: 199–215.

Lucassen, G., and Lubbers, M. 2012. Who fears what? Explaining far-right-wing preference in Europe by distinguishing perceived cultural and economic ethnic threats, *Comparative Political Studies* 45(5): 547–74.

Index